Ready-to-Run Delphi® 3.0 Algorithms

Ready-to-Run
Delphi® 3.0 Algorithms

ROD STEPHENS

WILEY COMPUTER PUBLISHING

John Wiley & Sons, Inc.
New York • Chichester • Weinheim • Brisbane • Singapore • Toronto

Publisher: Robert Ipsen
Editor: Carol A. Long
Assistant Editor: Kathryn A. Malm
Managing Editor: Marnie Wielage
Electronic Products, Associate Editor: Mike Sosa
Text Design & Composition: Benchmark Productions, Inc.

Designations used by companies to distinguish their products are often claimed as trademarks. In all instances where John Wiley & Sons, Inc., is aware of a claim, the product names appear in initial capital or ALL CAPITAL LETTERS. Readers, however, should contact the appropriate companies for more complete information regarding trademarks and registration.

This book is printed on acid-free paper. ∞

This publication is designed to provide accurate and authoritative information in regard to the subject matter covered. It is sold with the understanding that the publisher is not engaged in professional services. If professional advice or other expert assistance is required, the services of a competent professional person should be sought.

Library of Congress Cataloging-in-Publication Data:
Stephens, Rod, 1961–
    Ready-to-run Delphi 3.0 algorithms / Rod Stephens.
      p. cm.
    Includes index.
    ISBN 0-471-25400-2
    1. Delphi (Computer file) 2. Computer software--Developmnent.
    I. Title.
    QA76.76.D47S735   1998
    005.265--dc21   98-7019
                                    CIP

Printed in the United States of America
10 9 8 7 6 5 4 3 2 1

CONTENTS

INTRODUCTION

Programming for Windows has always been a daunting task. The Windows Application Programming Interface (API) provides a powerful but dangerous set of tools for building Windows applications. In a way, the API is like a bulldozer: If you use it properly, you can build amazing things, but without the proper skills and care, you will probably wreak havoc and destruction.

Delphi has helped change all that. Using a point-and-click interface, Delphi allows you to build complete applications quickly and easily. Using Delphi, you can write and test sophisticated applications with complex user interfaces without ever using the API directly. By freeing you from API worries, Delphi lets you concentrate on the details of your application.

Even though Delphi makes building a program's user interface much easier, you must write the rest of the application yourself. You must write the code that takes input from the interface, processes it, and presents the results. That is where algorithms come in.

Algorithms are formal instructions for performing complicated tasks on a computer. A searching algorithm, for example, might explain how to locate a particular customer record in a database of 10 million records. The quality of the algorithms you use can make the difference between locating needed data in seconds, hours, or not at all.

This book describes algorithms in Delphi. It contains many powerful algorithms, completely implemented in Delphi 3. It analyzes techniques for managing data structures such as lists, stacks, queues, and trees. It also describes algorithms to perform common programming tasks like sorting, searching, and hashing.

To use these algorithms successfully, you must do more than copy the code into your program and press F9. You must understand how different algorithms behave under different circumstances. You must also determine which circumstances apply in your situation. Finally, you must use that information to select the algorithm that best fits your needs.

This book describes algorithms in plain English. It explains their typical and worst-case behaviors so you will know what to expect when you use them in your programs. This approach will help you recognize worst-case behavior when it occurs so you can rewrite or replace the algorithm. Even the best algorithm will not help you if you use it under the wrong circumstances.

Each algorithm is also implemented in ready-to-run Delphi source code that you can easily plug into your programs. The code is provided on the accompanying CD-ROM, along with example applications. These examples show how a program can use the algorithms, and they demonstrate important characteristics of the algorithms themselves.

What This Package Includes

This book and CD-ROM package will provide you with the following:

A solid introduction to algorithms. After reading the book and running the example programs, you will be able to use sophisticated algorithms in your Delphi projects. You will be able to critically evaluate new algorithms written by you or others.

A large collection of source code that you can add to your programs. Using the code on the CD-ROM, you can quickly add powerful algorithms to your applications.

Complete, ready-to-run example programs that allow you to test the algorithms. You can use these programs to gain a deeper understanding of how the algorithms work. You can modify the programs to learn more about the algorithms, or you can use them as a basis for building your own applications.

Intended Audience

This book covers advanced Delphi programming topics. It does not teach Delphi itself. If you have a good understanding of the fundamentals of Delphi, you will be able to concentrate on the algorithms rather than becoming bogged down in the details of the language.

This book teaches important programming concepts that you can generalize to solve new problems. The algorithms use powerful programming techniques such as recursion, binary subdivision, dynamic memory allocation, and network data structures that you can apply to your unique problems.

Even if you have not yet mastered Delphi, you will be able to run the example programs and compare the performance of different algorithms. Most importantly, you will be able to select the correct algorithms for your needs and add them to your Delphi projects.

Delphi Version Compatibility

The best algorithms depend on fundamental programming concepts, not the idiosyncrasies of a particular version of a programming language. The code in this book was tested using Delphi version 3.0, but the language features used are generic and should be available in later versions of Delphi when they are released.

Programming languages often grow, but they rarely shrink. A remarkable example is the goto statement in the C language. This statement is awkward, dangerous, and almost never used by the vast majority of C programmers, but it has remained in the language since the 1970s. In fact, it was incorporated into C++ and more recently Java, even though the creation of a new language provided an ideal excuse to drop it.

Similarly, future versions of Delphi will continue to add new features to the language, but they are unlikely to remove the building blocks needed to implement the algorithms described in this book. Whatever they add, Delphi 4, 5, and 6 will surely provide classes, arrays, and record data types. Most, if not all, of the algorithms explained in this book should run unchanged for many years to come. If any changes are necessary, they will be posted at www.delphi-helper.com.

Chapter Overviews

Chapter 1, "Fundamental Concepts," covers those concepts you should understand before you begin to analyze complex algorithms. It explains the techniques you need to theoretically analyze the complexity of algorithms. Some algorithms that perform well in theory may not do as well in practice, however, so this chapter also deals with practical programming considerations like paging.

Chapter 2, "Lists," shows how to build several kinds of lists using arrays and pointers. These data structures are useful in many programs, and they are used throughout the rest of the book. Chapter 2 also tells how to generalize linked list techniques to build other, more complicated data structures such as trees and networks.

Chapter 3, "Stacks and Queues," describes two special kinds of lists: stacks and queues. These data structures are used in many algorithms including several described in later chapters. Chapter 3 ends by presenting a simulation that compares the performance of two kinds of queues that might be used at an airline check-in counter.

Chapter 4, "Arrays," explains several special kinds of arrays. Triangular, irregular, and sparse arrays allow you to use convenient array representations while reducing memory usage.

Chapter 5, "Recursion," discusses the powerful tool of recursion. Because recursion can be confusing and dangerous, Chapter 5 explains when recursion is appropriate and shows how you can remove it when necessary.

Chapter 6, "Trees," uses many of the techniques presented earlier, such as recursion and linked lists, to examine the more complicated topic of trees. This chapter covers different tree representations like the *fat node* and *forward star* representations. It describes several important tree algorithms such as tree traversal.

Chapter 7, "Balanced Trees," examines a more advanced topic. Balanced trees have certain properties that keep them evenly balanced and efficient. Balanced tree algorithms are surprisingly simple to describe but quite difficult to implement. This chapter uses one of the most powerful of these structures, a *B+tree,* to build a sophisticated database.

Chapter 8, "Decision Trees," discusses problems that can be described as searching for a solution within a decision tree. For even small problems, these trees can become enormous, so searching them as efficiently as possible is essential. This chapter compares several different techniques that make searching for solutions manageable.

Chapter 9, "Sorting," deals with what is probably the most heavily studied topic in algorithms. Sorting algorithms are interesting for several reasons. First, sorting is a common task in programming. Second, different sorting algorithms have their own strengths and weaknesses, so no single algorithm works best in all situations. Finally, sorting algorithms demonstrate a wide variety of important algorithmic techniques such as recursion, heaps, and the use of random numbers to minimize worst-case behavior.

Chapter 10, "Searching," examines a topic closely related to sorting. Once a list has been sorted, a program may need to locate items within the list. This chapter compares several methods for locating items in sorted lists as efficiently as possible.

Chapter 11, "Hashing," discusses techniques for storing and locating items even more quickly than is possible using trees or sorting and searching. The chapter covers several hashing techniques, including chaining, buckets, and several kinds of open addressing.

Chapter 12, "Network Algorithms," describes another category of algorithms. Some of these, like shortest-path calculations, apply directly to physical networks. The algorithms can also be used indirectly to solve other problems that may initially seem unrelated to networks. For example, shortest path algorithms can divide a network into districts or identify critical tasks in a project schedule.

Chapter 13, "Object-Oriented Techniques," explains object-oriented algorithms. These algorithms use an object-oriented approach to implement behaviors that are unnatural for "traditional" algorithms.

Appendix A, "Using the CD-ROM," describes the contents of the CD-ROM. It explains how you can load the example programs, and it tells how you can get help if you have trouble with the CD-ROM.

Appendix B, "List of Example Programs," summarizes the example programs provided on the CD-ROM. You can look through this list to see which programs demonstrate particular algorithmic techniques.

What's on the CD-ROM

The CD-ROM contains the Delphi 3 source code for the algorithms and example programs described in this book.

The example programs described in each chapter are contained in separate subdirectories. For example, programs demonstrating algorithms described in Chapter 3, "Stacks and Queues," are stored in the Ch3 directory. Appendix B lists the programs described in this book.

Hardware Requirements

To run and modify the example applications, you need a computer that is reasonably able to run Delphi 3. Almost any computer running any Windows operating system will do. You also need a compact disk drive to load the programs from the CD-ROM.

Algorithms run at different speeds on different computers with different configurations. A 200-megahertz Pentium Pro with 64Mb of memory will be faster than a 386-based computer with 4Mb of memory. You will quickly learn the limits of your hardware.

How to Use This Book

Chapter 1, "Fundamental Concepts," gives background material used later throughout the book so you should start there. You should read this material even if you do not need an in-depth understanding of the algorithms right away.

Chapter 2, "Lists," and Chapter 3, "Stacks and Queues," explain different kinds of lists used by programs later in the book, so you should read these chapters next.

Chapter 6, "Trees," discusses material that is used in Chapter 7, "Balanced Trees," in Chapter 8, "Decision Trees," and in Chapter 12, "Network Algorithms." You should read Chapter 6 before you tackle these later chapters. You can read the remaining chapters in any order.

Table I.1 shows three possible plans of study that you can use, depending on how broad you want your introduction to algorithms to be. The plan in the top row covers basic techniques and data structures that you will find helpful in your programs. The middle row also describes fundamental algorithms, like sorting and searching algorithms, which you may need to build more advanced programs.

The plan on the bottom shows one order in which you could cover the whole book. While Chapter 7, "Balanced Trees," and Chapter 8, "Decision Trees," follow logically from Chapter 6, "Trees," they are more difficult than some of the later chapters, so in this plan they are studied a little later. Chapter 7, "Balanced Trees," Chapter 12, "Network Algorithms," and Chapter 13, "Object-Oriented Techniques," are probably the most difficult chapters in the book, so they are left for last. Of course, you can also read the book in order from the front cover to the back cover if you like.

Table I.1 Plans of Study

Coverage	Chapters												
Basic techniques	1	2	3	4									
Fundamental algorithms	1	2	3	4	5	6	9	10	13				
In-depth coverage	1	2	3	4	5	6	9	10	11	8	12	7	13

FUNDAMENTAL CONCEPTS

This chapter presents background material that you should understand before you begin the serious study of algorithms. The chapter begins by asking, "What are algorithms?" Before you get deeply into programming details, it is worth spending a few moments to step back and consider exactly what algorithms are.

The chapter then introduces *complexity theory*, the formal study of the complexity of algorithms. Using complexity theory, you can evaluate the theoretical performance of algorithms. This approach lets you compare different algorithms to each other and predict their performance under different circumstances. The chapter gives several examples that show how to apply complexity theory to small problems.

Some algorithms that perform well in theory may not do as well in practice, however, so the chapter ends with a discussion of several real-world programming considerations. Excessive paging can ruin the performance of an otherwise fine application.

Once you have mastered the concepts in this chapter, you will be able to apply them to the algorithms throughout the rest of the book. You will even be able to use them to analyze programs of your own so you can judge their performance and anticipate problems before they turn into disasters.

What Are Algorithms?

An algorithm is a set of directions for performing a particular task. When you give someone instructions to fix a lawn mower, drive a car, or bake a cake, you create an algorithm. Of course, these sorts of everyday algorithms are described in imprecise terms like these:

```
Make sure the car is in park.
Make sure the parking brake is set.
Turn the key.
Etc.
```

You assume that the person following the instructions can handle the millions of little details such as unlocking the door, opening the door, sitting down behind the wheel, fastening the seat belt, finding the parking brake, and so forth.

When you write an algorithm for a computer, you cannot assume that the computer will understand anything you do not tell it explicitly. The computer has a very limited vocabulary (a programming language), and all your instructions must be phrased using that vocabulary. To deal with this situation, you need to use a more formal style for writing computer algorithms.

It is an interesting exercise to try to write an algorithm for a common, everyday task in a formal style. The car-driving algorithm, for example, might begin like this:

```
If the door is locked then:
    Insert the key in the lock
    Turn the key
    If the door is still locked then:
        Turn key the other way
Pull up on the door handle
Etc.
```

This piece of code only gets the door open; it does not even check that you are opening the correct door. If the lock is sticky and hard to open, or if the car has an anti-theft system, the algorithm can become extremely complicated.

Algorithms have been formalized for thousands of years. Around 300 B.C., Euclid wrote algorithms for bisecting angles, testing whether triangles were equal, and performing other geometric tasks. He started with a small vocabulary of axioms such as "parallel lines never intersect," and from those he built algorithms for complicated tasks.

This sort of formalized algorithm is appropriate for mathematical purposes where it must be shown that something is true or that some task can be accomplished, but the speed of the algorithm is unimportant. For problems where someone must actually execute the instructions, like sorting a million customer records using a computer, efficiency becomes a critical part of the problem.

Analyzing Algorithms—How Fast Is Fast?

Complexity theory is the study of the complexity of algorithms. There are several ways in which you can measure the complexity of an algorithm. Programmers usually focus on an algorithm's speed, but other factors are also important. How much memory, disk space, or other resources an algorithm uses can also be an issue. A fast algorithm will not be of much use if it requires more memory than your computer has available.

Space versus Time

Many algorithms provide a trade-off between space and time. You can solve the problem quickly, using a lot of memory, or more slowly, using less memory.

One type of shortest-path algorithm provides a good example. Given a network, like the network of streets in a city, you can write an algorithm to compute the shortest distance between any two points in the network. Instead of calculating these distances whenever you need them, you could precompute the shortest distances between every point and every other point and store the results in a table. When you need to know the shortest distance between any two points, you look the value up in the table.

This example would allow you to look up distances almost instantly, but it would require a huge amount of memory. The street network for a large city like Boston or Denver might contain a few hundred thousand points. The table needed to store all of the shortest-distance information would have more than 10 billion entries. In this example, the space versus time trade-off is clear: By using an additional 10 gigabytes of memory you can make the program much faster.

This special relationship between time and space gives rise to the idea of *space-time complexity*. In this sort of analysis, an algorithm is evaluated in terms of both time and space, and the trade-offs between them are studied.

This book concentrates mostly on time complexity, but it points out any unusual space requirements. Some algorithms, like the mergesort algorithm discussed in Chapter 9, "Sorting," require extra scratch space. Other algorithms, such as heapsort, also discussed in Chapter 9, require a fairly natural amount of space.

Big O Notation

When you compare different algorithms, it is important to understand how complexity relates to the size of the problem itself. One algorithm may need 1 second to sort a thousand numbers and 10 seconds to sort a million numbers. Another algorithm might need 2 seconds to sort a thousand numbers but only 5 seconds to sort a million. In that case, you cannot instantly declare one program better than the other; which is better depends on the data you are sorting.

Although it is interesting to know the exact speeds of each algorithm, it is more important to understand the relative behaviors of the algorithms for problems of different sizes. In this example, the first algorithm sorts small lists faster, but the second algorithm sorts large lists faster.

You can relate an algorithm's speed and size using *Big O* notation. An algorithm has complexity O(f(N)), pronounced *order F of N*, if the time required by the algorithm goes up at the same rate as the function f(N) when the problem size N gets large. For example, consider the following code that sorts N positive numbers:

```
for i := 1 to N do
begin
```

```
// Find the largest item in the list.
MaxValue := 0;
for j := 1 to N do
    if (Value[j] > MaxValue) then
    begin
        MaxValue := Value[J];
        MaxJ := J;
    end;

// Print the largest item we just found.
PrintValue(MaxValue);
// Zero the item so we do not pick it again.
Value[MaxJ] := 0;
end;
```

In this algorithm, the variable i loops from 1 to N. Each time i changes, the variable j also loops from 1 to N. For each of the N times the outer loop is executed, the inner loop is executed N times. The total number of times the inner loop is executed equals $N * N$ or N^2. This gives the algorithm complexity of $O(N^2)$ (order N-squared).

When calculating Big O values, you should use only the fastest-growing part of the runtime equation. Suppose an algorithm has a runtime given by $N^3 + N$. The Big O notation for that algorithm would be $O(N^3)$. Looking at only the fastest-growing part of the function allows you to study the behavior of the algorithm as the problem size N gets large.

When N is large for a procedure with runtime $N^3 + N$, the N^3 term dominates and the entire function starts to look like N^3. When N = 100, the difference between $N^3 + N = 1,000,100$ and $N^3 = 1,000,000$ is only 100, a 0.01 percent difference. Notice that this is true only for large N. When N = 2, the difference between $N^3 + N = 10$ and $N^3 = 8$ is 2, a 20 percent difference.

You should also ignore constant multiples in Big O notation. An algorithm with runtime $3 * N^2$ would be considered $O(N^2)$. This makes it easier to understand relative changes in the problem size. If you increase N by a factor of 2, the 2 is squared in the N^2 term, so the runtime would increase by a factor of roughly 4.

Ignoring constant multiples also makes it easier to count the steps executed by the algorithm. In the previous sorting example, the inner loop is executed N^2 times, but how many steps should you count for each inner loop? You could count only the if statement because only it is executed every time through the loop. You could calculate the total number of times the statements within the if are executed and count those, too. Then there are the statements inside the outer loop but outside the inner loop, like the PrintValue statement. Should those be counted, too?

Following these different counting methods you might decide the algorithm has N^2, $3 * N^2$, or $3 * N^2 + N$ complexity. With Big O notation, these are all the same. They all reduce to $O(N^2)$, so it does not matter exactly which statements you count.

Looking for Complexity

The most complex parts of a program are usually in program loops and procedure calls. In the previous sorting example, two loops executed all of the algorithm's statements.

When a procedure calls another procedure, you must think more carefully about how much work that other procedure is doing. If it is performing a constant amount of work, like printing a number, then you do not need to worry too much about it for Big O purposes. On the other hand, if it is executing $O(N)$ steps, then the function may be contributing significantly to the algorithm's complexity. If the procedure call is executed within a loop, the effect may be even greater.

For example, suppose a program has a procedure called Slow with $O(N^3)$ complexity and another procedure Fast with $O(N^2)$ complexity. The complexity of the program as a whole depends on how the two procedures are related.

If Fast calls Slow each time it runs through its loops, then the complexities of the procedures combine. The combined complexity is the product of the two. In this case, the complexity is $O(N^2)$ times $O(N^3)$ or $O(N^3 * N^2) = O(N^5)$. The following code fragment shows this sort of behavior:

```
procedure Slow;
var
     i, j, k : Integer;
begin
    for i := 1 to N do
        for j := 1 to N do
            for k := 1 to N do
                // Do something here.
end;

procedure Fast;
var
    i, j : Integer;
begin
    for i := 1 to N do
        for j := 1 to N do
            Slow; // Call procedure Slow.
end;

procedure RunBoth;
```

```
begin
    Fast;
end;
```

On the other hand, if the main program calls the procedures separately, their complexities add. In this case, the total complexity is $O(N^3) + O(N^2) = O(N^3)$ in Big O notation. The following code fragment has this complexity:

```
procedure Slow;
var
    i, j, k : Integer;
begin
    for i := 1 to N do
        for j := 1 to N do
            for k := 1 to N do
                // Do something here.
end;

procedure Fast;
var
    i, j : Integer;
begin
    for i := 1 to N do
        for j := 1 to N do
            // Do something here.
end;

procedure RunBoth;
begin
    Fast;
    Slow;
end;
```

Complexity of Recursive Algorithms

Recursive procedures are procedures that call themselves. They introduce complexity in a subtle way. In many recursive algorithms, it is the number of times recursion occurs that determines the complexity of the algorithm. While a recursive procedure may seem simple, it can contribute greatly to the program's complexity if it calls itself many times.

The following code fragment shows a procedure that contains only two statements. When called for input N, however, this procedure executes N times. That makes the complexity of this piece of code O(N).

```
procedure CountDown(N : Integer);
begin
```

```
    if (N <= 0) then exit;
    CountDown(N - 1);
end;
```

Multiple Recursion

A recursive algorithm that calls itself more than once is *multiply recursive*. Multiply recursive procedures can be harder to analyze than singly recursive algorithms, and they can contribute much more complexity.

The following procedure is similar to procedure CountDown described previously except it calls itself twice instead of once.

```
procedure DoubleCountDown(N : Integer);
begin
    if (N <= 0) then exit;
    DoubleCountDown(N - 1);
    DoubleCountDown(N - 1);
end;
```

Because the procedure calls itself twice, you might expect that it would have twice the runtime of procedure CountDown. That would give the procedure a runtime of $2 * O(N) = O(N)$. Unfortunately, the truth is more complicated.

If you let $T(N)$ be the number of times the procedure is executed with input N, it is easy to see that $T(0) = 1$. When the procedure is called with input 0, it simply exits.

For larger values of N, the procedure recursively calls itself twice with parameter $N - 1$. The number of times the procedure is executed is $1 + 2 * T(N - 1)$. Table 1.1 shows some of the values generated by the equations $T(0) = 1$ and $T(N) = 1 + 2 * T(N - 1)$. If you look closely at these values, you will see that $T(N) = 2^{(N + 1)} - 1$ giving the procedure a run time of $O(2^N)$. Even though procedures CountDown and DoubleCountDown look similar, DoubleCountDown requires many more steps to execute.

Indirect Recursion

A recursive procedure can also call itself indirectly by calling a second procedure that then calls the first. Indirect recursion can be even harder to analyze than multiple recursion. The Sierpinski curve algorithm discussed in Chapter 5, "Recursion,"

Table 1.1 Values of the Runtime Function for Procedure DoubleCountDown

N	0	1	2	3	4	5	6	7	8	9	10
T(N)	1	3	7	15	31	63	127	255	511	1023	2047

uses four procedures that are both multiply and indirectly recursive. Each of these procedures calls itself and the other three procedures up to four times. It is a fair amount of work to show that this algorithm runs in time $O(4^N)$.

Space Complexity of Recursive Algorithms

Space complexity is particularly important for some recursive algorithms. It is very easy to write a recursive procedure that allocates a little bit of memory each time it is called. That space can add up if the procedure enters a long series of recursive calls. For this reason, you should perform at least a casual space complexity analysis of recursive procedures to make sure they do not use huge amounts of memory.

The following procedure allocates more memory each time it is called. After one or two hundred recursive calls, the procedure uses up all of the computer's memory and the program stops with an "Out of memory" error.

```
procedure GobbleMemory;
var
    x : Pointer;
begin
    GetMem(x, 100000); // Allocate 100,000 bytes.
    GobbleMemory;
end;
```

Chapter 5, "Recursion," has much more to say about recursive algorithms.

Average Case and Worst Case

Big O notation is used as an upper bound on the complexity of algorithms. Just because a program has a certain Big O complexity does not mean the algorithm always takes that long. Given the right data, many algorithms take far less time than analysis indicates they might. For example, the following code shows a simple algorithm that locates an item within a list.

```
function LocateItem(target : Integer) : Integer;
var
    i : Integer;
begin
    for i := 1 to N do
        if (Value[i] = target) then break;
    Result := i;
end;
```

If the target item is at the end of the list, the algorithm will need to search all N items in the list before finding the item. That will take N steps so this is an O(N) algorithm. This is the longest the algorithm could possibly take so it is called the *worst case analysis* of the algorithm.

On the other hand, if the target number happens to be at the very beginning of the list, the algorithm will stop almost immediately. It will execute only a couple of steps before it finds the number and stops. This makes the algorithm's *best case* runtime a constant, or O(1). Generally, a best case like this one is not very interesting because it will be unlikely to occur in real life. It is more interesting to look at the algorithm's *average* or *expected case* behavior.

If the numbers in the list are initially mixed randomly, the target item could appear anywhere in the list. It could be near the end of the list, and it could be near the beginning. On the average, you would need to examine N / 2 of the items before finding the one you wanted. This makes the average case behavior of this algorithm O(N / 2), which is the same as O(N) in Big O notation.

For some algorithms, the worst case and expected case results are different. For example, the quicksort algorithm discussed in Chapter 9, "Sorting," has worst case behavior $O(N^2)$ but expected behavior $O(N * \log(N))$, which is much faster. Algorithms like quicksort go to great lengths to ensure that worst case behavior is as unlikely as possible.

Common Complexity Functions

Table 1.2 lists some of the functions that commonly occur in complexity calculations. The functions are listed in increasing order of growth, with the functions at the top of the list growing more slowly than the functions at the bottom. This means algorithms with runtime complexities involving functions near the top of the list will be faster than those with runtime complexities involving functions near the bottom.

Table 1.2 Common Complexity Functions

Function	Notes
f(N) = C	C is a constant
f(N) = log(log(N))	
f(N) = log(N)	
$f(N) = N^C$	C is a constant between 0 and 1
f(N) = N	
f(N) = N * log(N)	
$f(N) = N^C$	C is a constant greater than 1
$f(N) = C^N$	C is a constant greater than 1
f(N) = N!	i.e., 1 * 2 *...* N

It also means a complexity equation that contains more than one of these functions will reduce to the last one in the table when it comes to Big O notation. For example, $O(\log(N) + N^2)$ is the same as $O(N^2)$.

Whether an algorithm with a runtime shown in Table 1.2 is fast enough depends on how you use it. If you run the algorithm once per year on a fairly small data set, $O(N^2)$ performance is probably acceptable. If you run the algorithm interactively on large data sets with a user watching, $O(N)$ may not be fast enough.

Usually runtimes involving $N * \log(N)$ and smaller functions are very fast. Runtimes involving N^C for small C, like N^2, are acceptably fast if the amount of data is limited. Runtimes involving functions like C^N and $N!$ are so slow that these algorithms are usable only for very small problem sizes.

An interesting way to think about the relative sizes of these functions is to consider the time it would take to solve problems of different sizes. Table 1.3 shows how long it would take a computer executing 1 million algorithm steps per second to execute some slow algorithms. The table shows that only very small problems can be solved when the complexity is $O(C^N)$, and only the tiniest problems can be solved when the complexity is $O(N!)$. An $O(N!)$ problem where N is only 24 would take more time to solve than the current age of the universe.

Logarithms

Before reading further, you should review a little bit about logarithms because they play an important role in many algorithms. The logarithm of a number N in a base B is the power P that satisfies the equation $B^P = N$. For example, when you see the equation $\log_2(8)$ you should think, "2 to what power equals 8?" In this case, $2^3 = 8$, so $\log_2(8) = 3$.

You can convert between different log bases using the relationship $\log_B(N) = \log_C(N) / \log_C(B)$. If you wanted to convert $\log_2(N)$ into base 10, for example, you would have $\log_{10}(N) = \log_2(N) / \log_2(10)$. The value $\log_2(10)$ is a constant that is approximately 3.32. Because you ignore constant multipliers in Big O notation,

Table 1.3 Times to Execute Complex Algorithms

	N = 10	N = 20	N = 30	N = 40	N = 50
N^3	.001 sec	.008 sec	.027 sec	.064 sec	.125 sec
2^N	.001 sec	1.05 sec	17.9 min	1.27 days	35.7 years
3^N	.059 sec	58.1 min	6.53 years	$3.86 * 10^5$ years	$2.28 * 10^{10}$ years
$N!$	3.63 sec	$7.71 * 10^4$ years	$8.41 * 10^{18}$ years	$2.59 * 10^{34}$ years	$9.64 * 10^{50}$ years

you can ignore the $\log_2(10)$ term. In fact, for any base B, the value $\log_2(B)$ is a constant. That means for purposes of Big O notation, all log bases are the same. In other words, $O(\log_2(N))$ is the same as $O(\log_{10}(N))$ or $O(\log_B(N))$ for any B. Because all log bases are the same, the log base is usually omitted in Big O notation, so $O(\log_2(N))$ is written $O(\log(N))$.

Binary representations are natural in programming, so the logarithms used when analyzing runtimes are usually base 2. To make the notation easier, the chapters that follow assume that $\log(N)$ means $\log_2(N)$. When a different log base is needed, the base is written explicitly.

The Real World—Fast versus FAST

Even though it is useful to ignore small terms and constant multiples when studying complexity, it is often important to consider them when actually writing programs. These numbers become particularly important when the problem size is small and the constants are large.

For example, suppose you have two algorithms that can accomplish the same task. One runs in $O(N)$ time, and the other runs in $O(N^2)$ time. For large problems, the first algorithm will probably be faster.

Looking closely at the runtime functions, however, you may find that the first is $f(N) = 30 * N + 7000$ and the second is $f(N) = N^2$. In this case, the second algorithm will execute fewer steps for problems where N is under 100. If you know that your problem size will never exceed 100, you might be better off using the second approach.

On the other hand, not all algorithm steps are equally fast on a computer. If the first algorithm uses fast memory operations and the second uses slow disk accesses, the first algorithm might be faster in all cases.

A number of other factors further confuse the issue. The first algorithm might require a huge amount of memory that your computer may not have. The second algorithm may be much more complicated so it might take you days longer to implement, and it might become a debugging nightmare in the future. Real-life issues like these can sometimes make complexity analysis seem almost pointless.

Complexity analysis is still useful for understanding the general nature of an algorithm. The analysis usually shows you where the bulk of the computation takes place. Knowing which parts of the algorithm determine the overall performance lets you decide where improvements will give you the greatest benefit.

Sometimes the best way to determine which algorithm is better is to test them. When you compare algorithms like this, it is very important that you use data that is as similar to the real data as possible. Many algorithms behave quite differently when they execute on different sets of data. If you test the algorithms on unrealistic data, you may be unpleasantly surprised when you run the program in the real world.

Paging

A particularly important real-world consideration is *paging*. The Windows operating system reserves a certain amount of disk space that it can use for *virtual memory*. When all of your real memory fills up, Windows writes the contents of some of that memory onto the disk. This process is called *paging* because Windows writes the memory in chunks called *pages*. Windows then uses the real memory that was copied to the disk for other things. When a program needs to access items written to disk, the system copies them back into real memory.

Because accessing a disk is much slower than accessing real memory, paging can slow the performance of an application tremendously. If a program jumps back and forth across huge amounts of memory, the system will page often. All that reading and writing to the disk will slow the application.

Example program Pager allows you to allocate bigger and bigger arrays until the system begins paging. Enter the amount of memory you want the program to allocate in megabytes, and click the Page button. If you enter a small value like 1 or 2, the program will be able to allocate the array in real memory so the program will run quickly.

If you enter a value close to the amount of physical memory on your computer, the program will start to page. You will probably hear your disk drive start working overtime when this happens. You will also notice that the program takes much longer to run. A 10 percent increase in array size may result in a 100 percent increase in runtime.

Program Pager can access its memory in one of two ways. If you click the Page button, Pager examines its array from the beginning to the end. When the program visits part of the array, the system may have to page to load that part of the array into real memory. Once that page is in real memory, the program continues to visit that part of the array until it is finished with the entries on that page.

On the other hand, if you click the Thrash button, Pager accesses the memory randomly. By jumping randomly through the array, the program greatly increases the chances that the next item it needs has been paged to the disk. In that case, the system will need to page it back into real memory. This excessive paging is called *thrashing*.

Table 1.4 shows times required by program Pager to examine various amounts of memory on a 133-megahertz Pentium with 32Mb of real memory and a lot of other processes running. Your runtimes will be different and will depend on the kind of computer you have, the amount of real memory you have, the speed of your disk drives, and the sizes of other programs running on your system.

Initially, the time needed by the tests increases about as quickly as the memory allocated does. When paging begins, there is a sudden dramatic increase in runtime. Notice that the paging and thrashing tests have very similar behavior until paging occurs. When all of the memory allocated fits in real memory, it takes the same amount of time to access items in an orderly or random fashion. Once paging begins, however, random access to the memory is much less efficient.

Table 1.4 Runtimes in Seconds for Program Pager

Memory (Mb)	Paging	Thrashing
4	0.62	0.75
8	1.35	1.56
12	2.03	2.33
16	4.50	39.46

You can do a few things to minimize the effects of paging. Most importantly, do not waste memory. If you can keep memory usage to a reasonable level, you will never have to worry about paging. Remember that other programs including Windows also use memory while your program is running, so you will not be able to use all the physical memory on your computer. The computer that generated the data in Table 1.4 paged heavily when the program allocated 16Mb of memory even though it had 32Mb physically available.

Sometimes you can write your program's code so it deals with memory in natural chunks before moving on to other parts of memory. The mergesort algorithm described in Chapter 9, "Sorting," manipulates data in large chunks. Each of these chunks is sorted, and then the chunks are merged together. The orderly way mergesort moves through memory minimizes paging.

The heapsort algorithm, also described in Chapter 9, jumps freely from one part of its list to another. For very large lists, this will cause thrashing. On the other hand, mergesort requires extra storage space while heapsort does not. If the list is large enough, the extra storage mergesort uses may force it to page.

Summary

Analyzing the performance of algorithms lets you compare different algorithms. It allows you to predict how algorithms will behave under different circumstances. By pointing out the parts of an algorithm that contribute most to runtime, analysis helps you define the places where extra work may give the largest improvements.

Programming is full of trade-offs that are critical in real-world applications. One algorithm may be faster than another, but only if it can use a huge amount of extra memory. Another algorithm may be easy to implement and maintain, but it may be slower than a more complicated algorithm.

Once you have analyzed the available algorithms, understand how they behave under different circumstances, and know how they are influenced by real-world trade-offs, you can select the one most appropriate for your situation.

LISTS

Arrays are an indispensable programming tool. They allow you to manage large groups of objects quickly and easily in a uniform way. Unfortunately, arrays are also inflexible. Rearranging items within an array can be complicated and time consuming. To move an item from one end of an array to the other, for example, you need to rearrange the entire array. You must shift every item in the array over one position to fill in the spot left by the item being moved. Then you must place the moved item in its new location.

Dynamic data structures allow you to make this sort of change quickly and easily. With only a few steps, you can move an item from any position in the data structure to any other.

This chapter describes methods for creating dynamic lists in Delphi. Different kinds of lists have different properties. Some are simple and provide only limited functionality. Others, such as circular lists, doubly linked lists, and threaded lists, are more complex and support advanced data management features.

Later chapters use the techniques described here to build stacks, queues, arrays, trees, hash tables, and networks. Be sure you understand this chapter before you read the later material.

List Basics

In its simplest form, a list is a group of objects. It holds the objects and allows your program to examine them. If that is all you need a list to do, you can use an array to store the list. You can use a variable NumInList to keep track of the number of items in the list. Whenever your program needs to examine the items, it can use NumInList to determine how many items are present. It can then visit the items using a for loop and perform whatever actions are necessary.

If you have a program that can use this simple strategy, use it. This method is effective and, due to its simplicity, is easy to debug and maintain. Many programs are not this straightforward, however, and require more complicated versions of even simple objects like lists. The sections that follow discuss some of the ways you can build more powerful lists.

The first section describes ways to make lists that can grow and shrink over time. In some programs, you may not be able to determine beforehand how large a list might need to be. You can handle this situation with a list that can resize itself as needed.

The next section discusses *unordered lists* that allow you to remove items from any part of the list. Unordered lists give you more control over the list contents than simple lists do. They are also more dynamic because they allow you to change the contents of the list freely over time.

The following sections discuss *linked lists,* which use *pointers* to create an extremely flexible data structure. You can add or remove items from any part of a linked list with very little effort. These sections also describe some linked list variations such as circular, doubly linked, and threaded lists.

Simple Lists

If your program needs a list that never changes, you can build it easily using an array. It is then a simple matter to examine the items when necessary using a for loop.

Many programs use lists that grow and shrink over time. You could allocate an array big enough to handle the list at its largest, but that may not always work very well. You may not know ahead of time how large the list will become. There may also be a small chance that the list will become huge. In that case, allocating a gigantic array would be a waste of memory most of the time.

Resizing Arrays

Delphi does not allow you to resize arrays. Once an array is declared, its size is fixed. However, you can implement resizable arrays indirectly by using pointers.

First, use a type statement to define an array type with huge bounds. If you want the array indexes to start with 1, you can dimension the array with bounds from 1 to 1,000,000. Next, define a type that is a pointer to an object of this array type.

Use Delphi's GetMem function to allocate space for the array. This procedure's second argument indicates the size of the array in bytes. This value should be the number of items the array should hold times the size of each item. You should use Delphi's SizeOf function to determine the item size.

Use the FreeMem procedure to free the array's memory when the program no longer needs it.

Example program SizeArr demonstrates array resizing. Enter a number of items and click the Resize button to make the program resize an array. The following code fragment shows the program's most interesting pieces.

```
type
    // Define array type.
    TIntArray = array [1..1000000] of Integer;
```

```
    // Define pointer to array type.
    PIntArray = ^TIntArray;

    // <code omitted>...

// Resize the array.
procedure TSizeArrForm.CmdResizeClick(Sender: TObject);
var
    NumItems : Integer;      // Array item count.
    Items    : PIntArray;    // Array of items.
    i        : Integer;
    txt      : String;
begin
    // Allocate space for the array.
    NumItems := StrToInt(NumItemsText.Text);
    GetMem(Items, NumItems * SizeOf(Integer));

    // Fill the array with values.
    for i := 1 to NumItems do
    begin
        Items^[i] := i;
        txt := txt + IntToStr(Items^[i]) + ' ';
    end;
    ItemsLabel.Caption := txt;

    // Free the array.
    FreeMem(Items);
end;
```

Array resizing is a powerful technique, but it is a bit dangerous. When Delphi is working with the array, it does not know how large the array is. In program SizeArr, Delphi thinks it is working with a pointer to an array containing 1 million entries. If the program has actually allocated space for only 10 entries, Delphi cannot tell that accessing the 100th entry is a mistake. Instead of providing a compile time error saying the array index is out of bounds, the program will attempt to write into the 100th position in the array at runtime. In the best case, accessing this memory location will crash the program. In the worst case, it will cause a subtle bug that will be extremely hard to find.

A similar problem occurs if the program uses an incorrect lower bound for the array. For example, suppose the array type is defined as in the following code:

```
TIntArray = array [1..1000000] of Integer;
```

The program can cause problems if it tries to access the array's entry in position 0. This mistake is easy to make. When you declare a new array of type

PIntArray in a procedure, the array bounds are not shown in the declaration. You must remember how you defined the array type elsewhere in the program.

A program must explicitly free the array's memory when it is no longer needed. Delphi frees normal array memory when the array goes out of scope. For example, an array declared within a procedure is automatically freed when the procedure ends.

On the other hand, memory allocated using GetMem stays allocated until it is explicitly freed by FreeMem. If a procedure allocates memory using GetMem and does not free it using FreeMem, the memory will remain allocated and inaccessible until the program stops. This gives the program a *memory leak* that can use up a lot of system memory if the procedure is called many times.

Finally, a program will have problems if it tries to access memory that has been freed by FreeMem. If the program frees an array's memory and then accesses the array, it can crash or cause subtle bugs. You can reduce the chances of these problems by resetting the array pointer to nil after freeing its memory. Then if the program tries to access the array, it immediately generates an access violation instead of a subtle bug.

Despite these dangers, array resizing is a powerful technique. It allows you to manage lists that change in size at runtime with extremely good performance.

A Resizable List

Using resizable arrays, you can build a simple resizable list. To add an item to the list, create a new array that is one item larger than the old one. Copy the items from the old array into the new one and add the new item. Then free the old array and set the array pointer to indicate the new memory.

The following code shows a procedure that adds an item to a resizable array. You could write similar code to remove an item by making the array smaller.

```
var
    List     : PIntArray; // The array.
    NumItems : Integer;   // The number of items used.


procedure AddItem(new_item : Integer);
var
    new_array : PIntArray;
    i         : Integer;
begin
    // Create a new array.
    GetMem(new_array, (NumItems + 1) * SizeOf(Integer));

    // Copy the existing items into the new array.
    for i := 1 to NumItems do
        new_array^[i] := List^[i];
```

```
    // Save the new item.
    new_array^[NumItems + 1] := new_item;

    // Free the previously allocated memory.
    if (NumItems > 0) then FreeMem(List);

    // Make the array point to the new memory.
    List:= new_array;

    // Update the size.
    NumItems := NumItems + 1;
end;
```

This simple scheme works well for small lists, but it has a few drawbacks. First, the array must be resized frequently. To create a list of 1000 items, you would need to resize the array 1000 times. Even worse, as the list gets larger, resizing it takes longer because you must copy the growing list into the newly allocated memory.

To reduce the number of times the array must be resized, you can add extra entries to the array whenever you resize it. When you enlarge the array, add 10 entries instead of 1. When you add new items in the future, the array will contain unused entries where you can place the items without resizing. You need to resize the array only when it runs out of unused entries.

Similarly, you can avoid resizing each time you remove an item from the list. You can wait until there are at least 20 unused items in the array before resizing. When you do resize the array, be sure to leave 10 empty entries so you can add more items without being forced to resize again.

Note that the maximum number of unused items (20) should be larger than the minimum number (10). This minimizes the number of times you need to resize the array when you add and remove items.

With this scheme, the list will usually hold a few unused items. The number of these items is small, however, so not much memory is wasted. The unused items give you insurance against resizing the array when you later add and remove items from the list. In fact, if you repeatedly add and remove only one or two items, you might never need to resize the array.

The following code shows this strategy for enlarging a list.

```
var
    List          : PIntArray; // The array.
    NumItems      : Integer;   // The number of items used.
    NumAllocated : Integer;    // The number of items allocated.

procedure AddItem(new_item : Integer);
var
    new_array : PIntArray;
```

```
    i           : Integer;
begin
    // See if there's room.
    if (NumItems >= NumAllocated) then
    begin
        // Create a new array.
        NumAllocated := NumAllocated + 10;
        GetMem(new_array, NumAllocated * SizeOf(Integer));

        // Copy the existing items into the new array.
        for i := 1 to NumItems do
            new_array^[i] := List^[i];

        // Free the previously allocated memory.
        if (NumItems > 0) then FreeMem(List);

        // Make the array point to the new memory.
        List:= new_array;
    end;

    // Update the number of items.
    NumItems := NumItems + 1;

    // Save the new item.
    new_array^[NumItems] := new_item;
end;
```

For very large arrays, this may still not be a good solution. If you need a list holding 1000 items and you typically add 100 items at a time, you will still spend a large amount of time resizing the array. An obvious strategy for handling this situation is to increase the extra resize amount from 10 items to 100 or some even larger value. Then you could add 100 items at a time without frequent resizing.

A more flexible solution is to make the amount of extra space depend on the current size of the list. When the list is small, the extra space added is small. The array would be resized more often, but it does not take too long to resize a small array. When the list is large, the amount of extra space added is larger, so the array would be resized less often.

The following code tries to keep about 10 percent of the list array empty. When the array fills completely, the program enlarges it by 10 percent. If the amount of empty space in the array grows beyond about 20 percent of the array's size, the code makes the array smaller.

Whenever the program resizes the array, it always adds at least 10 items, even if 10 percent of the array size is smaller. This reduces the number of resizes necessary when the list is very small.

```
var
    List            : PIntArray;   // The array.
    NumItems        : Integer;     // The number of items used.
    NumAllocated : Integer;        // The number of items allocated.
    ShrinkWhen      : Integer;     // Shrink if NumItems < ShrinkWhen.

procedure ResizeList;
const
    WANT_FREE_PERCENT = 0.1;       // Try for 10% free space.
    MIN_FREE = 10;                 // Min unused space when resizing.
var
    want_free, new_size, i : Integer;
    new_array              : PIntArray;
begin
    // See how big the array should be.
    want_free := Round(WANT_FREE_PERCENT * NumItems);
    if (want_free < MIN_FREE) then want_free := MIN_FREE;
    new_size := NumItems + want_free;

    // Resize the array preserving the old values.
    // Create a new array.
    GetMem(new_array, new_size * SizeOf(Integer));

    // Copy the existing items into the new array.
    for i := 1 to NumItems do
        new_array^[i] := List^[i];

    // Free the previously allocated memory.
    if (NumAllocated > 0) then FreeMem(List);
    NumAllocated := new_size;

    // Make List point to the new memory.
    List := new_array;

    // Calculate ShrinkWhen. We resize the array if it
    // shrinks until NumItems < ShrinkWhen.
    ShrinkWhen := NumItems - want_free;
end;
```

The SimpleList Class

To use this simple list strategy, a program would need to know all the details of the list. It would need to keep track of the size of the array, the number of entries currently in use, and so forth. If the program needed to create more than one list, it would need multiple copies of all these values and duplicated code to manage the different lists.

Delphi's classes can greatly simplify this task. The TSimpleList class encapsulates this list scheme to make list management easy. The class provides Add and RemoveLast methods for the main program to use.

It also provides an Item function that returns the value of a specific item. Function Item also checks that the index of the requested item is within the bounds allocated by the array. If it is not, the function raises a range error. This makes the program stop instead of causing a subtle bug.

The ResizeList procedure is declared private within the TSimpleList class. This hides the procedure from the main program. Only the class needs to know how or when the list is resized.

Using the TSimpleList class, it is easy for an application to create more than one list. It simply declares objects of type TSimpleList and uses the class method Create to build the lists. The list objects each have their own variables so they can each manage their separate lists.

```
var
    list1, list2 : TSimpleList;

procedure MakeLists;
begin
    // Create the TSimpleList objects.
    list1 := TSimpleList.Create;
    list2 := TSimpleList.Create;
end;
```

Example program SimList demonstrates the TSimpleList class. Enter a value in the text box and click the Add button to make the program add the item to its list. The TSimpleList object resizes its array if necessary. Whenever the list is not empty, you can press the Remove button to remove the last item from the list.

When the TSimpleList object resizes its array, it displays a message box telling you how large the array is, how many items in the array are unused, and the value ShrinkWhen. When the number of items in use in the array falls below the value ShrinkWhen, the program resizes the array to make it smaller. Notice that, when the array is almost empty, ShrinkWhen sometimes becomes zero or negative. In that case, the array will not be resized even if you remove all the items from the list.

Program SimList adds 50 percent of the current array size as empty entries when it resizes the array, and it always keeps a minimum of one empty entry when it resizes. These values were chosen so that you could easily make the program resize the array. In a real application, the percentage of free memory should be smaller and the minimum number of free entries should be larger. Values more like 10 percent of the current list size and a minimum of 10 unused entries would make more sense.

Unordered Lists

In some applications you may need to remove items from the middle of the list, though you can still add new items at the end. This will be the case when the order of the items is not particularly important, but you may need to remove specific items from the list. This kind of list is called an *unordered list*. It is also sometimes called a *bag* or *sack*.

An unordered list should support these operations:

• Add an item to the list

• Remove a specific item from the list

• Determine whether a specific item is in the list

• Perform some operation (print, display, etc.) on all of the items in the list

You can easily modify the simple scheme presented in the previous section to handle this kind of list. When you remove an item from the middle of the list, you shift the remaining items one position to fill in the hole left behind. Figure 2.1 shows this operation graphically. Here the second item is removed from the list and the third, fourth, and fifth items are shifted to the left to fill in the hole.

Removing an item from an array in this way can take quite a bit of time, particularly if the item removed is near the beginning of the array. To remove the first item in an array containing 1000 entries, you would need to move 999 of the entries one position to the left. A simple *garbage collection* scheme will allow you to remove items much more quickly.

Instead of removing items from the list, mark them as not in use. If the items in the list are simple data types like integers, you might be able to use a specific *garbage value* to mark items. For integers, you might use the value –32,767. You assign this value to any item that is not in use. The following code fragment shows how to remove an item from this kind of integer list.

Figure 2.1 Removing an item from the middle of an array.

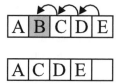

```
Const
     GARBAGE_VALUE = -32767;
```

```
// Mark the item as garbage.
procedure RemoveFromList(position : Integer);
begin
     List^[position] := GARBAGE_VALUE;
end;
```

If the items in the list are records, you can add a new IsGarbage field to the record. When you remove an item from the list, set the value of the item's IsGarbage field to True.

```
type
     MyRecord = record
          Name      : String * 20; // The data.
          IsGarbage : Boolean;     // Is this entry garbage?
     end;
```

```
// Mark the item as garbage.
procedure RemoveFromList(position : Integer);
begin
     List^[position].IsGarbage := True;
end;
```

To keep things simple, the rest of this section assumes that the data items are integers and that you can mark them with a garbage value.

Once the list contains entries marked as garbage, you must modify other procedures that use the list so they can skip the garbage values. For example, you might change a procedure that shows the items in the list like this:

```
// Show the items in the list.
procedure ShowItems;
var
     i : Integer;
begin
     For i := 1 to NumItems do
          if (List^[i] <> GARBAGE_VALUE) then  // If it's not garbage
               ShowMessage(IntToStr(List^[i])); // print it.
end;
```

After you use a garbage marking scheme for a while, the list may become full of garbage. Eventually, procedures like this one will spend more time skipping garbage entries than examining actual data.

To solve this problem, you can periodically run a *garbage collection routine*. This routine moves all of the nongarbage entries to the beginning of the array.

You can then add the remaining entries to the unused items at the end of the array. When you need to add more items to the list, you can reuse these entries to avoid resizing.

Adding the reclaimed garbage entries to the other unused entries may make the total amount of unused space quite large. In that case, you may want to resize the array to free some unused space.

```
procedure CollectGarbage;
var
    i, good : Longint;
begin
    good := 1; // The first good item goes here.
    for i := 1 to NumItems do
    begin
        // If not garbage, move it to its new location.
        if (not (List^[i] = GARBAGE_VALUE)) then
        begin
            if (good <> i) then
                List^[good] := List^[i];
            good := good + 1;
        end;
    end;

    // This is where the last good item is.
    NumItems := good - 1;
end;
```

When you perform garbage collection, you move items near the end of the list toward the beginning to fill in the space occupied by garbage entries. That means the positions of the items in the list may change during garbage collection. That in turn means other parts of the program cannot rely on the items in the list staying in their original positions. If other parts of the program must access items by their positions, you need to modify the garbage collection routine so it can update those other parts of the program. Generally, this sort of thing can be confusing and can lead to big maintenance problems later.

There are several ways you can decide when to run the garbage collector. One way is to wait until the array reaches a certain large size. For example, when a list contains 30,000 entries, you could run the garbage collector.

This method has some drawbacks. First, it uses a lot of memory. If you add and remove items frequently, you will fill a lot of array entries with garbage. If you waste enough memory like this, the program might spend time paging when the list could fit completely in real memory if you rearranged it sooner.

Second, if the list starts to fill with garbage, procedures that use it will become extremely inefficient. If an array of 30,000 items contains 25,000 pieces of garbage, a procedure like ShowItems described earlier would be terribly slow.

Finally, garbage collection for a very large array can take quite a bit of time, particularly if scanning the array causes your program to page. This may cause your program to freeze for several seconds while it cleans house.

To help solve this problem, you can create a new variable GarbageCount to keep track of the number of garbage items in the list. When a substantial fraction of the list's memory contains garbage, you can start garbage collection. In the following code, the MaxGarbage variable holds the maximum number of garbage entries the list is allowed to hold.

```
// Remove the last item from the list.
procedure Remove(index : Longint);
begin
    List^[index] := GARBAGE_VALUE;
    NumGarbage := NumGarbage + 1;
    if (NumGarbage > MaxGarbage) then CollectGarbage;
end;
```

Example program Garbage demonstrates these garbage collection techniques. It displays unused items in the list as <UNUSED> and entries marked as garbage with <GARBAGE>. The TGarbageList class the program uses is similar to the TSimpleList class used by program SimList, except it performs garbage collection.

Enter a value and click the Add button to add an item to the list. To remove an item, click on the item and then click the Remove button. When the list contains too much garbage, the program performs garbage collection.

Whenever the TGarbageList object resizes its list, it presents a message box that tells you the number of used and unused items in the list and the values of MaxGarbage and ShrinkWhen. If you remove enough items so that more than MaxGarbage items in the list contain garbage, the program runs the garbage collector. Once the garbage collector is finished, the program shrinks the array if it contains fewer than ShrinkWhen used items.

Program Garbage adds 50 percent of the current list size as empty entries when it must resize the array, and it always keeps a minimum of one empty entry when it resizes. These values were chosen so you can easily make the program resize the list. In a real program the percentage of free memory should be smaller and the minimum number of free entries should be larger. Values more like 10 percent free and a minimum of 10 entries would make more sense.

Linked Lists

Linked lists provide an alternative list management strategy. A linked list stores items in records or objects called *cells*. Each cell includes a pointer to the next cell in the list.

The cell record or class should define a NextCell variable that indicates the next cell in the linked list. It should also define variables to hold whatever data the program needs to manipulate. For example, in a linked list of employee records, these fields might store employee name, Social Security number, job title, and so forth. The definition of a TEmpCell record might look like the following:

```
type
    PEmpCell = ^TEmpCell;
    TEmpCell = record
        EmpName  : String * 20;
        SSN      : String * 11;
        JobTitle : String * 10;
        NextCell : PEmpCell;
    end;
```

A program uses the New statement to create new cells. It assigns their variable values and uses their NextCell variables to connect them.

The program should keep a pointer to the top of the list. So it can tell where the list ends, the program should set the NextCell value for last item to nil. For example, the following code fragment creates a list representing three employees.

```
var
    top_cell, cell1, cell2, cell3 : PEmpCell;
begin
    // Build the cells.
    New(cell1);
    cell1^.EmpName := 'Stephens';
    cell1^.SSN := '123-45-6789';
    cell1^.JobTitle := 'Author';

    New(cell2);
    cell2^.EmpName := 'Cats';
    cell2^.SSN := '234-56-7890';
    cell2^.JobTitle := 'Lawyer';

    New(cell3);
    cell3^.EmpName := 'Toole';
    cell3^.SSN := '345-67-8901';
    cell3^.JobTitle := 'Manager';

    // Connect the cells to make the linked list.
    cell1^.NextCell := cell2;
    cell2^.NextCell := cell3;
    cell3^.NextCell := nil;

    // Save a pointer to the top of the list.
    top_cell := cell1;
```

Figure 2.2 shows a schematic representation of this linked list. Boxes represent cells, and arrows represent pointers to objects. The small box with an X in it represents the value nil that marks the end of the list. Keep in mind that top_cell, cell1, cell2, and cell3 are not actually objects—they are pointers to objects.

The following code uses the linked list built by the previous example to show the names of the employees in the list. The variable ptr is used as a pointer to the items in the list. It starts at the top of the list. The code uses a while loop to move ptr through the list until it reaches the end. During each loop, the procedure prints the EmpName field for the cell pointed to by ptr. It then advances ptr to indicate the next cell in the list. Eventually, ptr reaches the end of the list and is set to nil, and the loop stops.

```
var
    ptr : PEmpCell;
begin
    ptr := top_cell;  // Start at the top of the list.
    while (ptr <> nil) do
    begin
        // Display this cell's EmpName field.
        ShowMessage(ptr^.EmpName);

        // Advance to the next cell in the list.
        ptr := ptr^.NextCell;
    end;
```

Using a pointer to point to another object is called *indirection* because you use the pointer to manipulate something indirectly. Indirection can be very confusing. Even for a simple arrangement like a linked list, it is sometimes hard to

Figure 2.2 A linked list.

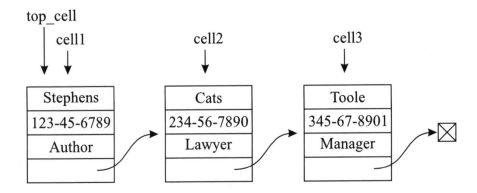

remember which pointer points to which object. In more complicated data structures such as trees and networks, a pointer may point to an object containing another pointer. With a couple of different pointers and several levels of indirection, you can easily become confused.

To make things a little easier, this book uses pictures such as Figure 2.2 to help you visualize the situation whenever possible. Many algorithms that use pointers are easy to describe using pictures like this one.

Adding Items to a Linked List

The simple linked list shown in Figure 2.2 has several important properties. First, it is very easy to add a new cell to the beginning of the list. Set the new cell's NextCell value so that it points to the current top of the list. Then set top_cell to point to the new cell. Figure 2.3 shows the picture corresponding to this operation. The Delphi code for this operation is quite simple:

```
new_cell^.NextCell := top_cell;
top_cell := new_cell;
```

Compare this to the code required to add a new item to the beginning of an array-based list. There you would need to move every entry in the array one space to make room for the new item. This O(N) operation could take a long time if the list is long. Using a linked list, you can insert a new item at the top of the list in just two steps.

It is also easy to insert a new item in the middle of a linked list. Suppose you want to insert a new item after the cell pointed to by variable after_me. Set the new cell's NextCell value to after_me^.NextCell. Then set after_me^.NextCell to point to the new cell. Figure 2.4 shows this operation graphically. Once again, the Delphi code is straightforward:

```
new_cell^.NextCell := after_me^.NextCell;
after_me^.NextCell := new_cell;
```

Figure 2.3 Adding an item to the top of a linked list.

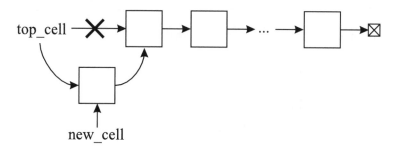

Figure 2.4 Adding an item to the middle of a linked list.

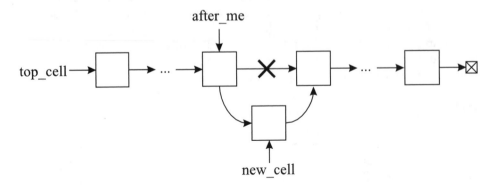

Removing Items from a Linked List

It is just as easy to remove an item from the top of a linked list as it is to add one:
Simply set top_cell to point to the next cell in the list. Figure 2.5 shows the picture corresponding to this operation. The source code for this operation is even simpler than the code for inserting an item.

```
top_cell := top_cell^.NextCell;
```

When top_cell is moved to the second item in the list, the program may no longer have any variable referencing the former first object. In that case, space for the object will remain allocated but inaccessible to the program. To prevent this, the program should save a pointer to the object in a temporary variable. After resetting top_cell, the program should use Dispose to free the object's memory.

```
target := top_cell;
top_cell := top_cell^.NextCell;
Dispose(target);
```

Removing an item from the middle of the list is also easy. Suppose you want to remove the item after the cell after_me. Simply set that cell's NextCell value to

Figure 2.5 Removing the top cell from a linked list.

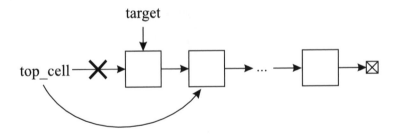

point to the following cell. Again you should use a temporary variable to dispose of the removed cell. Figure 2.6 shows this operation graphically. The Delphi code is straightforward:

```
target := after_me^.NextCell;
after_me^.NextCell := target^.NextCell;

Dispose(target);
```

Again you should compare this code to the code needed to perform the same operation using an array-based list. You can quickly mark a removed item as garbage, but this leaves garbage entries in the list. Procedures that manipulate the list must be complicated to take this into account. They may also be slowed by excessive garbage, and eventually you will need to run a garbage collector.

When you remove an item from a linked list, you create no gaps in the list. Procedures that manipulate the list still start from the top and follow the list to its end, so you do not need to modify those procedures.

Sentinels

The procedures for adding and removing items are different depending on whether you want to add or remove an item from the top or middle of the list. You can make both of these cases behave in the same way, and eliminate some redundant code, if you introduce a special *sentinel* cell at the very top of the list. The sentinel cell should never be removed. It contains no meaningful data—it is used only to mark the top of the list.

Now instead of having to deal with the odd case of adding an entry at the very top of the list, you can add the new item after the sentinel. Similarly, you do not need to worry about the special case of removing the first item in the list—you simply remove the item after the sentinel.

Using a sentinel makes a small difference now. Sentinels play important roles in many more complex algorithms. They allow a program to treat special cases, like dealing with the top of a list, as if they were nothing special. You can write and debug less code, and the algorithms are more consistent and easier to understand.

Table 2.1 compares the difficulty of performing some common operations using array-based lists with garbage collection and linked lists.

Figure 2.6 Removing an item from the middle of a linked list.

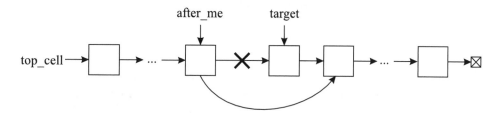

Table 2.1 Comparison of Array-Based Lists and Linked Lists

Operation	Array-Based	Linked
Add item at end	Easy	Easy
Add item at top	Hard	Easy
Add item in middle	Hard	Easy
Remove item from top	Easy	Easy
Remove item in middle	Easy	Easy
List nongarbage items	Medium	Easy

Linked lists are usually better, but the array-based list is superior in one area: memory usage. Linked lists require you to add an extra NextCell field to every data item. Each of these pointers takes an additional 4 bytes of memory. For very large lists, this may take up a lot of space.

Example program LList1 demonstrates a simple linked list with a sentinel. Enter a value in the text box, and click on an item in the list or on the sentinel. Then click the Add After button, and the program will add the new item after the one you selected. To remove an item from the list, click on an item and click the Remove After button.

Accessing Cells

The TLinkedList class used by program LList1 allows the main program to use the list much as it would use an array. For example, the Item procedure shown in the following code returns the value of an item given its position.

```
function TLinkedList.Item(index : Longint) : String10;
var
    cell_ptr : PLinkedListCell;
begin
    // Find the cell.
    cell_ptr := Sentinel.NextCell;
    while (index > 1) do
    begin
        index := index - 1;
        cell_ptr := cell_ptr^.NextCell;
    end;
    Item := cell_ptr^.Value;
end;
```

This procedure is fairly simple, but it does not take advantage of the list's linked structure. For example, suppose a program needs to examine each of the objects in the list in order. It could use the Item procedure to access the items one at a time, as shown in the following code.

```
var
    i : Integer;
begin
    for i := 1 to the_list.Count do
    begin
        // Do something with the_list.Item(i).
        :
    end;
```

Each time the Item procedure executes, it loops through the list looking for the next item. To find item I in the list, it must skip over $I - 1$ items. To examine every item in an N item list, it will skip over $0 + 1 + 2 + 3 + ... + N - 1 = N * (N - 1) / 2$ items. When N is large, the program will waste a large amount of time skipping items.

The TLinkedList class can make this operation faster using a different access scheme. It should use a private variable CurrentCell to keep track of its position in the list. It can then provide a CurrentItem function to return the value of the current cell. The MoveFirst and MoveNext procedures let the main program adjust the list's current position. The EndOfList function returns True when the current position has moved off the end of the list and CurrentCell is nil.

For example, the following code shows the MoveNext procedure.

```
procedure TLinkedList.MoveNext;
begin
    // If there's no current cell, do nothing.
    if (CurrentCell <> nil) then
        CurrentCell := CurrentCell.NextCell;
end;
```

Using these procedures, the main program can visit every item in the list using the following code. This code is slightly more complicated than the previous version, but it is much more efficient. Instead of skipping $N * (N - 1) / 2$ items to visit every cell in an N item list, this code skips no items. When the list contains 1000 items, this saves almost half a million steps.

```
the_list.MoveFirst

while (not the_list.EndOfList) do
begin
    // Do something with the_list.CurrentItem.
        :
    the_list.MoveNext
end;
```

Example program LList2 uses these new techniques to manage a linked list. The program is similar to program LList1 except that it accesses its list items more efficiently. For the small lists used by this program, the difference is unnoticeable. For a program that accesses every element in a large list, this version of the TLinkedList class is more efficient.

Linked List Variations

Linked lists play a part in many algorithms, and you will see them throughout the rest of this book. The following sections discuss a few specialized variations of linked lists.

Circular Linked Lists

Instead of setting the NextCell field of the last item in a list to nil, you could have it point back to the first item in the list. This makes a *circular list*, as shown in Figure 2.7.

Circular lists are useful when you need to loop through a set of data items indefinitely. At each step in the loop, the program simply moves a cell pointer to the next cell in the list. For example, suppose you had a circular list of items containing the names of the days of the week. Then a program could list the days of the month using the following code.

```
// Code to set up the list, etc. goes here.
      :
// Print a calendar for the month.
// first_day points to the cell for the first day of
// the month. num_days is the number of days in the month.
procedure ListMonth(first_day : PDayCell; num_days : Integer);
var
    ptr : PDayCell;
    i   : Integer;
begin
    ptr := first_day;
    for i := 1 to num_days do
```

Figure 2.7 A circular linked list.

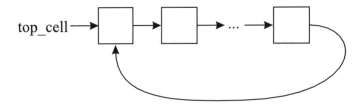

```
    begin
        PrintEntry(Format('%d : %s', [i, ptr^.Value]));
        ptr := ptr^.NextCell;
    end;
end;
```

Circular lists also allow you to reach the entire list starting from any position. This gives the list an appealing symmetry. The program can treat all the items in the list in pretty much the same way.

```
procedure ShowList(start_cell : PListCell);
var
    ptr : PListCell;
begin
    ptr := start_cell;
    repeat
        ShowMessage(ptr^.Value);
        ptr := ptr^.NextCell;
    until (ptr = start_cell);
end;
```

Doubly Linked Lists

You may have noticed during the discussion of linked lists that most operations were defined in terms of doing something *after* a particular cell in the list. Given a particular cell, it is easy to add a new cell after it, delete the cell after it, or list all the cells that come after it. It is not as easy to delete the cell itself, to insert a new cell before the cell, or to list the cells that come before it. With only a small change, however, you can make these operations easy, too.

Add a new pointer field to each cell pointing to the *previous* cell in the list. Using the new fields you can create a *doubly linked list* that lets you move forward and backward through the items. Now you can easily delete a cell, insert before a cell, and list cells in either direction. Figure 2.8 shows a picture of a doubly linked list.

A TDoubleListCell record type used for this kind of list might be defined by the following code:

```
type
    PDoubleListCell = ^TDoubleListCell;
    TDoubleListCell = record
        Value    : String * 20;
        NextCell : PDoubleListCell;
        PrevCell : PDoubleListCell;
    end;
```

Figure 2.8 A doubly linked list.

It is often useful to keep pointers to both the top and bottom of a doubly linked list. Then you can easily add items at either end of the list. It is also sometimes useful to have sentinels at both the top and bottom of the list. Then as you manipulate the list, you need not care whether you are working on the top, middle, or bottom of the list.

Figure 2.9 shows a doubly linked list with sentinels. In this picture, the sentinels' unused NextCell and PrevCell pointers are set to nil. Because the program recognizes the ends of the list by comparing cell pointers to the sentinels rather than by looking for the value nil, setting these values to nil is not absolutely necessary. It is still a good practice, however.

The code for inserting and removing items from a doubly linked list is similar to the code presented earlier for dealing with a singly linked list. The procedures need to be changed only slightly to handle the PrevCell pointers.

You can now write new procedures to add an item before or after a given item and to delete a particular item. For example, the following procedures add and remove cells in a doubly linked list. Notice that these procedures do not need to access either of the list's sentinels. All they need are pointers to the node to be added or removed and a node near the point of insertion.

```
procedure Remove(target : PDoubleListCell);
var
    after_target, before_target : PDoubleListCell;
begin
    after_target := target^.NextCell;
    before_target := target^.PrevCell;
    before_target^.NextCell := after_target;
    after_target^.PrevCell := before_target;
end;
```

Figure 2.9 A doubly linked list with sentinels.

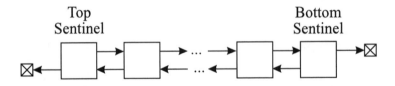

```
procedure AddAfter(new_cell, after_me : PDoubleListCell);
var
    before_me : PDoubleListCell;
begin
    before_me := after_me^.NextCell;
    after_me^.NextCell := new_cell;
    new_cell^.NextCell := before_me;
    before_me^.PrevCell := new_cell;
    new_cell^.PrevCell := after_me;
end;

procedure AddBefore(new_cell, before_me : PDoubleListCell);
var
    after_me : PDoubleListCell;
begin
    after_me := before_me^.PrevCell;
    after_me^.NextCell := new_cell;
    new_cell^.NextCell := before_me;
    before_me^.PrevCell := new_cell;
    new_cell^.PrevCell := after_me;
end;
```

Example program DblList manipulates a doubly linked list. It allows you to add items before or after a selected item, and it lets you delete a selected item.

Threaded Lists

In some applications, it is useful to traverse a linked list using more than one possible ordering. In different parts of an application you might want to list employees ordered by their last names, salaries, Social Security numbers, or job classifications.

Normal linked lists allow you to examine the items in one order only. Using a PrevCell pointer, you can create a doubly linked list that allows you to move forward or backward through the list. You can extend this idea further by adding more pointers to the data structure to allow you to display the list in still other orders.

The set of links that makes up one of these orderings is called a *thread*. Do not confuse this term with the multiprocessing threads provided by Windows NT.

A list can contain any number of threads, though at some point, the extra work of maintaining the threads is not worth the effort. A thread ordering employees by last name would make sense if your application uses that ordering frequently. A thread ordering employees by middle initial would probably not be useful because your program would probably never use it.

Some orderings do not make good threads. A thread ordering employees by gender, for example, would not be a good thread because the ordering is easy to obtain without it. To list the employees ordered by gender without the thread, you simply traverse the list along any other thread while printing out the names of the female employees. Then you traverse the list again printing out the names of the male employees. You would need only two passes through the list to produce this ordering.

Compare this to the case where you want to list employees ordered by their last names. If the list did not include a last name thread, you would have to search the list for the name that came first, then search for the name that came second, and so forth. This is an $O(N^2)$ process that is much less efficient than the $O(N)$ method for ordering employees by gender.

Generally, an ordering will make a good thread if you need to use it often and if it would be hard to build the same ordering whenever you need it. An ordering will make a bad thread if it is easy to recreate.

Example program Threads demonstrates a simple threaded employee list. Fill in the last name, first name, Social Security number, job class, and gender fields for a new employee. Then click the Add button to add the new employee to the list.

The program contains threads that order the list by employee last name forward and backward, by Social Security number, and by job classification forward and backward. You can use the option buttons to select the thread by which the program displays the list. Figure 2.10 shows program Threads listing employees ordered by name.

Figure 2.10 Program Threads.

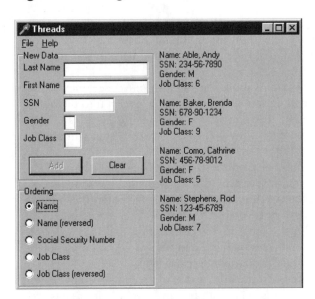

The TThreadedList class used by program Threads uses cells defined by the following code:

```
TThreadedListCell = record
    // The data.
    LastName     : String[20];
    FirstName    : String[20];
    SSN          : String[11];
    Gender       : String[1];
    JobClass     : Integer;

    // Thread pointers.
    NextName      : PThreadedListCell;
    PrevName      : PThreadedListCell;
    NextSSN       : PThreadedListCell;
    NextJobClass  : PThreadedListCell;
    PrevJobClass  : PThreadedListCell;
end;
```

The TThreadedList class encapsulates the threaded list. When the program uses the Add procedure, the list updates all of its threads. For each thread, the program must insert the new item in its proper order. To insert a record with last name "Smith," for example, the program loops through the list using the NextName thread until it finds an item with a name that should come after "Smith." It then inserts the new entry in the NextName thread before that item.

Sentinels play an important role in finding where new entries belong in the threads. The class constructor initializes the top and bottom sentinels' pointers so they point to each other. It sets the data values for the top sentinel so they come before any valid real entries for all the threads.

For example, The LastName variable can contain string values. The empty string "" comes alphabetically before all valid string values, so the program sets the top sentinel's LastName value to the empty string.

Similarly, the constructor sets the data values for the bottom sentinel to be bigger than any valid values in all of the threads. Because "~" comes alphabetically after all other visible ASCII characters, the program sets the bottom sentinel's LastName value to "~~~~~~~~~~~~~~~~~~~~."

By giving the sentinels these LastName values, the program avoids the need to check for special cases where a new item should be inserted at the top or bottom of the list. All valid new values will fall between the sentinels' LastName values, so the program will always find the new item's correct position without worrying about searching past the bottom sentinel and falling off the list.

The following code shows how the TThreadedList class inserts a new item in the threads. Because the LastName and PrevName threads use the same key, the program can update them at the same time. Similarly, it can update the NextJobClass and PrevJobClass threads at the same time.

```
procedure TThreadedList.Add(new_last_name, new_first_name,
    new_ssn, new_gender : String; new_job_class : Integer);
var
    cell_ptr, new_cell : PThreadedListCell;
    combined_name      : String;
begin
    // Create the new cell.
    New(new_cell);
    new_cell.LastName  := new_last_name;
    new_cell.FirstName := new_first_name;
    new_cell.SSN := new_ssn;
    new_cell.Gender := new_gender;
    new_cell.JobClass := new_job_class;

    // Insert in the name threads.
    // Find the cell after this one.
    cell_ptr := @TopSentinel;
    combined_name := Format('%s, %s',
        [new_last_name, new_first_name]);
    while (Format('%s, %s', [cell_ptr^.LastName, cell_ptr^.FirstName])
        < combined_name) do
            cell_ptr := cell_ptr^.NextName;
    new_cell^.NextName := cell_ptr;
    new_cell^.PrevName := cell_ptr^.PrevName;
    new_cell^.PrevName^.NextName := new_cell;
    cell_ptr^.PrevName := new_cell;

    // Insert in the SSN thread.
    // Find the cell before this one.
    cell_ptr := @TopSentinel;
    while (cell_ptr^.NextSSN^.SSN < new_ssn) do
        cell_ptr := cell_ptr^.NextSSN;
    new_cell^.NextSSN := cell_ptr^.NextSSN;
    cell_ptr^.NextSSN := new_cell;

    // Insert in the job class threads.
    // Find the cell before this one.
    cell_ptr := @TopSentinel;
    while (cell_ptr^.JobClass < new_job_class) do
        cell_ptr := cell_ptr^.NextJobClass;
    new_cell^.NextJobClass := cell_ptr;
    new_cell^.PrevJobClass := cell_ptr^.PrevJobClass;
    new_cell^.PrevJobClass^.NextJobClass := new_cell;
```

```
    cell_ptr^.PrevJobClass := new_cell;

    NumItems := NumItems + 1;
end;
```

For this to work, the program must ensure that the new cell's values always lie between the sentinel values. For example, if a user somehow managed to enter a name value greater than the bottom sentinel's name value, the loop would run past the bottom sentinel. The program would then crash when it tried to access the value cell_ptr^.LastName when cell_ptr was set to nil.

Other Linked Structures

Using pointers you can build many other useful kinds of linked structures such as trees, irregular arrays, sparse arrays, graphs, and networks. A cell can contain any number of pointers to other cells. For example, you could use a cell containing two pointers, one to a right child cell and one to a left child cell, to create a binary tree. A BinaryCell record can be defined as in the following code:

```
type
    PBinaryCell = ^TBinaryCell;
    TBinaryCell = record
        LeftChild  : PBinaryCell;
        RightChild : PBinaryCell;
    end;
```

Figure 2.11 shows a tree built from this kind of cell. Chapter 6, "Trees," has much more to say about trees.

A cell can even contain a linked list of cells, each containing a pointer to another cell. This allows a program to link a cell to any number of other cells. Figure 2.12 shows examples of other linked data structures. You will see structures like these later, particularly in Chapter 12, "Network Algorithms."

Figure 2.11 A binary tree.

Figure 2.12 Linked structures.

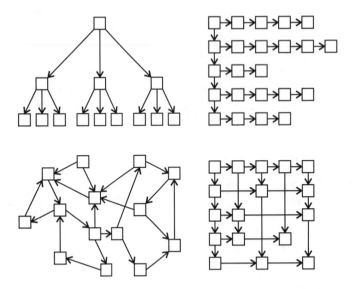

Summary

Using pointers, you can build flexible data structures such as linked lists, circular linked lists, and doubly linked lists. These lists allow you to add and remove items quickly from any position in the list.

By adding extra pointers to a cell class, you can extend the ideas used by doubly linked lists to create threaded lists. Extending these ideas still further, you can create more exotic data structures including sparse arrays, trees, hash tables, and networks. These are described in detail in the following chapters.

3

STACKS AND QUEUES

This chapter continues the discussion of lists started in Chapter 2, "Lists," by describing two special kinds of lists: stacks and queues. A stack is a list in which items are added and removed from the same end of the list. A queue is a list in which items are added to one end and removed from the other. Many algorithms, including several presented in later chapters, use stacks and queues.

Stacks

A *stack* is an ordered list where items are always added and removed from the same end of the list. You can think of a *stack* as a stack of objects on the floor. You can add items to the top and remove them from the top, but you cannot add or remove an item from the middle of the pile.

Because of their Last-In-First-Out behavior, stacks are sometimes called *LIFO lists* or *LIFOs*. For historical reasons, adding an item to a stack is called *pushing* the item onto the stack, and removing an item from a stack is called *popping* the item off the stack.

The first array-based implementation of a simple list described at the beginning of Chapter 2, "Lists," is a stack. You use a counter to keep track of where the top of the list is. You then use that counter to add and remove items from the top of the list.

The only minor change made here is that Pop, the function that removes an item from the stack, returns the value of the removed item. This makes it a little easier for other procedures to retrieve an item and remove it from the stack in one step. Other than this change, the following code is similar to the list code presented in Chapter 2.

```
// Push an item onto the stack.
procedure TArrayStack.Push(value : String10);
begin
    // Make sure there's room for the new item.
    if (NumItems >= NumAllocated) then ResizeStack;
    NumItems := NumItems + 1;
```

```
        Stack^[NumItems] := value;
end;
```

```
// Pop the last item from the stack.
function TArrayStack.Pop : String10;
begin
    if (NumItems < 1) then
        raise EInvalidOperation.Create(
            'The stack is empty.');

    Result := Stack^[NumItems];
    NumItems := NumItems - 1;
    if (NumItems < ShrinkWhen) then ResizeStack;
end;
```

All of the previous discussion about lists also applies to this sort of stack implementation. In particular, you can save time if you do not resize the array every time you push or pop an item. Example program AStack uses several array-based stacks. Using the program, you can push and pop items onto and off of each of the stacks.

Programs often use stacks to hold a sequence of items that the program will manipulate until the stack is empty. Operating on one item might cause others to be pushed onto the stack, but eventually, they will all be removed. A simple example is an algorithm to reverse the order of the items in an array. Here each item is pushed onto the stack in order. Then each item is popped off the stack in reverse order and written back into the array.

```
procedure ReverseArray;
var
    the_stack : TArrayStack;
    i         : Integer;
begin
    // Create the stack.
    the_stack := TArrayStack.Create;

    // Push the items onto the stack.
    for i := 1 to NumItems do
        the_stack.Push(the_array[i]);

    // Pop the items from the stack back into the array.
    for i := 1 to NumItems do
        the_array[i] := the_stack.Pop;
end;
```

In this example, the stack may change length many times before it is eventually emptied. If you know ahead of time how big the array needs to be, you can avoid these resizings by making the stack big enough to hold all the items at the start. Instead of resizing the stack as it grows and shrinks, you can allocate it at the beginning and destroy it when you are finished.

The following code lets you preallocate a stack if you know how large it must be. The Pop function does not resize the array. When the program finishes using the stack, it should use the FreeStack procedure to deallocate all of the stack's memory at once.

```
// Make an array big enough for the stack.
procedure TArrayStack.PreallocateStack(entries : Integer);
begin
    NumAllocated := entries;
    GetMem(Stack, NumAllocated * SizeOf(Longint));
end;


// Free the Stack array.
procedure TSimpleStack.FreeStack;
begin
    NumAllocated := 0;
    FreeMem(Stack);
end;


// Push an item onto the stack.
procedure TArrayStack.Push(value : String10);
begin
    // Make sure there's room for the new item.
    if (NumItems >= NumAllocated) then
        raise EInvalidOperation.Create(
            'The stack is full.');

    NumItems := NumItems + 1;
    Stack^[NumItems] := value;
end;


// Pop the last item from the stack.
function TArrayStack.Pop : String10;
begin
    if (NumItems < 1) then
        raise EInvalidOperation.Create(
            'The stack is empty.');

    Result := Stack^[NumItems];
    NumItems := NumItems - 1;
end;
```

This sort of stack implementation is quite efficient. The stack does not waste much memory, and it does not waste time resizing frequently.

Linked List Stacks

You can manage two stacks in the same array by placing one at the top of the array and the other at the bottom. Keep separate Top counters for the two stacks, and make the stacks grow toward each other, as shown in Figure 3.1. This method allows the two stacks to grow into the same memory until they bump into each other when the array is completely full.

Unfortunately, resizing these sorts of stacks is not very efficient. You must allocate a new stack array and copy all of the items from the old array into the new one. For large stacks, this can be time consuming. This method is also difficult to extend for more than two stacks.

Linked lists provide a more flexible method for building multiple stacks. To push an item onto a stack, you insert it at the top of its linked list. To pop an item off a stack, you remove the first item from the linked list. Because all items are added and removed from the top of the list, you do not need sentinels or doubly linked lists to implement this sort of stack. Linked list stacks also do not require complicated array reallocation schemes like array-based stacks. The following code shows the Push and Pop routines used by a linked list stack class.

```
// Add an item to the stack.
procedure TStack.Push(new_value : String10);
var
    new_cell : PStackCell;
begin
    // Create the new cell.
    New(new_cell);
    new_cell^.Value := new_value;

    // Insert the cell at the top of the stack.
    new_cell^.NextCell := Top;
    Top := new_cell;
end;
```

Figure 3.1 Two stacks in the same array.

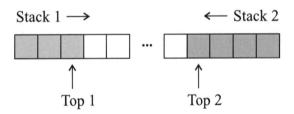

```
// Remove the first item from the stack.
function TStack.Pop : String10;
var
    target : PStackCell;
begin
    if (Top = nil) then
        raise EInvalidOperation.Create(
            'Cannot pop items from an empty stack.');

    // Save the return value;.
    target := Top;
    Pop := target^.Value;

    // Remove the first cell from the stack.
    Top := target^.NextCell;

    // Free the target cell's memory.
    Dispose(target);
end;
```

The main drawback to linked list stacks is that they require extra memory for the cells' NextCell pointers. A single array-based stack containing N integers requires only 2 * N bytes of memory (2 bytes per integer). The same stack implemented as a linked list would require an additional 4 * N bytes of memory for the NextCell pointers, tripling the memory needed by the stack.

Example program LStack uses several stacks implemented as linked lists. Using the program, you can push and pop items onto and off of each of the lists.

Queues

A *queue* is an ordered list where items are added at one end of the list and removed from the other. A group of people waiting in a store checkout line is a queue. New arrivals enter at the back of the line. When a customer reaches the front of the line, the cashier helps that customer. Due to their First-In-First-Out nature, queues are sometimes called *FIFO lists* or *FIFOs*.

You can implement queues in Delphi using techniques similar to the ones used to implement simple stacks. Allocate an array and keep counters that indicate where the top and bottom of the queue are. QueueFront indicates the index of the item at the front of the queue. QueueBack indicates where the next new item should be added to the queue. As items enter and leave the queue, you resize the queue array when new items run to the end of the array.

As is the case with lists, you can improve performance by adding more than one new item whenever you enlarge the array. You can also save time by shrinking the array only when it contains a large number of unused entries.

In a simple list or stack, you add items to one end of the array and remove them from the same end. If the list stays roughly the same size, you might not have to resize it too often. On the other hand, because you add items at one end of a queue and remove them from the other, you must occasionally rearrange a queue even if its total size stays the same.

```
// Add an item to the queue.
procedure TArrayQueue.EnterQueue(new_value : String10);
begin
    // Make sure there's room for the new item.
    if (AddHere >= NumAllocated) then ResizeQueue;
    Queue^[AddHere] := new_value;
    AddHere := AddHere + 1;
end;


// Remove the last item from the list.
function TArrayQueue.LeaveQueue : String10;
begin
    if (QueueEmpty) then
        raise EInvalidOperation.Create(
            'No items to remove.');

    LeaveQueue := Queue^[RemoveHere];
    RemoveHere := RemoveHere + 1;
    if (RemoveHere > ResizeWhen) then ResizeQueue;
end;


// Resize the queue.
procedure TArrayQueue.ResizeQueue;
const
    WANT_FREE_PERCENT = 0.5; // Try for 50% free space.
    MIN_FREE = 2;            // Min unused space when resizing.
var
    want_free, new_size, i : Longint;
    new_array              : PQueueArray;
begin
    // See how big the array should be.
    new_size := AddHere - RemoveHere;
    want_free := Round(WANT_FREE_PERCENT * new_size);
    if (want_free < MIN_FREE) then want_free := MIN_FREE;
    new_size := new_size + want_free;

    // Create a new array.
    GetMem(new_array, new_size * SizeOf(String10));
```

```
// Copy the existing items into the new array.
for i := RemoveHere to AddHere - 1 do
    new_array^[i - RemoveHere] := Queue^[i];
AddHere := AddHere - RemoveHere;
RemoveHere := 0;

// Free the previously allocated memory.
if (NumAllocated > 0) then FreeMem(Queue);
NumAllocated := new_size;

// Make Queue point to the new memory.
Queue := new_array;

// We resize when RemoveHere > ResizeWhen.
ResizeWhen := want_free;
end;
```

Example program ArrayQ uses this method to implement a simple queue. Enter a string and click the Enter button to add a new item to the end of the queue. Click the Leave button to remove the top item from the queue.

As you run the program, notice that the queue requires resizing when you add and remove items from the queue, even if the total queue size does not change much. In fact, the queue will resize even if you repeatedly add and remove a single item.

Circular Queues

The queues described in the previous section require occasional rearrangement even if the total queue size does not change much. The queue will require rearrangement even if you repeatedly add and remove a single item.

If you know in advance how large a queue might need to be, you can avoid all this reorganizing by creating a *circular queue*. The idea is to treat the queue's array as if it wraps around to form a circle. You treat the last item in the array as if it comes just before the first item. Figure 3.2 shows a circular queue.

A program can use variable RemoveHere to hold the index of the item that has been in the queue the longest. It can use variable AddHere to hold the index of the position in the queue array where the next item should be added.

Unlike in the previous implementation, when the program updates QueueFront and QueueBack, it should use the Mod operator to make the indexes stay within the bounds of the array. For example, the following code adds an item to the queue.

```
Queue^[AddHere] := new_value;
AddHere := (AddHere + 1) mod NumAllocated;
```

Figure 3.2 A circular queue.

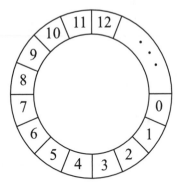

Figure 3.3 shows the process of adding a new item to a circular queue that can hold four entries. Here the item C is added at the position indicated by AddHere. AddHere is then advanced to point to the next entry in the array.

Similarly when a program removes an item from the queue, it should update RemoveHere with code like this:

```
LeaveQueue  := Queue^[RemoveHere];
RemoveHere  := (RemoveHere + 1) mod NumAllocated;
```

Figure 3.4 shows the process of removing an item from a circular queue. The first item, in this case the item A, is removed from the front of the queue, and RemoveHere is updated so that it indicates the next item in the array.

Telling the difference between a full queue and an empty one can be a little tricky with circular queues. In both cases, RemoveHere will equal AddHere. Figure 3.5 shows two circular queues, one empty and one full.

Figure 3.3 Adding an item to a circular queue.

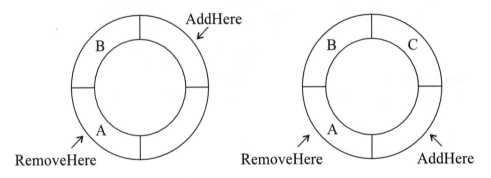

Figure 3.4 Removing an item from a circular queue.

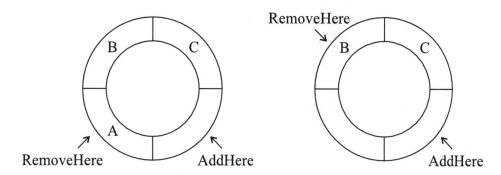

An easy way to solve this problem is to keep track of the number of items in the queue using a separate variable NumItems. This count tells whether there are any items to remove from the queue and whether there is room in the queue to add new items.

The following code uses all of these techniques to manage a circular queue.

```
// Add an item to the queue.
procedure TCircleQueue.EnterQueue(new_value : String10);
begin
    if (NumItems >= NumAllocated) then ResizeQueue;

    Queue^[AddHere] := new_value;
    AddHere := (AddHere + 1) mod NumAllocated;
    NumItems := NumItems + 1;
end;
```

Figure 3.5 Empty and full circular queues.

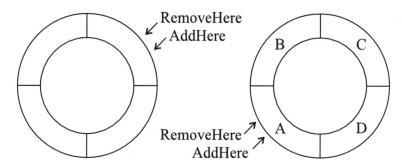

```
// Remove the top item from the queue.
function TCircleQueue.LeaveQueue : String10;
begin
    if (QueueEmpty) then
        raise EInvalidOperation.Create(
            'No items to remove.');

    LeaveQueue := Queue^[RemoveHere];
    RemoveHere := (RemoveHere + 1) mod NumAllocated;
    NumItems := NumItems - 1;
    if (NumItems < ShrinkWhen) then ResizeQueue;
end;

// Return true if the queue is empty.
function TCircleQueue.QueueEmpty : Boolean;
begin
    QueueEmpty := (NumItems <= 0);
end;
```

As is the case with array-based lists, you can resize this array if the queue fills completely or if the array contains too much unused space. Resizing a circular queue, however, is more difficult than resizing an array-based list or stack.

When you resize the array, the list of items currently in the queue may wrap around the end of the array. If you simply enlarge the array, the newly inserted items will be at the end of the array so that they will fall into the middle of the list. Figure 3.6 shows what would happen if you enlarged the array in this way.

Similar problems occur if you simply shrink the array. If the items wrap past the end of the array, you will lose the items at the end of the array that are near

Figure 3.6 Incorrectly enlarging a circular queue.

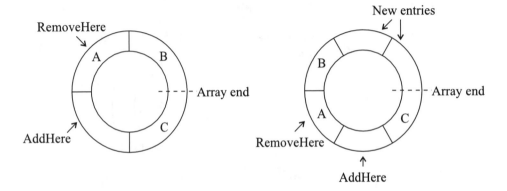

the front of the queue. To avoid these difficulties, you must be certain you copy the queue entries into their correct positions in the new queue array.

```
// Resize the queue.
procedure TCircleQueue.ResizeQueue;
const
    WANT_FREE_PERCENT = 0.5;  // Try for 50% free space.
    MIN_FREE = 2;             // Min unused space when resizing.
var
    want_free, new_size, i : Integer;
    new_array              : PCircleQueueArray;
begin
    // Create the new array.
    want_free := Round(WANT_FREE_PERCENT * NumItems);
    if (want_free < MIN_FREE) then want_free := MIN_FREE;
    new_size := NumItems + want_free;
    GetMem(new_array, new_size * SizeOf(String10));

    // Copy the items into positions new_array[0]
    // through new_array[NumItems - 1].
    for i := 0 to NumItems - 1 do
        new_array^[i] :=
            Queue^[(i + RemoveHere) mod NumAllocated];

    // Free the previously allocated memory.
    if (NumAllocated > 0) then FreeMem(Queue);
    NumAllocated := new_size;

    // Make Queue point to the new memory.
    Queue := new_array;

    RemoveHere := 0;
    AddHere := NumItems;

    // We will resize when NumItems < ShrinkWhen.
    ShrinkWhen := NumAllocated - 2 * want_free;
    if (ShrinkWhen < 3) then ShrinkWhen := 0;
end;
```

Example program CircleQ demonstrates this technique for implementing a circular queue. Enter a string and click the Enter button to add a new item to the queue. Click the Leave button to remove the top item from the queue. The program will resize its queue array when necessary.

Although resizing the queue is a bit of work, resizing will happen infrequently if the total number of items in the queue does not change much. If you set the resizing parameters correctly, you may never need to resize the array.

Linked List-Based Queues

A completely different approach to implementing queues is to use doubly linked lists. You can use sentinels to keep track of the top and bottom of the list. Add new items to the queue just before the bottom sentinel and remove items leaving the queue from just after the top sentinel. Figure 3.7 shows a doubly linked list used as a queue.

It is easy to add and remove items from a doubly linked list, so you never need complicated resizing algorithms. This method also has the advantage that it is a bit more intuitive than the circular array queue. It has the drawback that it requires extra memory to hold the linked list's NextCell and PrevCell pointers. This makes linked list queues a bit less space efficient than circular queues.

Example program LinkedQ manages a queue using a doubly linked list. Enter a string and click the Enter button to add the new item to the bottom of the queue. Click the Leave button to remove the top item from the queue.

Priority Queues

Each item in a *priority queue* has an associated priority. When the program needs to remove an item from the queue, it selects the item with the highest priority. It does not matter how the items in a priority queue are stored, as long as the program can always find the highest priority item when it is needed.

Some operating systems use priority queues for job scheduling. In the UNIX operating system, each process can have a different priority. When the computer is ready to run, it selects the highest priority process that is ready to execute.

Figure 3.7 A linked list queue.

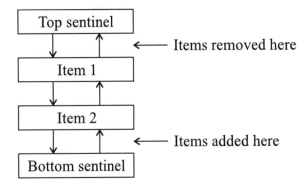

Lower priority processes must wait until all of the higher processes have finished or are blocked, waiting for some external event like a data read on a disk drive.

Air traffic control also uses a priority queue concept. Planes that are trying to land and are running out of fuel have top priority. Other planes trying to land have second priority. Planes on the ground have third priority because they are in a safer position than planes in the air. Over time, some of the priorities might change because planes trying to land will eventually run low on fuel.

One simple way to build a priority queue is to keep all the items in a list. When you need to remove an item from the queue, you can search the list to see which item has the highest priority. To add an item to the queue, you place the new item at the top of the list. Using this method, it takes one step to add a new item to the queue. If the queue holds N items, it takes O(N) steps to locate and remove the highest priority item from the queue.

A slightly better scheme is to use a linked list and keep the items sorted in order of decreasing priority. The TPriorityCell data type for the list might use the following declaration:

```
type
    String10 = String[10];
    PPriorityQCell = ^TPriorityQCell;
    TPriorityQCell = record
        Value    : String10;        // The data.
        Priority : Longint;         // The item's priority.
        NextCell : PPriorityQCell;  // The next cell.
    end;
```

To add an item to the queue, search through the list until you find the position where the new item belongs and insert it at that position. To make it easier to find the item's correct position, you can use top and bottom sentinels with appropriate priorities. For example, if the items will have priorities between 0 and 100, you could give the top sentinel priority 101 and the bottom sentinel priority –1. Any real priorities will fall between these values.

Figure 3.8 shows a priority queue implemented using a linked list.

Figure 3.8 A linked list priority queue.

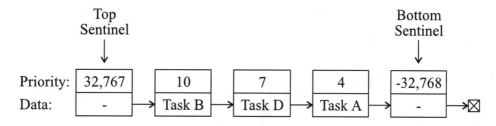

The following code fragment shows the heart of this search routine.

```
var
    new_cell, cell_ptr, next_cell : PPriorityQCell;
begin
        :
    // See where the new cell belongs.
    cell_ptr := @TopSentinel;
    next_cell := cell_ptr^.NextCell;
    while (next_cell^.Priority > new_priority) do
    begin
        cell_ptr := next_cell;
        next_cell := cell_ptr^.NextCell;
    end;

    // Insert the new cell.
    cell_ptr^.NextCell := new_cell;
    new_cell^.NextCell := next_cell;
        :
```

To remove the highest priority item from the list, you simply remove the item after the top sentinel. Because the list is kept sorted in priority order, the top item always has the highest priority.

Adding a new item to this queue takes an average of N / 2 steps. Sometimes the new item will go near the top of the list, and sometimes it will go near the bottom, but on average it will fall somewhere in the middle. The previous simple list-based priority queue required O(1) step to insert a new item into the queue and O(N) steps to remove the highest priority items from the queue. The sorted linked list version requires O(N) steps to add an item to the queue and O(1) step to remove the top item. Both versions require O(N) steps for one of these operations, but the sorted linked list queue needs only N / 2 steps on the average.

Example program PriorQ uses a sorted linked list to manage a priority queue. Fill in priority and data values and click the Enter button to add a new item to the priority queue. Click the Leave button to remove the highest priority item from the queue.

With some extra work, you can build a priority queue where insertion and deletion both take O(log(N)) steps. For very large queues, the added speed is worth the extra effort. This sort of priority queue uses the *heap* data structure used by the sorting algorithm heapsort. Heaps and heap-based priority queues are discussed in more detail in Chapter 9, "Sorting."

Multi-Headed Queues

Another interesting type of queue is the *multi-headed queue*. Items enter the queue at the rear as usual, but the queue has more than one *front end* or *head*. The program may remove items from any of the heads.

An everyday example of a multi-headed queue is the customer service counter at a bank. All of the customers stand in a single line, but they are served by several tellers. The next available teller serves the customer at the front of the line. This sort of queue seems fair because the tellers serve customers in their order of arrival. It is also efficient because all of the tellers stay busy as long as any customers are waiting in the queue.

Compare this sort of queue to the multiple single-headed queues used in a grocery store. Here people are not necessarily served in arrival order. One person in a slow line may wait longer than someone who arrived later but got in a faster line. The cashiers may not always be busy either because one line could empty completely while people wait in other lines.

Generally, multi-headed queues are more efficient than multiple single-headed queues. The latter are used in grocery stores because shopping carts take up a lot of space. A multi-headed queue would force customers to stand in a single line that would take up a lot of room. When a cashier was available, the customer at the front of the line would need to maneuver a bulky shopping cart across the front of the store to the cashier. This could be difficult. In a bank, on the other hand, the customers do not have large shopping carts to push around, so it is easy for them to stand in a single line.

Some airport check-in counters have a combination of both situations. Their customers have large amounts of baggage to push around, but the airline still uses a multi-headed queue. They are willing to give up the extra space needed to create a large single line for their customers.

It is easy to build a multi-headed queue using a normal single-headed queue. Store the items representing customers or whatever in a normal single-headed queue. When an agent (teller, cashier, etc.) becomes available, remove the first item from the front of the queue and assign it to that agent.

A Queue Simulation

Suppose you are in charge of designing a check-in counter for a new airline terminal and you want to compare a single multi-headed queue to multiple single-headed queues. You would need some sort of model of customer behavior. For this example, you might make the following assumptions:

- Each customer requires between two and five minutes at the counter.

- When customers arrive in multiple single-headed queues, they enter the queue that is currently the shortest.

- Customers arrive at roughly a constant rate.

Example program HeadedQ runs a simulation to model this situation. You can modify a number of simulation parameters including the following:

- Number of customers arriving per hour

- Minimum and maximum time needed by customers

- Number of clerks available
- Milliseconds the program pauses between simulation steps

When you run the simulation, the program shows you the elapsed simulated time, the average and maximum amounts of time customers have to wait for service, and the percentage of time the clerks are busy.

As you experiment with different parameters, you will notice several interesting things. First, the multi-headed queue gives lower average and maximum waiting times for the customers. It also keeps the clerks slightly busier than the single-headed queue.

Both kinds of queue have a threshold beyond which customer waiting times increase dramatically. Suppose you indicate that customers need between 2 and 10 minutes each, or 6 minutes on average. If you specify 60 customers per hour, then the clerks must provide about 6 * 60 = 360 minutes of service per hour to satisfy all of the customers. Because each clerk can provide 60 minutes of service per hour, the program needs 6 clerks to satisfy the customers.

If you run program HeadedQ with those parameters, you will find that the queues do quite well. The multi-headed queue has an average wait time of only a few minutes. If you add another clerk so there is a total of 7, the average and maximum wait times decrease dramatically. The average wait for the multi-headed queue drops to about a tenth of a minute.

On the other hand, if you decrease the number of clerks to 5, the average and maximum waiting times show a large increase. The times also increase over time. The longer the simulation runs, the longer the waits become.

Table 3.1 shows the average and maximum wait times for the 2 different kinds of queues. Here the program ran for 3 simulated hours and assumed 60 customers per hour requiring between 2 and 10 minutes each.

The multi-headed queue also seems more fair than the single-headed queues because customers are served in arrival order. Figure 3.9 shows the HeadedQ program after it has run for two simulated hours. In the multi-headed queue, customer 93 is next in line. All the customers who arrived before customer 93 have

Table 3.1 Waiting Times (Minutes) in Single- and Multi-Headed Queues

Clerks	Multi-Headed Queue		Single-Headed Queue	
	Avg Time	Max Time	Avg Time	Max Time
5	11.37	20	12.62	20
6	1.58	5	3.93	13
7	0.11	2	0.54	6

Figure 3.9 Program HeadedQ.

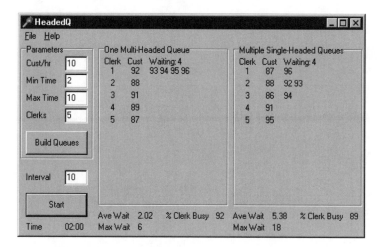

already been, or are currently being, served. In the single-headed queue, customer 95 is being served. Customers 92, 93, and 94 are still waiting even though they arrived before customer 95.

Summary

Different stack and queue implementations offer different features. Array-based stacks and circular queues are simple and efficient, particularly if you know in advance how large a stack or queue will need to be. Linked lists provide more flexibility if the size must change frequently. Once you know your application's requirements, you can pick the stack or queue structure that best meets your needs.

ARRAYS

4

This chapter describes array data structures. Using Delphi, you can easily build arrays of standard or user-defined data types. Using a pointer to an array, you can even redimension the array later using the GetMem statement. These features make Delphi's arrays very useful.

Some programs use specialized types of arrays that are not directly supported by Delphi. These include triangular arrays, irregular arrays, and sparse arrays. This chapter explains how you can use flexible array structures that can greatly reduce your program's memory usage.

Triangular Arrays

Some programs need values for only half the entries in a two-dimensional array. For example, suppose you have a map with 10 cities on it numbered from 0 to 9. You can use an array to make an *adjacency matrix* indicating whether there is a highway between any pair of cities. The A[i, j] entry is True if there is a highway between city i and city j.

In this case, half of the array would contain duplicated data because A[i, j] = A[j, i]. Also, A[i, i] would be meaningless because you do not need to take a highway from city i to itself. The only entries you really need in this array are the A[i, j] in the lower-left corner where i > j. Alternatively, you could use the entries in the upper-right corner. Because these entries form a triangle, this sort of array is called a *triangular array*.

Figure 4.1 shows a triangular array. Entries with meaningful data are indicated by Xs. Entries that are meaningful but duplicated by other entries are left blank. The meaningless diagonal entries A[i, i] are indicated by dashes.

For a small array, the space wasted by using a normal two-dimensional array to hold this data is not too important. If the map holds many cities, the wasted space can be large. For N cities there will be N * (N – 1) / 2 duplicated entries and N entries like A[i, i] that are not meaningful. If the map contains 1000 cities, the array will hold more than half a million unnecessary entries.

You can avoid wasting this space by creating a one-dimensional array B and then packing the meaningful entries of array A into array B. Place the entries in

Figure 4.1 A triangular array.

-				
X	-			
X	X	-		
X	X	X	-	
X	X	X	X	-

array B one row at a time, as shown in Figure 4.2. Notice that the array indexes are numbered starting from 0. This makes the equations that follow a little simpler.

To make this triangular array representation easier to use, you can write functions to translate between the indexing schemes used by arrays A and B. The equation for converting from A[i, j] to B[x] is:

```
x := Round(i * (i - 1) / 2) + j; // For i > j.
```

For example, if you plug in i = 2 and j = 1, you get x = 2 * (2 – 1) / 2 + 1 = 2. This means that A[2, 1] maps into position 2 in the B array as shown in Figure 4.2. Remember, the arrays are numbered starting with 0.

This equation holds only when i > j. The values for the other entries in array A are not stored in array B because they are redundant or not meaningful. If you

Figure 4.2 Packing a triangular array into a one-dimensional array.

Array A:

A[1, 0]			
A[2, 0]	A[2, 1]		
A[3, 0]	A[3, 1]	A[3, 2]	
A[4, 0]	A[4, 1]	A[4, 2]	A[4, 3]

Array B:

A[1, 0]	A[2, 0]	A[2, 1]	A[3, 0]	A[3, 1]	A[3, 2]	...

need to compute the value of A[i, j] where i < j, you should instead calculate the value of A[j, i].

This equation is not easy to compute. It requires a subtraction, an addition, a multiplication, and a division. If a program must execute the function very frequently, it will pay a slight penalty in execution speed. This is an example of a space versus time trade-off. Packing a triangular array into a one-dimensional array saves memory. Storing the data in a two-dimensional array takes more memory but is faster.

Diagonal Entries

Some programs use triangular arrays that include the diagonal entries A[i, i]. In this case, you need to make only two changes to the index translation equation. First, the translation should not reject cases where i = j. It should also add 1 to i before calculating the index in array B.

```
i := i + 1;
x := Round(i * (i - 1) / 2) + j; // For i > j.
```

Using the preceding equations, you can write a Delphi function to translate between the coordinates of the two arrays.

```
// Convert the i and j indexes in two-dimensional array A
// into the x index in one-dimensional array B.
function TTriangularArray.AtoB(i, j : Integer) : Integer;
var
    tmp : Integer;
begin
    if ((i < 0) or (i >= Rows) or
        (j < 0) or (j >= Rows))
    then
        raise EInvalidOperation.CreateFmt(
            'Indices %d and %d are not between %d and %d.',
            [i, j, 0, Rows - 1]);

    if ((not UseDiagonal) and (i = j)) then
        raise EInvalidOperation.Create(
            'This array does not contain diagonal values.');

    // Make i bigger than j.
    if (i < j) then
    begin
        tmp := i;
        i := j;
        j := tmp;
```

```
    end;

    if (UseDiagonal) then i := i + 1;
    AtoB := Round(i * (i - 1) / 2) + j;
end;
```

Example program Triang uses this function to demonstrate triangular arrays. It stores strings in a TTriangularArray object for each of the valid entries in array A. It then retrieves the values to display an image of the array. If you click the With Diagonal option button, the program stores labels for the diagonal entries in array A. If you click the Without Diagonal option button, it does not.

Irregular Arrays

Some programs need an array with an irregular size and shape. A two-dimensional array might need six items in the first row, three in the second, four in the third, and so forth. One example where this would be useful is in storing a number of polygons, each consisting of a different number of points. The array should look like the picture shown in Figure 4.3.

Arrays in Delphi cannot have ragged edges like this. A program could use an array large enough to hold every row, but that would leave many entries in the array unused. For the example shown in Figure 4.3, the array would be declared using var Polygons : array [1..3, 1..6] of TPoint, and four entries would remain unused.

There are several other ways you can store irregular arrays.

Forward Star

One way to avoid wasting space is to pack the data into a one-dimensional array B. Unlike triangular arrays, irregular arrays do not come with formulas for calculating how items map between the arrays. To handle this problem, you can create another array A that holds the offsets of each row in the one-dimensional array B.

To make it easier to locate the points in array B that correspond to each row, you can add a sentinel entry at the end of the array A that points *just beyond* the

Figure 4.3 An irregular array.

Polygon 1	(2, 5)	(3, 6)	(4, 6)	(5, 5)	(4, 4)	(4, 5)
Polygon 2	(1, 1)	(4, 1)	(2, 3)			
Polygon 3	(2, 2)	(4, 3)	(5, 4)	(1, 4)		

last item in array B. Then the points that make up polygon i are in array B at positions A[i] through A[i + 1] − 1. For example, a program can list the entries that make up row i using the following code:

```
for j := A[i] to A[i + 1] - 1 do
    // List entry B[j].
        :
```

This method is called *forward star.* Figure 4.4 shows the forward star representation of the irregular array shown in Figure 4.3. In this figure, the sentinel has been shaded so that it is easy to see.

You can easily generalize this method to form irregular arrays of higher dimensions. You might use a three-dimensional forward star representation to store a set of pictures, each with a different number of polygons, each consisting of many points.

Figure 4.5 shows a schematic picture of a three-dimensional forward star data structure. The two sentinels are shaded so that they are easy to see. The sentinels point one position beyond the end of the real data in the following array.

These forward star representations require very little unused storage. The only "wasted" space is contained in the entries for the sentinels.

Listing the points that make up a polygon is fast and easy using a forward star data structure. Saving and loading forward star data in files is also easy. On the other hand, updating arrays in a forward star format is quite difficult. Suppose you want to add a new point to the first polygon in Figure 4.4. You would need to shift all the entries to the right of the new point one position to make room for the new entry. Then you would need to add one to all the entries that came after the first in array A to account for the new point. Finally, you would insert the new item. Similar difficulties occur when you remove a point from the first polygon.

Figure 4.6 shows the forward star representation from Figure 4.4 after one point has been added to the first polygon. The entries that were updated are shaded. As the picture shows, almost every item in both arrays has been modified.

Figure 4.4 The forward star representation of an irregular array.

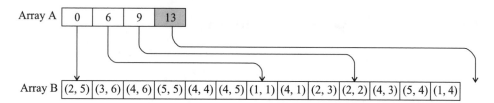

Figure 4.5 Three-dimensional forward star.

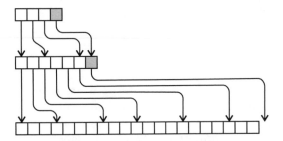

Irregular Linked Lists

Another method for creating irregular arrays is to use linked lists. Each cell contains a pointer to the next cell at its level of the hierarchy plus a pointer to the list of cells below it in the hierarchy. A polygon cell, for example, would contain a pointer to the next polygon and a pointer to its first point cell.

The following code shows variable type declarations you could use to build a linked list of pictures, each containing a linked list of polygons, each containing a linked list of points.

```
type
    PPictureCell = ^TPictureCell;
    TPictureCell = record
        NextPicture  : PPictureCell; // The next picture.
        FirstPolygon : PPolygonCell; // The first polygon in this
                                     // Picture.
    end;

    PPolygonCell = ^TPolygonCell;
    TPolygonCell = record
        NextPolygon : PPolygonCell;  // The next polygon.
        FirstPoint  : PPointCell;    // The first point in this
                                     // polygon.
    end;
```

Figure 4.6 Adding a point in forward star.

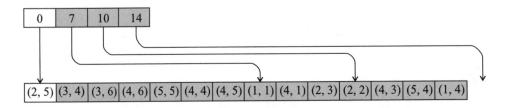

```
PPointCell = ^TPointCell;
TPointCell = record
    X, Y       : Integer;           // The point's coordinates.
    NextPoint : PPointCell;         // The next Point.
end;
```

Using these linked techniques, it is easy to add and remove pictures, polygons, or points from any position in the data structure.

Example program Poly, shown in Figure 4.7, uses a similar approach. It allows you to build a linked list of TPolylineCells, each containing a linked list of TPointCells. Use the left mouse button to draw polylines. Each time you click the left mouse button, the program adds a new point to the polyline. Click the right mouse button to finish a polyline and prepare to start another.

Sparse Arrays

Many applications call for large arrays that contain only a few nonzero elements. A connectivity matrix for an airline, for example, might contain a 1 in position A[i, j] if there is a flight between city i and city j. Many airlines service hundreds of cities, but the number of flights they actually run is much smaller than the N^2 possible combinations. Figure 4.8 shows a small airline flight map, in which the airline has flights between only 11 of the 100 possible pairs of cities.

You could build the connectivity matrix for this example using a 10 by 10 array, but the array would be mostly empty. You can avoid wasting this space by

Figure 4.7 Program Poly.

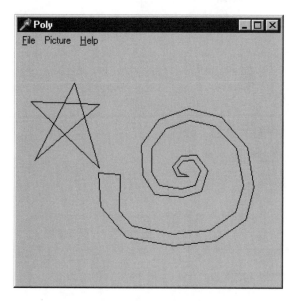

Figure 4.8 An airline flight map.

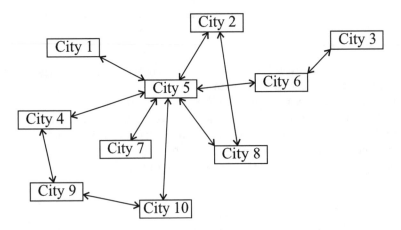

using pointers to build a sparse array. Each row in the array is represented by a linked list of cells representing the nonempty entries in the row. Sentinels for each row list are kept in an array.

Figure 4.9 shows the sparse connectivity matrix corresponding to the flight map shown in Figure 4.8.

The following code shows how a program might define the cell data type used to store the row lists.

Figure 4.9 A sparse connectivity matrix.

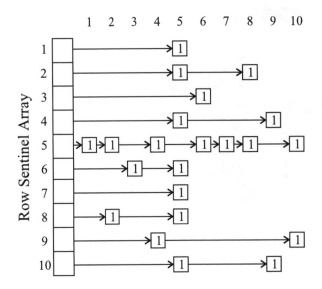

```
type
    String10 = String[10];

    PSparseCell = ^TSparseCell;
    TSparseCell = Record
        Col      : Longint;      // The column number.
        Value    : String10;     // The data value.
        NextCell : PSparseCell;  // The next cell in the row.
    end;
    TCellArray = array[0..100000000] of TSparseCell;
    PCellArray = ^TCellArray;
```

Array Indexing

Normal array indexing like A[i, j] will not work on this sort of structure. You can make indexing easier by writing procedures that set and get the values in the array. If the array represents a matrix, you might also want procedures to add, multiply, and perform other matrix operations.

A special value DEFAULT_VALUE represents an empty array entry. The procedure that gets array entries should return DEFAULT_VALUE when it is called to retrieve the value of an entry not contained in the array. Similarly, the procedure that sets values should remove a cell from the array if its value is set to DEFAULT_VALUE.

The particular value that DEFAULT_VALUE should have depends on the nature of the application. For an airline connectivity matrix, empty entries might have the value False. Then you can set A[i, j] True if there is a connection between cities i and j.

The GetValue function in the TSparseArray class returns the value of an entry in the array. The function starts at the first cell in the indicated row and moves through the row's linked list of cells. If it finds a cell with column value equal to the target column, it has found the required cell. Because the cells are kept in order within the row list, the function can stop looking if it ever finds a cell with column value larger than the target column.

```
// Return an array entry's value.
function TSparseArray.GetValue(r, c : Longint) : String10;
var
    cell_ptr : PSparseCell;
begin
    if ((r < 0) or (c < 0)) then
        raise EInvalidOperation.Create(
            'Row and column must be at least zero.');

    // See if we have a sentinel for this row.
    if (r > Max_Row) then
```

```
        GetValue := DEFAULT_VALUE
    else begin
        // Find a cell with column >= c.
        cell_ptr := RowSentinel^[r].NextCell;
        while (cell_ptr^.Col < c) do
            cell_ptr := cell_ptr^.NextCell;

        // If we did not find it, return DEFAULT_VALUE.
        if (cell_ptr^.Col = c) then
            GetValue := cell_ptr.Value
        else
            GetValue := DEFAULT_VALUE;
    end;
end;
```

The SetValue procedure assigns a new value to a cell. It searches through the row list for the entry's row until it finds an entry with column greater than or equal to the target column.

If the new value equals DEFAULT_VALUE, the procedure removes the cell from the row list; otherwise if it found the cell, the procedure updates the cell's value. If it did not find the cell, the procedure creates a new one.

```
// Set an array entry's value.
procedure TSparseArray.SetValue(r, c : Longint; new_value : String10);
var
    cell_ptr, next_ptr : PSparseCell;
    i                  : Longint;
    new_array          : PCellArray;
    bottom_sentinel    : PSparseCell;
begin
    if ((r < 0) or (c < 0)) then
        raise EInvalidOperation.Create(
            'Row and column must be at least zero.');

    // See if we need to make the sentinel array bigger.
    if (r > Max_Row) then
    begin
        // Copy the old values into a new array.
        GetMem(new_array, (r + 1) * SizeOf(TSparseCell));
        for i := 0 to Max_Row do
            new_array^[i] := RowSentinel^[i];

        // Free the old array.
        if (Max_Row >= 0) then FreeMem(RowSentinel);
        RowSentinel := new_array;
```

```
        // Create new sentinels.
        for i := Max_Row + 1 to r do
        begin
            New(bottom_sentinel);
            bottom_sentinel^.Col := 2147483647;
            bottom_sentinel^.NextCell := nil;
            RowSentinel^[i].NextCell := bottom_sentinel;
            RowSentinel^[i].Col := -1;
        end;
        Max_Row := r;
    end;

    // Find a cell with column >= c.
    cell_ptr := @RowSentinel^[r];
    next_ptr := cell_ptr^.NextCell;
    while (next_ptr^.Col < c) do
    begin
        cell_ptr := next_ptr;
        next_ptr := cell_ptr^.NextCell;
    end;

    // If the value is the default value...
    if (new_value = DEFAULT_VALUE) then
    begin
        // If we found a cell for this column, remove it.
        if (next_ptr^.Col = c) then
        begin
            cell_ptr^.NextCell := next_ptr^.NextCell;
            Dispose(next_ptr);
        end;
    end else begin
        // The value is not the default value.
        // If we did not find the cell, create a new cell.
        if (next_ptr^.Col <> c) then
        begin
            New(next_ptr);
            next_ptr^.Col := c;
            next_ptr^.NextCell := cell_ptr^.NextCell;
            cell_ptr^.NextCell := next_ptr;
        end;

        // Save the new value.
        next_ptr^.Value := new_value;
    end;
end;
```

Example program Sparse, shown in Figure 4.10, uses the TSparseArray class to manage a sparse array. Using the program, you can set and fetch array entries. DEFAULT_VALUE is blank for this program, so if you set the value of an entry to a blank string, the program removes the entry from the array.

Very Sparse Arrays

Some arrays contain so few nonblank entries that many rows are completely empty. In that case, it is better to store row sentinels in a linked list instead of an array. That allows the program to omit empty rows completely. Figure 4.11 shows a 100 by 100 array that contains only 7 nonempty entries.

Modifying the previous code to handle this sort of array is fairly straightforward. Most of the code remains the same, and you can use the same TSparseCell data type for the array entries. Instead of using an array to store the row sentinels, however, you store them in their own linked list. The list is made up of TRowCell records. These records each have a pointer to the next row record and to the top sentinel for a row linked list.

```
TRowCell = Record
    Row        : Longint;
    FirstCell  : PSparseCell;
    NextRow    : PRowCell;
end;
```

To locate an item in the array, the program first looks through the linked list of TRowCells until it finds the row it needs. It then looks through the row linked list until it finds the correct column.

```
// Return an array entry's value.
function TVerySparseArray.GetValue(r, c : Longint) : String10;
var
    row_ptr : PRowCell;
```

Figure 4.10 Program Sparse.

Figure 4.11 A very sparse array.

```
        col_ptr : PSparseCell;
begin
    if ((r < 0) or (c < 0)) then
        raise EInvalidOperation.Create(
            'Row and column must be at least zero.');

    // Find the row cell.
    row_ptr := TopSentinel^.NextRow;
    while (row_ptr^.Row < r) do
        row_ptr := row_ptr^.NextRow;

    // See if we found the row we need.
    Result := DEFAULT_VALUE;
    if (row_ptr^.Row <> r) then exit;

    // Find the column cell.
    col_ptr := row_ptr^.FirstCell^.NextCell;
    while (col_ptr^.Col < c) do
        col_ptr := col_ptr^.NextCell;

    // See if we found the column we need.
    if (col_ptr^.Col <> c) then exit;

    // We found it.
    Result := col_ptr^.Value;
end;
```

Example program VSparse uses this code to demonstrate a very sparse array. Using the program, you can set and fetch array entries. DEFAULT_VALUE is blank for this program, so if you set the value of an entry to a blank string, the program removes the entry from the array.

Summary

Some programs use arrays that contain very few interesting elements. Using Delphi's normal arrays to store mostly empty cells would waste a lot of space. Using triangular, irregular, sparse, and very sparse arrays, you can create powerful array representations that take up much less memory.

5

RECURSION

R ecursion is a powerful programming technique that allows you to break a problem into smaller and smaller pieces until the pieces are small enough to handle easily.

After you have gained some experience with recursion, you will find it all around you. In fact, many programmers who have recently mastered recursion get carried away and begin applying it in situations where it is unnecessary and even harmful.

The first sections of this chapter discuss factorials, Fibonacci numbers, and greatest common divisors. These provide good examples of bad uses of recursion— nonrecursive versions of these programs are much more efficient. These examples are interesting and easy to understand, however, so they are worth discussing.

Next, the chapter examines some examples where recursion is more appropriate. The Hilbert and Sierpinski curves use recursion properly and efficiently.

The final sections of this chapter explain why factorials, Fibonacci numbers, and greatest common divisors are better without recursion. These sections explain when you should avoid recursion, and they show ways to eliminate recursion when necessary.

What Is Recursion?

Recursion occurs when a function or procedure calls itself. A recursive routine can call itself *directly* like this:

```
function Factorial(num : Longint) : Longint;
begin
    Factorial := num * Factorial(num - 1);
end;
```

A recursive routine can also call itself *indirectly* by calling a second routine that calls the first.

```
procedure Ping(num : Integer);
begin
```

```
      Pong(num - 1);
end;

procedure Pong(num : Integer);
begin
     Ping(num div 2);
end;
```

Recursion is useful for solving problems that naturally break into smaller instances of the same problem. You can think of the tree shown on the left in Figure 5.1, for example, as a "trunk" with two smaller trees attached. This leads to a naturally recursive procedure for drawing trees.

```
procedure DrawTree;
begin
     Draw a "trunk"
     Draw a smaller tree rotated -45 degrees
     Draw a smaller tree rotated 45 degrees
end;
```

Even though recursion can make some problems easier to understand, people do not naturally think recursively. People tend to break big tasks into smaller tasks that can be performed one at a time in order until all are finished. To paint a fence, you might start at the left side and work your way to the right until you are done. You probably do not think in terms of recursively painting the left half of the fence and then recursively painting the right half.

To think recursively you need to break tasks into large subtasks, which you can then recursively break into smaller subtasks. At some point, the subtasks become small enough to handle directly. When the subtasks are complete, the larger tasks they make up are also complete. When all of the subtasks are complete, the original task is finished.

Figure 5.1 A tree made of two smaller trees.

Recursive Factorials

The factorial of a number N is written N! (pronounced N *factorial*). The value of 0! is defined to be 1. Other values are defined by:

```
N! = N * (N - 1) * (N - 2) * ... * 2 * 1
```

As mentioned in Chapter 1, "Fundamental Concepts," this function grows extremely quickly. Table 5.1 shows the first 10 values of the factorial function.

You can also define the factorial function recursively.

```
0! = 1
N! = N * (N - 1)! for N > 0.
```

It is easy to translate this definition into a recursive function.

```
function Factorial(num : Integer) : Integer;
begin
    if (num <= 0) then
        Factorial := 1
    else
        Factorial := num * Factorial(num - 1);
end;
```

This function first checks to see if the number is less than or equal to 0. The factorial is not defined for numbers less than 0, but the function safeguards itself by checking for this condition anyway. If the function checked only to see if the number was equal to 0, it would enter an infinite recursion if the number was negative.

If the input value is less than or equal to 0, the function returns the value 1. Otherwise, the value of the function is the number times the factorial of the number minus 1.

Two things ensure that this recursive function eventually stops. First, on each subsequent call, the value of the parameter num is smaller. Second, the value of num is bounded below by 0. When the value of num reaches 0, the function ends the recursion. The condition, like num <= 0, that causes a recursion to end is called the *base case* or the *stopping case*.

Whenever a program calls a procedure, the system stores certain values in a stack similar to those described in Chapter 3, "Stacks and Queues." Because this

Table 5.1 Values of the Factorial Function

N	1	2	3	4	5	6	7	8	9	10
N!	1	2	6	24	120	720	5040	40,320	362,880	3,628,800

stack is so important, it is called simply *the stack*. If a recursive function calls itself too many times, it may use up all of the stack space and crash with a stack overflow error.

The number of times a function can call itself before using all the stack space depends on how much memory the computer has and how much data the program places on the stack. In Delphi, a function can usually call itself many times before causing a stack overflow. In one test, a program was able to recurse 2356 times before it used up all of the stack space.

Runtime Analysis

The factorial function takes only a single argument: the number for which it is to compute the factorial. Complexity analysis usually examines runtime as a function of the *size* of the problem or the *number of inputs*. Because there is only one input in this case, that calculation could be a little strange.

For this reason, algorithms that take a single parameter are usually evaluated in terms of the *number of bits required to store the input value* rather than the number of inputs. In some sense, this is the size of the input because it takes that many bits to store the input value. This, however, is not a very intuitive way to think about the problem. Also, in theory, a computer could store the input N in $\log_2(N)$ bits, but in reality it probably stores N in some fixed number of bits. For example, a long integer is stored in 32 bits whether its value is 1 or 2,147,483,647.

For these reasons this chapter analyzes this sort of algorithm in terms of the input's *value* rather than its *size*. If you want to rewrite the results in terms of the size of the input, you can do so using the fact that $N = 2^M$, where M is the number of bits needed to store N. If the runtime of an algorithm is $O(N^2)$ in terms of the input value N, it is $O((2^M)^2) = O(2^{2*M}) = O((2^2)^M) = O(4^M)$ in terms of the input size M.

For this particular algorithm, the factorial function is called for N, N – 1, N – 2, and so on until the input parameter reaches 0 and the recursion ends. If the initial input is N, the function is called a total of N + 1 times, so its runtime is $O(N)$. The runtime is $O(2^M)$ in terms of the size of the input M.

$O(N)$ functions grow pretty slowly, so you might expect good performance from this algorithm. In fact, that is the case. The function runs into trouble only when it exhausts the stack by executing too many recursions or when the value of N! becomes too large to fit in an integer and the program generates an overflow error.

Because N! grows very quickly, overflow happens first unless you are using the stack heavily for other things. Using the small integer data type, overflow occurs for 8! because 8! = 40,320 is larger than the largest possible small integer, 32,767. To allow the program to compute approximate values for larger numbers, you can modify the function so it uses doubles instead of integers. Then the largest number for which the algorithm can compute N! is 170! $\approx$ 7.257E + 306.

Example program Facto1 demonstrates the recursive factorial function. Enter a number and click the Compute button to make the program recursively compute factorials.

Recursive Greatest Common Divisor

The *greatest common divisor* (GCD) of two numbers is the largest integer that divides the two numbers evenly. The GCD of 12 and 9, for example, is 3, because 3 is the largest integer that divides both 12 and 9 with no remainder. Two numbers are *relatively prime* if their GCD is 1.

The eighteenth-century mathematician Euler discovered an interesting fact:

```
If A divides B evenly, GCD(A, B) = A.
Otherwise GCD(A, B) = GCD(B mod A, A).
```

You can use this fact to compute GCDs quickly. For example:

```
GCD(9, 12) = GCD(12 mod 9, 9)
           = GCD(3, 9)
           = 3
```

At each step, the numbers being compared get smaller because 1 <= B Mod A < A if A does not divide B evenly. If the arguments continue to decrease, A will eventually reach the value 1. Because 1 evenly divides any number B, the recursion must stop. At some point, A will divide B evenly so the recursion will eventually stop.

Euler's discovery leads naturally to a simple recursive algorithm for computing GCDs.

```
function Gcd(A, B : Longint) : Longint;
begin
    if (B mod A = 0) then    // If A divides B evenly, we're done.
        Gcd := A
    else                     // Otherwise recurse.
        Gcd := Gcd(B mod A, A);
end;
```

Runtime Analysis

To analyze the runtime of this algorithm, you must determine how quickly A decreases. Because the function stops if A reaches the value 1, the rate at which A decreases gives an upper bound on how long the algorithm can run. It turns out that every second time the function Gcd is called, the parameter A decreases by at least a factor of 1 / 2.

To see why, assume A < B. This is always true after the first call to Gcd.

If B mod A <= A / 2, the next call to Gcd will have the first parameter reduced by at least a factor of 1 / 2, and the proof is done.

Suppose this is not the case. Suppose B mod A > A / 2. The first recursive call to Gcd will be Gcd(B mod A, A).

Plugging the values B mod A and A into the function in place of A and B makes the second recursive call Gcd(A mod (B Mod A), B mod A).

But we have assumed that B mod A > A / 2. Then B mod A will divide into A exactly once, leaving a remainder of A – (B mod A). Because B mod A is greater than A / 2, the value A – (B mod A) must be less than A / 2. This shows that the first parameter in the second recursive call to Gcd is smaller than A / 2, and the proof is done.

Now suppose N is the original value of the parameter A. After two calls to Gcd, the value of parameter A will have been reduced to, at most, N / 2. After four calls, the value will be no more than (N / 2) / 2 = N / 4. After six calls, the value will be at most (N / 4) / 2 = N / 8. In general, after 2 * K calls to Gcd, the value of parameter A will be at most $N / 2^K$.

Because the algorithm must stop when the value of the parameter A reaches 1, it can continue only until $N / 2^K = 1$. This happens when $N = 2^K$ or when $K = \log_2(N)$. Because the algorithm is running for 2 * K steps, this means the algorithm must stop after, at most, $2 * \log_2(N)$ steps. Ignoring the constant multiplier, this means that the algorithm runs in O(log(N)) time.

This algorithm is typical of many recursive algorithms that run in O(log(N)) time. Each time it executes a certain fixed number of steps, in this case 2, it halves the problem size. More generally, if an algorithm decreases the problem size by a factor of at least 1 / D after every S steps, the problem will require $S * \log_D(N)$ steps.

Because you can ignore the constant multipliers and log bases in Big O notation, any algorithm that runs in $S * \log_D(N)$ time is an O(log(N)) algorithm. This does not necessarily mean you can completely ignore these constants when actually implementing an algorithm. An algorithm that reduces the problem size by a factor of 1 / 10 every step will probably be faster than an algorithm that reduces it by 1 / 2 every five steps. Still, they both have runtimes O(log(N)).

O(log(N)) algorithms are generally very fast, and the GCD algorithm is no exception. To find that the GCD of 1,736,751,235 and 2,135,723,523 is 71, for example, the function is called only 17 times. In fact, this algorithm can compute values for the largest possible long integer data type value 2,147,483,647 practically instantly. The Delphi mod operator cannot handle values larger than this, so that is the practical limit to this algorithm.

Example program Gcd1 uses this algorithm to recursively compute greatest common divisors. Enter values for A and B and click the Compute button, and the program will compute the GCD of the two numbers.

Recursive Fibonacci Numbers

You can define Fibonacci numbers recursively with the equations:

```
Fib(0) = 0
Fib(1) = 1
Fib(N) = Fib(N - 1) + Fib(N - 2)        for N > 1.
```

The third equation recursively uses the Fib function twice, once with input N – 1 and once with input N – 2. This makes it necessary to have two base cases for the recursion: Fib(0) = 0 and Fib(1) = 1. If you had only one, the function could slip past the base case and call itself recursively forever. For example, if you knew only that Fib(0) = 0, the computation of Fib(2) would look like this:

```
Fib(2) = Fib(1) + Fib(0)
       = [Fib(0) + Fib(-1)] + 0
       = 0 + [Fib(-2) + Fib(-3)]
       = [Fib(-3) + Fib(-4)] + [Fib(-4) + Fib(-5)]
       Etc.
```

You easily can translate this definition of Fibonacci numbers into a recursive function.

```
function Fibo(n : Double) : Double;
begin
    if (n <= 1) then
        Fibo := n
    else
        Fibo := Fibo(n - 1) + Fibo(n - 2);
end;
```

Runtime Analysis

The analysis of this algorithm is tricky. First, consider the number of times the algorithm reaches one of the base cases n <= 1. Let G(N) be the number of times the algorithm reaches a base case for input N. When N <= 1, the function reaches the base case once and requires no recursion.

If N > 1, the function recursively computes Fib(N – 1) and Fib(N – 2) and is then finished. In the initial call to the function, the base case is not reached—it is reached only by other, recursive calls. The total number of times the base case is reached for input N is the number of times it is reached for input N – 1 plus the number of times it is reached for input N – 2. You can write these three facts as:

```
G(0) = 1
G(1) = 1
G(N) = G(N - 1) + G(N - 2)          for N > 1.
```

This recursive definition is very similar to the definition of the Fibonacci numbers. Table 5.2 shows some values for G(N) and Fib(N). It is easy to see from these numbers that G(N) = Fib(N + 1).

Next consider the number of times the algorithm reaches the recursive step. When N <= 1, the function does not reach this step. When N > 1, the function reaches this step once and then recursively computes Fib(N – 1) and Fib(N – 2).

Table 5.2 Values of Fibonacci Numbers and G(N)

N	0	1	2	3	4	5	6	7	8
Fib(N)	0	1	1	2	3	5	8	13	21
G(N)	1	1	2	3	5	8	13	21	34

Let H(N) be the number of times the algorithm reaches the recursive step for input N. Then H(N) = 1 + H(N – 1) + H(N – 2). The defining equations for H(N) are:

```
H(0) = 0
H(1) = 0
H(N) = 1 + H(N - 1) + H(N - 2)          for N > 1.
```

Table 5.3 shows some values for Fib(N) and H(N). From these numbers, you can see that H(N) = Fib(N + 1) – 1.

Combining the results for G(N) and H(N) gives the total runtime for the algorithm.

```
Runtime      = G(N) + H(N)
             = Fib(N + 1) + Fib(N + 1) - 1
             = 2 * Fib(N + 1) - 1
```

Because Fib(N + 1) >= Fib(N) for all values of N, you know that:

```
Runtime >= 2 * Fib(N) - 1
```

In Big O notation, this simplifies to O(Fib(N)). It is interesting that this function is not only recursive, but that it also is used to compute its own runtime.

To understand the speed at which the Fibonacci function grows, it helps to know that $Fib(M) > \emptyset^{M-2}$ for a certain constant $\emptyset$, which is roughly 1.6. This means that the runtime is at least as big as the exponential function $O(\emptyset^M)$. Like other exponential functions, this function grows more quickly than polynomial functions and less quickly than factorial functions.

Because the runtime function grows very quickly, this algorithm is quite slow for large inputs. In fact, the algorithm is so slow that it is impractical to compute values of Fib(N) for N much larger than 40. Table 5.4 shows the runtimes for this algorithm with different inputs on a 133-megahertz Pentium.

Table 5.3 Values of Fibonacci Numbers and H(N)

N	0	1	2	3	4	5	6	7	8
Fib(N)	0	1	1	2	3	5	8	13	21
H(N)	0	0	1	2	4	7	12	20	33

Table 5.4 Fibonacci Program Runtimes

M	30	32	34	36	38	40
Fib(M)	832,040	2.18E + 6	5.70E + 6	1.49E + 7	3.91E + 7	1.02E + 8
Time (secs)	1.32	3.30	8.66	22.67	59.35	155.50

Example program Fibo1 uses this recursive algorithm to calculate Fibonacci numbers. Enter an integer and click the Compute button. Be sure to start with small numbers until you know how long your computer will take to make the computation.

Recursive Hilbert Curves

Hilbert curves are *self-similar* curves that are naturally defined recursively. Figure 5.2 shows Hilbert curves where the maximum depths of recursion are 1, 2, and 3.

You create a Hilbert curve, or any other self-similar curve, by breaking up a large curve into smaller pieces. You then use the curve itself, properly sized and rotated, to build those pieces. You may break those pieces into smaller pieces and so on until the process reaches some desired depth of recursion. The depth of the curve is defined to be the greatest depth of recursion the procedure reaches.

The Hilbert procedure controls its recursion using a depth parameter. When the procedure recursively calls itself, it decreases the depth parameter by 1. When the procedure is called with depth 1, it draws the simple depth 1 curve shown on the left in Figure 5.2 and exits. This is the base case for the recursion.

For example, the Hilbert curve of depth 2 is made up of four Hilbert curves of depth 1. Similarly, a Hilbert curve of depth 3 is made up of four Hilbert curves of depth 2, each consisting of four Hilbert curves of depth 1. Figure 5.3 shows Hilbert curves of depths 2 and 3. The smaller curves making up the larger ones are drawn with bold lines.

Figure 5.2 Hilbert curves.

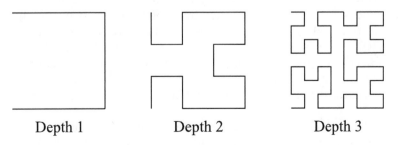

Depth 1   Depth 2   Depth 3

Figure 5.3 Hilbert curves made from smaller Hilbert curves.

The following code draws a depth 1 Hilbert curve.

```
with DrawArea.Canvas do
begin
    LineTo(PenPos.X + Length, PenPos.Y);
    LineTo(PenPos.X,          PenPos.Y + Length);
    LineTo(PenPos.X - Length, PenPos.Y);
end;
```

This code assumes that the current drawing position begins at the upper-left corner of the drawing area and that Length is the desired length for each line segment.

You can sketch the method for drawing a Hilbert curve of greater depth as follows:

```
procedure Hilbert(Depth : Integer);
begin
    if (Depth = 1) then
        Draw a depth 1 Hilbert curve
    else
        Draw and connect the four curves Hilbert(Depth - 1)
end;
```

You must complicate this method slightly so the Hilbert procedure can tell which direction it is heading and whether it is drawing clockwise or counterclockwise. It needs to know this to decide which kinds of Hilbert curves to use.

You can give the procedure this information by adding parameters dx and dy to indicate the direction of the first line in the curve. If the curve is of depth 1, the procedure draws its first line as in LineTo(PenPos.X + dx, PenPos.Y + dy). If the curve has greater depth, the procedure connects the first two smaller subcurves using LineTo(PenPos.X + dx, PenPos.Y + dy). In either case, the procedure can use dx and dy to pick the direction in which it should draw the lines making up the curve.

The Delphi code for drawing Hilbert curves is short but tricky. You may need to step through it several times for curves of depth 1 and 2 to see exactly how dx and dy change to produce the different parts of the curve.

```
procedure THilblForm.DrawHilbert(depth, dx, dy : Integer);
begin
    with DrawArea.Canvas do
    begin
        if (depth > 1) then DrawHilbert(depth - 1, dy, dx);
        LineTo(PenPos.X + dx, PenPos.Y + dy);
        if (depth > 1) then DrawHilbert(depth - 1, dx, dy);
        LineTo(PenPos.X + dy, PenPos.Y + dx);
        if (depth > 1) then DrawHilbert(depth - 1, dx, dy);
        LineTo(PenPos.X - dx, PenPos.Y - dy);
        if (depth > 1) then DrawHilbert(depth - 1, -dy, -dx);
    end;
end;
```

Runtime Analysis

To analyze this procedure's runtime, you must determine the number of times the Hilbert procedure calls itself. Each time the procedure recurses, it calls itself four times. If $T(N)$ is the number of times the procedure is executed when it is called for depth N, then:

```
T(1) = 1
T(N) = 1 + 4 * T(N - 1)          for N > 1.
```

If you expand the definition of $T(N)$ a few times you get:

$$
\begin{aligned}
T(N) &= 1 + 4 * T(N - 1) \\
     &= 1 + 4 * (1 + 4 * T(N - 2)) \\
     &= 1 + 4 + 16 * T(N - 2) \\
     &= 1 + 4 + 16 * (1 + 4 * T(N - 3)) \\
     &= 1 + 4 + 16 + 64 * T(N - 3) \\
     &= \ldots \\
     &= 4^0 + 4^1 + 4^2 + 4^3 + \ldots + 4^K * T(N - K)
\end{aligned}
$$

Expanding this equation until you reach the base case $T(1) = 1$ gives:

$$T(N) = 4^0 + 4^1 + 4^2 + 4^3 + \ldots + 4^{N-1}$$

You can use the following mathematical formula to simplify this equation.

$$X^0 + X^1 + X^2 + X^3 + \ldots + X^M = (X^{M+1} - 1) / (X - 1)$$

Using this formula, the equation becomes:

$$
\begin{aligned}
T(N) &= (4^{(N-1)+1} - 1) / (4 - 1) \\
     &= (4^N - 1) / 3
\end{aligned}
$$

Ignoring the constants, this procedure runs in time $O(4^N)$. Table 5.5 shows the first several values for the runtime function. If you look closely at the numbers, you will see that they agree with the recursive definition.

Table 5.5 Number of Recursive Calls to the Hilbert Procedure

N	1	2	3	4	5	6	7	8	9
T(N)	1	5	21	85	341	1365	5461	21,845	87,381

This algorithm is typical of many recursive algorithms that run in $O(C^N)$ time for some constant C. Each time the Hilbert procedure is called, it increases the problem size by a factor of 4. More generally, if an algorithm increases the problem size by a factor of at least C each time it executes a certain fixed number of steps, the algorithm will have $O(C^N)$ runtime.

This is exactly the opposite of the GCD algorithm's behavior. The Gcd function decreases the problem size by a factor of at least 1 / 2 every second time it is called, so it has $O(\log(N))$ runtime. The Hilbert curve procedure increases the problem size by a factor of 4 each time it is called, so it has $O(4^N)$ runtime.

The function $(4^N - 1) / 3$ is an exponential function that grows *very* quickly. In fact, this function grows so quickly that you might suspect that this is not a very efficient algorithm. This algorithm definitely takes a lot of time, but there are two reasons why this is not necessarily bad.

First, any other algorithm that draws Hilbert curves cannot be much faster. Hilbert curves contain a *lot* of line segments, and any algorithm that draws them all will take a long time. Each time the Hilbert procedure is called, it draws three lines. Let L(N) be the total number of lines drawn in a depth N Hilbert curve. Then $L(N) = 3 * T(N) = 4^N - 1$, so L(N) is also $O(4^N)$. Any algorithm that draws Hilbert curves must draw $O(4^N)$ lines, so it must execute $O(4^N)$ steps. There are other algorithms for drawing Hilbert curves, but they all take about as much time as this algorithm.

The second fact that indicates this algorithm might not be too bad is that a depth 9 Hilbert curve contains so many lines it turns most computer monitors completely black. This is not surprising because this curve contains 262,143 line segments. This means you will probably never want to display a Hilbert curve of depth 9 or greater anyway. At some depth beyond 9, you would reach the limits of your computer, but you reach the limits of what you might reasonably want to display first.

The conclusion is that Hilbert curves are just plain hard to draw. Drawing a quarter of a million lines is a lot of work, and it will take a while no matter how clever your algorithm is.

Example program Hilb1, shown in Figure 5.4, uses this recursive algorithm to draw Hilbert curves. When you run the program, be sure to keep the depth of recursion small (under 6) until you have seen how long the program takes on your computer.

Figure 5.4 Program Hilb1.

Recursive Sierpinski Curves

Like Hilbert curves, Sierpinski curves are self-similar curves that are naturally defined recursively. Figure 5.5 shows Sierpinski curves with depths 1, 2, and 3.

The Hilbert curve algorithm uses a single procedure to draw Hilbert curves. Sierpinski curves are easier to draw using four separate procedures that work together. These procedures are named SierpA, SierpB, SierpC, and SierpD. The procedures are indirectly recursive—each procedure calls the others, which then call the first. They draw the top, left, bottom, and right portions of a Sierpinski curve, respectively.

Figure 5.5 Sierpinski curves.

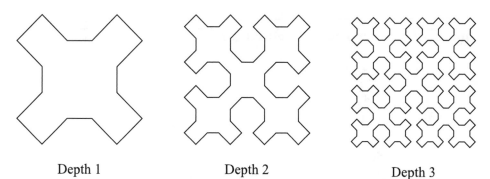

Depth 1   Depth 2   Depth 3

Figure 5.6 shows how these procedures work together to form a Sierpinski curve of depth 1. The subcurves are shown with arrows to indicate the direction in which they are drawn. Segments used to connect the four subcurves are drawn with dashed lines.

Each of the four basic curves is composed of a diagonal line segment, followed by a vertical or horizontal segment, followed by another diagonal line segment. When the depth of recursion is greater than 1, you must break each of these curves into smaller pieces. You do this by breaking each of the curves' two diagonal line segments into two subcurves.

For example, to break up a type A curve, break the first diagonal line segment into a type A curve followed by a type B curve. Then draw the horizontal line segment for the original type A curve unchanged. Finish by breaking the second diagonal line segment into a type D curve followed by a type A curve. Figure 5.7 shows how a depth 2 type A curve is built from depth 1 curves. The subcurves are drawn with bold lines so they are easy to see.

Figure 5.8 shows how a complete depth 2 Sierpinski curve is built from four depth 1 subcurves. Each of the subcurves is circled with dashed lines.

If you use arrows like ↗ and ↖ to indicate the types of lines that connect the subcurves (the thin lines in Figure 5.8), then you can list the recursive relationships among the four types of curves, as shown in Figure 5.9.

The procedures that draw the Sierpinski subcurves are all very similar, so only one is shown here. The relationships shown in Figure 5.9 indicate the drawing operations you should perform to draw each of the different types of curves. You can follow the relationships for a type A curve in the following code. You can use the other relationships to determine how to modify the code to draw the other types of curves.

```
procedure TSierp1Form.SierpA(depth, dist : Integer);
begin
    with DrawArea.Canvas do
    begin
        if (depth = 1) then
        begin
```

Figure 5.6 The parts of a Sierpinski curve.

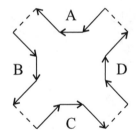

Figure 5.7 Breaking up a type A curve.

```
        LineTo(PenPos.X - dist, PenPos.Y + dist);
        LineTo(PenPos.X - dist, PenPos.Y + 0   );
        LineTo(PenPos.X - dist, PenPos.Y - dist);
    end else begin
        SierpA(depth - 1, dist);
        LineTo(PenPos.X - dist, PenPos.Y + dist);
        SierpB(depth - 1, dist);
        LineTo(PenPos.X - dist, PenPos.Y + 0   );
        SierpD(depth - 1, dist);
        LineTo(PenPos.X - dist, PenPos.Y - dist);
        SierpA(depth - 1, dist);
    end;
  end;
end;
```

In addition to procedures that draw each of the four basic curves, you need a procedure that uses the four of them to create the completed Sierpinski curve.

Figure 5.8 A Sierpinski curve made from smaller Sierpinski curves.

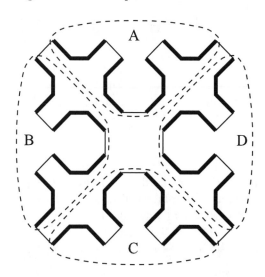

Figure 5.9 Recursive relationships among Sierpinski curves.

A: A ↙ B ← D ↖ A
B: B ↘ C ↓ A ↙ B
C: C ↗ D → B ↘ C
D: D ↖ A ↑ C ↗ D

```
procedure TSierp1Form.DrawSierp(depth, dist : Integer);
begin
    with DrawArea.Canvas do
    begin
        SierpB(depth, dist);
        LineTo(PenPos.X + dist, PenPos.Y + dist);
        SierpC(depth, dist);
        LineTo(PenPos.X + dist, PenPos.Y - dist);
        SierpD(depth, dist);
        LineTo(PenPos.X - dist, PenPos.Y - dist);
        SierpA(depth, dist);
        LineTo(PenPos.X - dist, PenPos.Y + dist);
    end;
end;
```

Runtime Analysis

To analyze the runtime of this algorithm, you must determine how many times each of the four curve drawing procedures is called. Let $T(N)$ be the number of times any one of the four basic curve procedures or the main DrawSierp procedure is called when drawing a depth N curve.

When the depth of the curve is 1, each type of curve is drawn once. Adding 1 for the main Sierpinski procedure gives $T(1) = 5$.

Each time one of the curve procedures recurses, it calls itself or another of the procedures four times. Because these procedures are all pretty much the same, $T(N)$ is the same no matter which procedure is called first. This makes sense because Sierpinski curves are symmetrical and contain the same number of each type of curve. The recursive equations for $T(N)$ are:

```
T(1) = 5
T(N) = 1 + 4 * T(N - 1)        for N > 1.
```

These equations are almost the same as the ones used to compute the runtime for the Hilbert curve algorithm. The only difference is that $T(1) = 1$ for the Hilbert curve. Comparing a few values for these equations shows that $T_{Sierpinski}(N) = T_{Hilbert}(N + 1)$. The last section showed that $T_{Hilbert}(N) = (4^N - 1) / 3$, so $T_{Sierpinski}(N) = (4^{N+1} - 1) / 3$, which is also $O(4^N)$.

Like the Hilbert curve algorithm, this algorithm runs in $O(4^N)$ time, but that is not necessarily bad. The Sierpinski curve requires $O(4^N)$ lines, so no algorithm can draw a Sierpinski curve in less than $O(4^N)$ time.

The Sierpinski curve also completely fills most computer screens for depths of 9 or greater. At some depth beyond 9, you would reach the limits of your computer, but you reach the limits of what you might reasonably want to display first.

Example program Sierp1, shown in Figure 5.10, uses this recursive algorithm to draw Sierpinski curves. When you run the program, be sure to keep the depth of recursion small (under 6) until you know how long the program takes on your computer.

Dangers of Recursion

Recursion can be a powerful technique for decomposing large problems, but it has a few dangers. This section takes a look at some of these dangers and explains when recursion is appropriate and when it is not. The sections that follow explain techniques for removing recursion when it might cause problems.

Infinite Recursion

The most obvious danger of recursion is infinite recursion. If you do not build your algorithm properly, the function may slip past your base case and run forever. The easiest way to make this mistake is to forget the base case, as is done in

Figure 5.10 Program Sierp1.

the following bad version of the factorial function. Because the function does not test to see if the base case is reached, it will recursively call itself forever.

```
function BadFactorial(num : Integer) : Integer;
begin
    BadFactorial := num * BadFactorial(num - 1);
end;
```

A function will also recurse infinitely if its base case does not stop all of the possible paths of the recursion. In the following incorrect version of the factorial function, the function will recurse forever if the input is not an integer or if it is less than 0. These values are not valid inputs for the factorial function, so you could require that the program using this function check that the inputs are valid. It is better, however, for the function to protect itself.

```
function BadFactorial2(num : Double) : Double;
begin
    if (num = 0) then
        BadFactorial2 := 1
    else
        BadFactorial2 := num * BadFactorial2(num - 1);
end;
```

The following version of the Fibonacci function shows a trickier example. Here the base case stops only some paths of recursion. This function has the same problems with noninteger and negative values that BadFactorial2 has.

```
function BadFib(num : Double) : Double;
begin
    if (num = 0) then
        BadFib := 0
    else
        BadFib := BadFib(num - 1) + BadFib(num - 2);
end;
```

A final problem related to infinite recursion is that "infinite" really only means "until you run out of stack space." Even correctly written recursive procedures will sometimes run out of stack space and fail. The following function, which computes the sum $N + (N - 1) + ... + 2 + 1$, exhausts the computer's stack space for large values of n. The largest value of n that will work depends on your computer's configuration.

```
function BigAdd(n : Double) : Double;
begin
    if (n <= 1) then
        BigAdd := 1
    else
```

```
        BigAdd := n + BigAdd(n - 1);
end;
```

Example program BigAdd1 demonstrates this algorithm. See how large an input you can give the program before it exhausts the stack on your computer.

Wasted Space

Wasted space is another danger of recursion. Each time your program executes a procedure call, the computer allocates space for the variables local to the new procedure. If you have a complicated chain of recursive calls, the computer will spend a considerable amount of time and memory allocating and deallocating these variables during the recursion. Even if this does not cause the program to run out of stack space, the time spent managing the variables can be significant.

There are several ways you can minimize this overhead. First, do not use lots of unnecessary variables. The following version of the BigAdd function runs out of stack space sooner than the previous version. The statement a[Random(99)] := 1 prevents the compiler from optimizing and removing the array.

```
function BigAdd(n : Double) : Double;
var
    a : array [0..99] of Longint;
begin
    a[Random(99)] := 1;
    if (n <= 1) then
        BigAdd := 1
    else
        BigAdd := n + BigAdd(n - 1);
end;
```

You can also reduce stack use by declaring variables globally. If you declare variables outside of the procedure, the computer will not need to allocate new memory each time the procedure is called.

Logical Misuse

A more subtle danger of recursion is logical misuse. Here you use recursion when it is not the best way to do the job. The factorial, Fibonacci, GCD, and BigAdd functions presented earlier do not really need to be recursive. Better, nonrecursive versions of these functions are described a little later in this chapter.

In the cases of the factorial and GCD functions, the unnecessary recursion is mostly harmless. Both of these functions are quite fast, and they will execute for relatively large input values. Unless you have used up a lot of stack space in some other part of your program, these functions will not be limited by the size of the stack.

On the other hand, recursion destroys the Fibonacci algorithm. To compute Fib(N), the algorithm first computes Fib(N − 1) and Fib(N − 2). But to compute Fib(N – 1), it must compute Fib(N – 2) and Fib(N – 3). Here, Fib(N – 2) is being computed twice.

The earlier analysis of this algorithm showed that Fib(1) and Fib(0) are computed a total of Fib(N + 1) times during the computation of Fib(N). Fib(30) = 832,040, so to compute Fib(29) you actually compute the same values for Fib(0) and Fib(1) a total of 832,040 times. The Fibonacci algorithm wastes a tremendous amount of time computing these intermediate values again and again.

The BigAdd function has a different problem. Although it runs quite quickly, it enters a deep recursion that may exhaust the stack space. The function could calculate values for much larger inputs if it did not overflow the stack first.

The factorial function has a similar problem. On input N, both the BigAdd and factorial functions recurse to a depth of N function calls. The factorial function cannot accept inputs as large as the BigAdd function can. The value of 170! ≈ 7.257E + 306 is the largest value that fits in a double variable, so that is the largest value the function can compute. While the function is headed for deep recursion, it causes double precision overflow before it overflows the stack.

When to Use Recursion

This discussion may lead you to think that all recursion is bad. That is definitely not the case. Many algorithms are naturally recursive. Even though it is possible to rewrite any algorithm so it does not contain recursion, many are harder to understand, analyze, debug, and maintain when they are written nonrecursively.

The following sections present methods for removing recursion from any algorithm. Some of the resulting nonrecursive algorithms are still fairly easy to understand. The nonrecursive factorial, GCD, Fibonacci, and BigAdd functions are relatively straightforward.

On the other hand, the nonrecursive versions of the Hilbert and Sierpinski algorithms are quite complicated. They are harder to understand and more difficult to maintain than the recursive versions. They are presented to show you techniques you could use to remove recursion from complicated algorithms, not because they are better than the recursive versions.

If an algorithm is naturally recursive, write it recursively. If all goes well, you will not encounter any of the problems described here. If you do run into some of these problems, you can rewrite the algorithm without recursion using the techniques presented in the following sections. Rewriting an algorithm is often easier than writing it nonrecursively in the first place.

Tail Recursion

Recall the functions presented earlier to compute factorials and greatest common divisors. Recall also the BigAdd function that exhausts the stack for relatively small inputs.

```
function Factorial(num : Integer) : Integer;
begin
    if (num <= 0) then
        Factorial := 1
    else
        Factorial := num * Factorial(num - 1);
end;

function Gcd(A, B : Longint) : Longint;
begin
    if (B mod A = 0) then
        Gcd := A
    else
        Gcd := Gcd(B mod A, A);
end;

function BigAdd(n : Double) : Double;
begin
    if (n <= 1) then
        BigAdd := 1
    else
        BigAdd := n + BigAdd(n - 1);
end;
```

In all of these functions, the last thing before the end of the function is the recursive step. This sort of recursion at the end of a routine is called *tail recursion* or *end recursion.*

Because nothing occurs in the routine after the recursive step, there is an easy way to remove the recursion. Instead of calling the function recursively, the routine resets its own parameters to match the ones it would normally pass into the recursive call. It then starts over from the beginning.

Consider this general recursive procedure:

```
procedure Recurse(A : Integer);
begin
    // Do stuff here, calculate B, etc.
    Recurse(B);
end;
```

You can rewrite this procedure without recursion as:

```
procedure NoRecurse(A : Integer);
begin
    while (not done) do
    begin
```

```
        // Do stuff here, calculate B, etc.
        A := B;
    end;
end;
```

This process is called *tail recursion removal* or *end recursion removal*. The process does not change the program's runtime. The recursive steps have just been replaced with passes through a while loop.

Tail recursion removal does eliminate procedure calls, however, and it may increase an algorithm's speed. More importantly, this method decreases the use of the stack. Algorithms like the BigAdd function that are limited by their depths of recursion will benefit greatly.

Some compilers remove tail recursion automatically. Delphi does not. Otherwise, the simple BigAdd function presented in the previous section would not exhaust the stack.

With tail recursion removal, rewriting the factorial, GCD, and BigAdd functions nonrecursively is easy.

```
function Factorial(num : Integer) : Integer;
begin
    Result := 1;
    while (num > 1) do
    begin
        Result:= Result * num;
        num := num - 1; // Prepare for the recursion.
    end;
end;


function Gcd(A, B : Longint) : Longint;
var
    b_mod_a : Longint;
begin
    b_mod_a := b mod a;
    while (b_mod_a <> 0) do
    begin
        // Prepare the arguments for the recursion.
        B := A;
        A = b_mod_a;
        b_mod_a := b mod a;
    end;
    Result := A;
end;


function BigAdd(n : Double) : Double;
```

```
begin
    Result := 1;
    while (n > 1) do
    begin
        Result := Result + N;
        n := n - 1;
    end;
end;
```

For the factorial and GCD algorithms, there is little practical difference between the recursive and nonrecursive versions. Both are fast, and both can handle problems that are reasonably large.

For the BigAdd algorithm, however, the difference is significant. The recursive version exhausts the stack for reasonably small inputs. Because the nonrecursive version does not use up the stack, it should be able to compute values for N up to about 10^{154}. Beyond that point, the double data type will overflow. Of course, running the algorithm for 10^{154} steps will take a long time, so you may not want to try such a large example. Notice also that this function is the same as the value of the more easily calculated function N * (N + 1) / 2.

Example programs Facto2, Gcd2, and BigAdd2 demonstrate these nonrecursive algorithms.

Nonrecursive Fibonacci Numbers

Unfortunately, the recursive algorithm for computing Fibonacci numbers does not contain only tail recursion. The algorithm uses two recursive calls to itself to calculate a value. The second call comes after the first finishes. Because the first call does not come at the very end of the function, it is not tail recursion, so it cannot be removed using tail recursion removal.

Perhaps this is just as well because the recursive Fibonacci algorithm is limited by the fact that it computes too many intermediate values rather than by its depth of recursion. Tail recursion removal decreases depth of recursion, but it does not change the algorithm's runtime. Even if tail recursion removal applied to the Fibonacci algorithm, it would still be extremely slow.

The trouble with this algorithm is that it recomputes the same values many times. The values Fib(1) and Fib(0) are computed a total of Fib(N + 1) times when the algorithm computes Fib(N). To compute Fib(29), the algorithm computes the same values for Fib(0) and Fib(1) a total of 832,040 times.

Whenever an algorithm recomputes the same values many times, you should look for a way to avoid the duplicate computations. A straightforward and mechanical way to do this is to build a table of the calculated values. When you need an intermediate value, you can look it up in the table rather than recomputing it.

In this example, you can build a table to store the values of the Fibonacci function Fib(N) for N less than 1477. For N >= 1477, the double precision variables used by the function overflow. The following code shows the Fibonacci function with this change.

```
Const
    MAX_FIB = 1476; // The largest value we can compute.

var
    FiboValues : Array[0..MAX_FIB] of Double;

function Fibo(n : Integer) : Double;
begin
    // Compute the value if it is not in the table.
    if (FiboValues[n] < 0.0) then
        FiboValues[n] := Fibo(n - 1) + Fibo(n - 2);
    Fibo := FiboValues[n];
end;
```

When the program begins, it should initialize each entry in the FibValues array to –1. It should then set the values of FibValues[0] to 0 and FibValues[1] to 1. These values establish the base case for the recursion.

When the function executes, it checks the array to see if it has already stored the value it needs. If not, it recursively calculates the value as before and stores the new value in the array for later use.

Example program Fibo2 uses this method for calculating Fibonacci numbers. The program can quickly compute Fib(N) for N up to 100 or 200. If you try to calculate Fib(1476), however, the program enters a chain of recursion 1476 levels deep. While this may not exhaust your system's stack, it is usually a good idea to avoid recursion this deep.

An alternative method for filling in the table of Fibonacci numbers avoids this deep recursion. When the program initializes the FibValues array, it precomputes all of the Fibonacci numbers.

```
// Initialize the lookup table.
procedure TFiboForm.FormCreate(Sender: TObject);
var
    i : Integer;
begin
    FiboValues[0] := 0;
    FiboValues[1] := 1;
    for i := 2 to MAX_FIB do
        FiboValues[i] :=
            FiboValues[i - 1] + FiboValues[i - 2];
end;
```

```
// Look up Fibonnaci numbers in a table.
function Fibo(n : Integer) : Double;
begin
    Fibo := FiboValues[n];
end;
```

This method takes a certain amount of time to create the lookup array. Once the array is ready, it takes only a single step to access a value in the array. Neither the initialization procedure nor function Fib uses recursion, so neither will exhaust the stack space. Example program Fibo3 demonstrates this approach.

One more method for computing Fibonacci numbers is worth mentioning. The first recursive definition of the Fibonacci function uses a top-down approach. To get a value for Fib(N), the algorithm recursively computes Fib(N – 1) and Fib(N – 2) and adds them together.

Procedure InitializeFibValues, on the other hand, works from the bottom up. It starts with the values of Fib(0) and Fib(1). It then uses smaller values to compute larger ones until the table is full.

You can use this same bottom-up strategy to compute the value of the Fibonacci function directly each time you need a value. This method takes longer than looking values up in an array, but it does not require the extra array memory. This is an example of a space versus time trade-off. Using extra space to store a table of values makes the algorithm faster.

```
function Fibo(n : Integer) : Double;
var
    fib_i, fib_i_minus_1, fib_i_minus_2 : Double;
    i                                   : Integer;
begin
    if (n <= 1) then
        Fibo := n
    else begin
        fib_i := 0;          // Prevent compiler warning.
        fib_i_minus_2 := 0;  // Initially fib(0).
        fib_i_minus_1 := 1;  // Initially fib(1).
        for i := 2 to n do
        begin
            fib_i := fib_i_minus_1 + fib_i_minus_2;
            fib_i_minus_2 := fib_i_minus_1;
            fib_i_minus_1 := fib_i;
        end;
        Fibo := fib_i;
    end;
end;
```

This version takes O(N) steps to calculate Fib(N). This is more than the single step the previous version required, but it is much faster than the original O(Fib(N)) steps. On a 133-megahertz Pentium, the original recursive algorithm took more than 155 seconds to calculate Fib(40) ≈ 1.02E + 8. The new algorithm takes no noticeable time to determine that Fib(1476) ≈ 1.31E + 308. Example program Fibo4 uses this method to compute Fibonacci numbers.

Avoiding More General Recursion

The factorial, GCD, and BigAdd functions can be simplified by tail recursion removal. The Fibonacci function can be simplified using a lookup table or by reformulating the problem in a bottom-up way.

Some recursive algorithms are so complicated that these methods are difficult or impossible. It would be hard to come up with nonrecursive algorithms for drawing Hilbert and Sierpinski curves from scratch. Other recursive algorithms are more complicated than those.

Earlier sections showed that any algorithm that draws Hilbert or Sierpinski curves must use $O(N^4)$ steps, so the original recursive implementations are pretty good. They are about as fast as possible and their depths of recursion are reasonable. Still, you may come across other complicated algorithms that have large depths of recursion but do not yield to tail recursion removal. In that case, converting a recursive algorithm into a nonrecursive one is still possible. The basic approach is to think about the way the computer performs recursion and then mimic the steps the computer follows. The new algorithm will perform a fake recursion instead of making the computer do all the work.

Because the new algorithm follows pretty much the same steps the computer follows, you might wonder if speed will increase. Chances are it will not. The computer can perform the tasks it needs for recursion more quickly than you can mimic them. Handling these details yourself gives you more control over the allocation of local variables, however, and allows you to avoid great depth of recursion.

Normally when you make a procedure call, the computer does three things. First, it saves any information it needs to resume execution when the procedure returns. Second, it prepares for the call and transfers control to the procedure. Third, when the called procedure ends, the computer restores the information it saved in the first step and transfers control back to the appropriate point in the program. When you convert a recursive procedure into a nonrecursive one, you perform these three steps yourself.

Consider the following generalized recursive procedure:

```
procedure Recurse(num : Integer);
begin
    <code block 1>
    Recurse(<parameters>)
    <code block 2>
end;
```

Because there is code after the recursive step, you cannot use tail recursion removal on this procedure.

Begin by labeling the first lines in code blocks 1 and 2. You will use these labels to determine where to resume execution when a fake recursion returns. You will use the labels only to help understand what the algorithm is doing—they are not actually part of the Delphi code. In this example, the labels are:

```
    procedure Recurse(num : Integer);
    begin
1        <code block 1>
         Recurse(<parameters>);
2        <code block 2>
    end;
```

Use a special label 0 to indicate that a fake recursion is ending. Now you can rewrite the procedure without recursion, like this:

```
procedure Recurse(num : Integer);
var
    pc : Integer;    // Tells us where to resume execution.
begin
    pc := 1;         // Start at the beginning.
    repeat           // Loop infinitely.
        case pc of
            1:       // Execute code block 1.
                begin
                    <code block 1>
                    if (the base case has been reached) then
                            // Skip the recursion and go to code
                            // block 2.
                        pc := 2
                    else begin
                            // Save variables needed after the
                            // recursion.
                            // Save pc = 2. This is where we will
                            // resume execution after the recursion
                            // returns.
                            // Set variables needed by the
                            // recursive call.
                            // For example, num = num - 1.
                            :
                            // Go to code block 1 to start the
                            // recursion.
                        pc := 1;
                    end;
```

```
              end;
    2:    // Execute code block 2.
          begin
              <code block 2>
              pc := 0;
          end;
    0:    // A recursion is ending.
          begin
              if (this is the last recursion) then break;
                  // Otherwise restore pc and other variables
                  // saved before the recursion.
                      :
          end;
      end; // End case.
   until (False); // End infinite loop.
end;
```

The variable pc, which stands for *program counter*, tells the procedure what step it should execute next. For example, when pc = 1, the procedure should execute code block 1.

When the procedure reaches the base case, it does not recurse. Instead, it changes pc to 2 so it will continue execution with code block 2.

If the procedure has not yet reached the base case, it prepares to mimic recursion. To do this, it saves the value of any local variables it will need later when the fake recursion ends. It also saves the value of pc for the code segment it should execute after the fake recursion returns. In this example, the procedure executes code block 2 next, so it saves 2 as the next value for pc. The easiest way to save the values of the local variables and pc is to use stacks like the ones described in Chapter 3, "Stacks and Queues."

A concrete example should make this easier to understand. Consider a slightly rewritten version of the factorial function. It is rewritten here as a procedure that returns its value through a variable, rather than as a function, to make things a little easier.

```
        procedure Factorial(num, value : Integer);

        var
            partial : Integer;
        begin
1           if (num <= 1) then
                value := 1
            else begin
                Factorial(num - 1, partial);
2               value := num * partial;
            end;
        end;
```

After the procedure returns from the recursion, it needs to know the original value of num so it can perform the multiplication value := num * partial. Because it needs access to the value of num after the recursion returns, it must save pc and num before starting the recursion.

The following procedure saves these values in two array-based stacks. When preparing for recursion, the procedure pushes num and pc onto the stacks. When a fake recursion finishes, the procedure pops the most recently added values from the stacks. The following code shows a nonrecursive version of the factorial procedure.

```
procedure Factorial(num, value : Integer);
var
    num_stack : array [1..200] of Integer;
    pc_stack  : array [1..200] of Integer;
    stack_top : Integer;    // The top of the stack.
    pc        : Integer;
begin
    stack_top := 0;
    pc := 1;
    repeat    // Loop infinitely.
        case pc of
            1:
                begin
                    if (num <= 1) then   // This is the base case.
                    begin
                        value := 1;
                        pc := 0;          // End this recursion.
                    end else             // Recurse.
                        // Save num and the next pc.
                        stack_top := stack_top + 1;
                        num_stack[stack_top] := num;
                        pc_stack[stack_top] := 2;  // Resume at 2.
                        // Start the recursion.
                        num := num - 1;
                        // Transfer control back to the start.
                        pc := 1;
                    end;
                end;
            2:
                begin
                    // Variable value holds the result of the
                    // recently finished recursion. Multiply it
                    // by num.
                    value := value * num;
                    // Return from a recursion.
```

```
                            pc := 0;
                end;
          0:
                begin
                    // End a recursion.
                    // If the stacks are empty, we are done
                    // with the original call to the procedure.
                    if (stack_top <= 0) then break;
                    // Otherwise restore local variables and pc.
                    num := num_stack[stack_top];
                    pc := pc_stack[stack_top];
                    stack_top := stack_top - 1;
                end;
            end; // End case.
        until (False); // End looping infinitely.
end;
```

Like tail recursion removal, this technique mimics the behavior of the recursive algorithm. The procedure has replaced each recursive call with an iteration in the repeat loop. Because the steps executed are the same, the overall runtime of the algorithm is unchanged.

As is the case with tail recursion removal, this technique removes the need for the algorithm to recurse deeply, possibly exhausting the stack.

Nonrecursive Hilbert Curves

The factorial example in the previous section turned a simple but inefficient recursive factorial function into a complicated and inefficient nonrecursive procedure. For the factorial function, a much better nonrecursive algorithm was presented earlier in the chapter.

Finding a simple nonrecursive version for more complicated algorithms can be difficult. The techniques of the previous section are useful when the algorithm is multiply recursive or calls itself indirectly.

For a more interesting example of recursion removal, consider the recursive Hilbert curve algorithm.

```
procedure THilb1Form.DrawHilbert(depth, dx, dy : Integer);
begin
    with DrawArea.Canvas do
    begin
        if (depth > 1) then DrawHilbert(depth - 1, dy, dx);
        LineTo(PenPos.X + dx, PenPos.Y + dy);
        if (depth > 1) then DrawHilbert(depth - 1, dx, dy);
        LineTo(PenPos.X + dy, PenPos.Y + dx);
```

```
        if (depth > 1) then DrawHilbert(depth - 1, dx, dy);
        LineTo(PenPos.X - dx, PenPos.Y - dy);
        if (depth > 1) then DrawHilbert(depth - 1, -dy, -dx);
    end;
end;
```

The following code shows the numbering of the first lines in each code block between the recursive steps. These include the first line of the procedure and any other places where the program might have to resume execution after a fake recursion returns.

```
    procedure THilb1Form.DrawHilbert(depth, dx, dy : Integer);
    begin
        with DrawArea.Canvas do
        begin
1           if (depth > 1) then DrawHilbert(depth - 1, dy, dx);
2           LineTo(PenPos.X + dx, PenPos.Y + dy);
            if (depth > 1) then DrawHilbert(depth - 1, dx, dy);
3           LineTo(PenPos.X + dy, PenPos.Y + dx);
            if (depth > 1) then DrawHilbert(depth - 1, dx, dy);
4           LineTo(PenPos.X - dx, PenPos.Y - dy);
            if (depth > 1) then DrawHilbert(depth - 1, -dy, -dx);
        end;
    end;
```

Each time the nonrecursive procedure begins a fake recursion, it must save the values of the local variables depth, dx, and dy, as well as the next value for pc. When it returns from a fake recursion, it restores these values. To make these operations a little easier, you can write a pair of auxiliary procedures to push and pop these values from a group of stacks.

```
const
    STACK_SIZE = 10; // Maximum depth of recursion.

type
  THilb2Form = class(TForm)
    // Code omitted...
        :
  private
    pc_stack, depth_stack : Array[1..STACK_SIZE] of Integer;
    dx_stack, dy_stack    : Array[1..STACK_SIZE] of Integer;
    top_of_stack          : Integer;
    // More code omitted...
        :
  end;
```

```
// Push values onto the stacks.
procedure THilb2Form.PushValues(pc, depth, dx, dy : Integer);
begin
    top_of_stack := top_of_stack + 1;
    depth_stack[top_of_stack] := depth;
    dx_stack[top_of_stack] := dx;
    dy_stack[top_of_stack] := dy;
    pc_stack[top_of_stack] := pc;
end;

// Pop values off of the stacks.
procedure THilb2Form.PopValues(var pc, depth, dx, dy : Integer);
begin
    depth := depth_stack[top_of_stack];
    dx := dx_stack[top_of_stack];
    dy := dy_stack[top_of_stack];
    pc := pc_stack[top_of_stack];
    top_of_stack := top_of_stack - 1;
end;
```

The following code shows the nonrecursive version of the Hilbert procedure.

```
procedure THilb2Form.DrawHilbert(depth, dx, dy : Integer);
var
    pc, tmp : Integer;
begin
    pc := 1;
    with DrawArea.Canvas do
        while (True) do
        begin
            Case pc of
            1:
                begin
                    if (depth > 1) then // Recurse.
                    begin
                        // Save the current values.
                        PushValues(2, depth, dx, dy);
                        // Prepare for the recursion.
                        depth := depth - 1;
                        tmp := dx;
                        dx := dy;
                        dy := tmp;
                        pc := 1; // Go to start of recursive call.
```

```
                           end else begin  // Base case.
                                   // We have recursed deeply enough.
                                   // Continue with code block 2.
                               pc := 2;
                           end;
                       end;
               2:
                   begin
                       LineTo(PenPos.X + dx, PenPos.Y + dy);
                       if (depth > 1) then // Recurse.
                       begin
                               // Save the current values.
                               PushValues(3, depth, dx, dy);
                               // Prepare for the recursion.
                               depth := depth - 1;
                               // dx and dy remain the same.
                               pc := 1  // Go to start of recursive call.
                       end else begin // Base case.
                               // We have recursed deeply enough.
                               // Continue with code block 3.
                               pc := 3;
                       end;
                   end;
               3:
                   begin
                       LineTo(PenPos.X + dy, PenPos.Y + dx);
                       if (depth > 1) then // Recurse.
                       begin
                               // Save the current values.
                               PushValues(4, depth, dx, dy);
                               // Prepare for the recursion.
                               depth := depth - 1;
                               // dx and dy remain the same.
                               pc := 1;  // Go to start of recursive call.
                       end else begin // Base case.
                               // We have recursed deeply enough.
                               // Continue with code block 4.
                               pc := 4;
                       end;
                   end;
               4:
                   begin
```

```
                LineTo(PenPos.X - dx, PenPos.Y - dy);
                if (depth > 1) then  // Recurse.
                begin
                        // Save the current values.
                    PushValues(0, depth, dx, dy);
                        // Prepare for the recursion.
                    depth := depth - 1;
                    tmp := dx;
                    dx := -dy;
                    dy := -tmp;
                    pc := 1; // Go to start of recursive call.
                end else begin // Base case.
                        // We have recursed deeply enough.
                        // This is the end of this recursive
                        // call.
                    pc := 0;
                end;
            end;
        0: // Return from recursion.
            begin
                if (top_of_stack > 0) then
                    PopValues(pc, depth, dx, dy)
            else
                    // The stack is empty. We are done.
                break;
        end; // End case pc of.
      end; // End while (True).
    end; // End with DrawArea.Canvas do.
end;
```

The runtime for this algorithm would be quite tricky to analyze directly. Because the techniques for converting recursive procedures into nonrecursive ones do not change the algorithm's runtime, this procedure has the same $O(N^4)$ runtime as the previous version.

Example program Hilb2 demonstrates this nonrecursive algorithm for drawing Hilbert curves. Be sure to draw simple curves (depth under 6) until you know how long the program will take on your computer.

Nonrecursive Sierpinski Curves

The Sierpinski algorithm presented earlier is both multiply and indirectly recursive. Because the algorithm consists of four subroutines that call each other, you cannot number the important lines as you can with the Hilbert curve algorithm. You can deal with this problem by rewriting the algorithm a bit first.

The recursive version of this algorithm consists of four subroutines: SierpA, SierpB, SierpC, and SierpD. Procedure SierpA looks like this:

```
procedure TSierp1Form.SierpA(depth, dist : Integer);
begin
    with DrawArea.Canvas do
    begin
        if (depth = 1) then
        begin
            LineTo(PenPos.X - dist, PenPos.Y + dist);
            LineTo(PenPos.X - dist, PenPos.Y + 0   );
            LineTo(PenPos.X - dist, PenPos.Y - dist);
        end else begin
            SierpA(depth - 1, dist);
            LineTo(PenPos.X - dist, PenPos.Y + dist);
            SierpB(depth - 1, dist);
            LineTo(PenPos.X - dist, PenPos.Y + 0   );
            SierpD(depth - 1, dist);
            LineTo(PenPos.X - dist, PenPos.Y - dist);
            SierpA(depth - 1, dist);
        end;
    end;
end;
```

The other three subroutines are similar. Combining these four procedures into a single procedure is not difficult.

```
procedure DrawSubcurve(depth, dist, func : Integer);
begin
    case func of
        1:
            // <SierpA code>.
        2:
            // <SierpB code>.
        3:
            // <SierpC code>.
        4:
            // <SierpD code>.
    end;
end;
```

The func parameter tells the procedure which piece of code to execute. The program can now replace calls to the subroutines with calls to SierpAll using the appropriate value for func. For example, a call to SierpA would be replaced with a call to SierpAll where func is set to 1.

The new procedure is massively recursive, calling itself in 16 different places. This procedure is much larger than the Hilbert procedure, but otherwise, it has a similar structure, and you can apply the same techniques for making it nonrecursive.

You can use the first digit of the pc labels to indicate which general piece of code to execute. Number lines within the SierpA code 11, 12, 13, and so on. Number lines in the SierpB code 21, 22, 23, and so forth.

Now you can label the key lines of code within each section. For the SierpA code, the key lines are:

```
        // SierpA code.
        with DrawArea.Canvas do
        begin
11          if (depth = 1) then
            begin
                LineTo(PenPos.X - dist, PenPos.Y + dist);
                LineTo(PenPos.X - dist, PenPos.Y + 0   );
                LineTo(PenPos.X - dist, PenPos.Y - dist);
            end else begin
                SierpA(depth - 1, dist);
12              LineTo(PenPos.X - dist, PenPos.Y + dist);
                SierpB(depth - 1, dist);
13              LineTo(PenPos.X - dist, PenPos.Y + 0   );
                SierpD(depth - 1, dist);
14              LineTo(PenPos.X - dist, PenPos.Y - dist);
                SierpA(depth - 1, dist);
            end;
        end;
```

A typical fake recursion from the SierpA code into the SierpB code looks like this:

```
PushValues(depth, 13)     // Resume at step 13 when done.
depth := depth - 1;
pc := 21;                 // Transfer to the start of the SierpB
                          // code.
```

The label 0 is reserved to indicate a return from a fake recursion. The following code shows part of the nonrecursive version of SierpAll. The code for the SierpB, SierpC, and SierpD code is similar to the code for SierpA, so it is omitted. You can find all the code on the CD-ROM.

```
procedure TSierpinskiForm.DrawSubcurve(depth, pc, dist : Integer);
begin
    with DrawArea.Canvas do
    begin
```

```
while (true) do
begin
    case pc of
    // **********
    // * SierpA *
    // **********
    11:
        begin
            if (depth <= 1) then
            begin
                LineTo(PenPos.X - dist, PenPos.Y + dist);
                LineTo(PenPos.X - dist, PenPos.Y + 0   );
                LineTo(PenPos.X - dist, PenPos.Y - dist);
                pc := 0;
            end else begin
                PushValues(12, depth); // Run SierpA.
                depth := depth - 1;
                pc := 11;
            end;
        end;
    12:
        begin
            LineTo(PenPos.X - dist, PenPos.Y + dist);
            PushValues(13, depth); // Run SierpB.
            depth := depth - 1;
            pc := 21;
        end;
    13:
        begin
            LineTo(PenPos.X - dist, PenPos.Y + 0);
            PushValues(14, depth); // Run SierpD.
            depth := depth - 1;
            pc := 41;
        end;
    14:
        begin
            LineTo(PenPos.X - dist, PenPos.Y - dist);
            PushValues(0, depth); // Run SierpA.
            depth := depth - 1;
            pc := 11;
        end;

    // SierpB, SierpC, and SierpD code omitted.
        :
```

```
//  ****************
//  * End recursion *
//  ****************
0:
        begin
            if (top_of_stack <= 0) then break;  // Done.
            PopValues(pc, depth);
        end;
    end; // case pc of.
  end; // while (true) do.
 end; // End with DrawArea.Canvas do.
end;
```

As is the case with the Hilbert curve algorithm, converting the Sierpinski curve algorithm into a nonrecursive format does not change the algorithm's runtime. The new algorithm mimics the behavior of the recursive algorithm that runs in $O(N^4)$ time, so the new version also has $O(N^4)$ runtime.

The nonrecursive version would allow a greater depth of recursion, but it is not practical to draw Sierpinski curves with depth greater than 8 or 9 anyway. These facts make the recursive algorithm the better algorithm.

Example program Sierp2 uses this nonrecursive algorithm to draw Sierpinski curves. Draw only simple curves (depth under 6) until you know how long the program will take on your computer.

Summary

You must watch for three main dangers in recursive algorithms:

Infinite recursion. Make sure your algorithm has a solid base case that stops all recursive paths.

Deep recursion. If the algorithm recurses too deeply, it will exhaust the stack. Minimize stack use by reducing the number of variables the procedure allocates or by allocating variables globally. If the procedure still exhausts the stack, rewrite the algorithm nonrecursively using tail recursion removal.

Inappropriate recursion. Usually this occurs when an algorithm like the recursive Fibonacci algorithm calculates the same intermediate values many times. If your program has this problem, try to rewrite the algorithm in a bottom-up way. If the algorithm does not lend itself to a bottom-up approach, create a lookup table of intermediate values.

Not all recursion is bad. Many problems are naturally recursive. In these cases, a recursive algorithm will be easier to understand, debug, and maintain than a nonrecursive one. The Hilbert and Sierpinski curve algorithms demonstrate appropriate recursion. Both are naturally recursive and are much easier to understand in their recursive forms.

If you have an algorithm that is naturally recursive but you are not sure if the recursive version will cause problems, write it recursively and see. There may be no problem. If there is, it will probably be easier to translate the recursive algorithm into a nonrecursive one than to come up with the nonrecursive version from scratch.

TREES

6

Chapter 2, "Lists," explains ways to create dynamic, linked data structures like those shown in Figure 6.1. These kinds of data structures are called *graphs*. Chapter 12, "Network Algorithms," discusses graph and network algorithms in some detail. This chapter examines a special kind of graph called a *tree*.

This chapter first defines trees and explains some tree terminology. It then describes several methods for implementing different kinds of trees in Delphi.

The sections that follow examine tree traversal algorithms for trees stored using these different formats. The chapter finishes by discussing some specialized types of trees including sorted trees, threaded trees, tries, and quadtrees.

Chapter 7, "Balanced Trees," and Chapter 8, "Decision Trees," explain two more advanced tree topics.

Figure 6.1 Graphs.

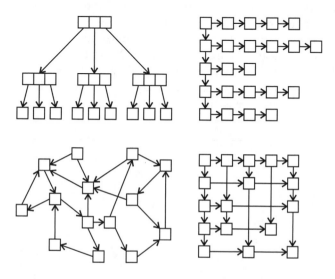

Definitions

You can define a tree recursively as either:

- An empty structure

- A *node,* called the *root* of the tree, connected to zero or more *subtrees*

Figure 6.2 shows a tree. Here the root node A is connected to three *subtrees* starting at nodes B, C, and D. Those nodes are connected to subtrees with roots E, F, and G, and those nodes are connected, in turn, to the subtrees with roots H, I, and J.

Tree terminology is a hodgepodge of terms borrowed from botany and genealogy. From botany come terms like *node* to describe where a branch might occur, *branch* to describe a link connecting two nodes, and *leaf* to describe a node that has no branches leaving it.

From genealogy come terms that describe relationships. When one node is directly above another, the upper node is called the *parent* and the lower node is called the *child.* The nodes along the path from a node upward to the root are that node's *ancestors.* For example, in Figure 6.2 the nodes E, B, and A are all ancestors of node I. The nodes below another node in the tree are that node's *descendants.* The nodes E, H, I, and J in Figure 6.2 are all descendants of node B. Occasionally, people even refer to nodes that have the same parent as *sibling* (brother or sister) nodes.

There are also a few tree terms that do not come from botany or genealogy. An *internal node* is a node that is not a leaf. A node's *degree* is the number of children the node has. The degree of a tree is the largest degree of all the nodes in the tree. The degree of the tree shown in Figure 6.2 is three, because the nodes with the largest degree, nodes A and E, have three children.

The *depth* of a node is 1 plus the number of the node's ancestors. In Figure 6.2, node E has depth 3. The *depth* or *height* of a tree is the greatest depth of all of its nodes. The depth of the tree shown in Figure 6.2 is 4.

A degree 2 tree is called a *binary* tree. Degree 3 trees are sometimes called *ternary* trees. Beyond that, trees of degree N are usually called *N-ary* trees. A degree 12 tree, for example, is called a 12-ary tree, not a "dodecadary" tree. Some people prefer to avoid odd terminology and simply say "tree of degree 12."

Figure 6.3 illustrates some of these tree terms.

Figure 6.2 A tree.

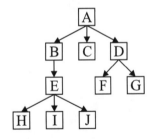

Figure 6.3 Parts of a ternary (degree 3) tree.

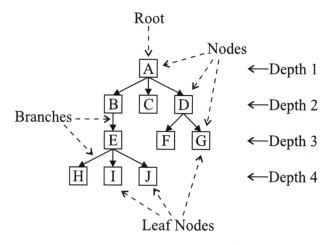

Tree Representations

Now that you know some basic tree terminology, you can think about ways to implement trees in Delphi. One approach is to create a different class for each type of node in the tree. To build the tree shown in Figure 6.3, you would define data structures for nodes that have zero, one, two, or three children. This approach would be rather inconvenient. In addition to managing four different node data types, you would need to place some sort of indicators in the classes so you could tell what kind of nodes their children were. Algorithms that manipulate these trees would need to be able to work with all the different kinds of nodes.

Fat Nodes

A simpler solution is to define a single node type with enough child pointers to represent any of the nodes you need. I call this the *fat node* method because some nodes will be larger than they really need to be.

The tree shown in Figure 6.3 has degree 3. To build this tree using the fat node method, you would define a single class that contains pointers to three child nodes. The following code shows how a TTernaryNode data type might define these pointers.

```
type
    PTernaryNode = ^TTernaryNode;
    TTernaryNode = record
        LeftChild   : PTernaryNode;
        MiddleChild : PTernaryNode;
        RightChild  : PTernaryNode;
    end;
```

With this data type you can build a tree using the nodes' child entries to link the nodes together. The following code fragment builds the top two levels of the tree shown in Figure 6.3.

```
var
    A, B, C, D : PTernaryNode;
begin
    // Allocate the nodes.
    GetMem(A, SizeOf(TTernaryNode));
    GetMem(B, SizeOf(TTernaryNode));
    GetMem(C, SizeOf(TTernaryNode));
    GetMem(D, SizeOf(TTernaryNode));

    // Connect the nodes.
    A^.LeftChild := B;
    A^.MiddleChild := C;
    A^.LeftChild := D;
        :
```

Example program Binary, shown in Figure 6.4, uses a fat node strategy to manage a binary tree. It uses the TBinaryNode class to store node information instead of a record data type. When you click on a node, the program enables the Add Left button if the node has no left child. It enables the Add Right button if the node has no right child. It enables the Remove button if the node is not the root node. If you click the Remove button, the program removes that node and all of its descendants.

Figure 6.4 Program Binary.

Because this program allows you to create nodes with zero, one, or two children, it uses a fat node representation. You could easily extend this example for
trees of higher degree.

Child Lists

If the degrees of the nodes in a tree vary greatly, the fat node strategy wastes a lot
of space. To build the tree shown in Figure 6.5 using fat nodes, you would need
to give every node six child pointers, even though only one node actually needed
all six of them. The tree's representation would require 72 child pointers, only 11
of which would actually be used.

Some programs add and remove nodes, so node degrees change while the program is running. In this case, the fat node strategy will not work. You can represent these dynamic trees by keeping the nodes' children in lists. There are several
strategies you might use for making the child lists.

One approach is to use a node class that has a resizable public array of child
nodes, as in the following code. Then you can use array-based list techniques to
manage the children.

```
type
    PNAryNodeArray = ^TNAryNodeArray;
    TNAryNode = class(TObject)
        private
        public
            NumChildren : Integer;
            Children    : PNAryNodeArray;
                :
    end;
    TNAryNodeArray = array [1..100000000] of TNAryNode;
```

Figure 6.5 A tree with nodes of widely varying degree.

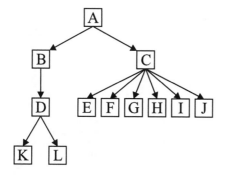

Example program NAry, shown in Figure 6.6, uses this strategy to manage an N-ary tree much as program Binary manage a binary tree. In this program, however, you can add as many children as you like to each node.

To avoid making the program's user interface more complicated than necessary, program NAry always adds new nodes at the end of the parent's child collection. You could modify the program to allow the insertion of children in the middle of a node's child collection, but the user interface would be more complicated.

An alternative approach is to store a node's child pointers in linked lists. Each node contains a pointer to its first child. It also contains a pointer to the next child at its level of the tree. Those links form a linked list of the node's siblings, so I call this technique a *linked sibling* representation. See Chapter 2, "Lists," for more information about linked lists.

Forward Star

The forward star representation introduced in Chapter 4, "Arrays," provides a compact array-based representation of trees, graphs, and networks. To store a tree using forward star, an array FirstLink holds the index of the first branch leaving each node. Another array, ToNode, gives the node to which the branch leads.

A sentinel entry at the end of the FirstLink array points just beyond the last entry in the ToNode array. This makes it easy to determine which branches leave each node. The branches leaving node i are those numbered FirstLink[i] through FirstLink[i + 1] – 1.

Figure 6.7 shows a tree and its forward star representation. The links out of node 3 (labeled D) are the links FirstLink[3] through FirstLink[4] – 1. FirstLink[3] = 9 and FirstLink[4] = 11, so these are the links numbered 9 and 10. The ToNode entries for these links are ToNode[9] = 10 and ToNode[10] = 11, so the children of node 3 are nodes 10 and 11. These are the nodes labeled K and L. This means the links leaving node D go to nodes K and L.

Figure 6.6 Program NAry.

Figure 6.7 A tree and its forward star representation.

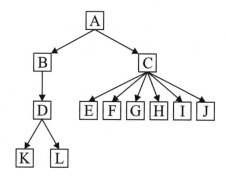

FirstLink:

Index	0	1	2	3	4	5	6	7	8	9	10	11	12
Label	A	B	C	D	E	F	G	H	I	J	K	L	
FirstLink	0	2	3	9	11	11	11	11	11	11	11	11	11

ToNode:

Index	0	1	2	3	4	5	6	7	8	9	10
ToNode	1	2	3	4	5	6	7	8	9	10	11

The forward star representation of a tree is compact and array based. That makes it easy to read and write to files. The array operations used by forward star can also be faster than the pointer operations used by some representations.

It is partly for these reasons that much of the literature about network algorithms uses a forward star representation. Many articles about shortest path calculations, for example, assume that the data is in a format similar to forward star. If you ever research these algorithms in journals like *Management Science* or *Operations Research,* you will need to understand forward star.

Using forward star, you can quickly find the links leaving a particular node. On the other hand, forward star is extremely difficult to modify. To add a new child to node A in Figure 6.7, you would have to update almost every entry in both the FirstLink and ToNode arrays. First, you would move every entry in the ToNode array one position to the right to make room for the new link. Next, you would insert the new ToNode entry, pointing to the new node. Finally, you would run through the FirstLink array updating each entry so that it pointed to the new position of the corresponding ToNode entry. Because you moved all of the ToNode entries one position to the right to make room for the new link, you would need to add 1 to the affected FirstLink entries.

Figure 6.8 shows this tree after the new node has been added. The items that have been modified are shaded so they are easy to see.

Removing a node from the beginning of a tree's forward star representation is just as hard as adding one. If the node you are removing has children, the process becomes even more time consuming because you need to remove the children as well.

The relative simplicity of a class with an array or linked list of child pointers makes that representation better if you need to modify the tree frequently. It is usually easier to understand and debug procedures that modify that representation. On the other hand, forward star sometimes gives better performance for complicated tree algorithms. It is also a standard data structure discussed in the literature, so you need to be familiar with it if you want to do further research into tree and network algorithms.

Example program FStar uses a forward star representation to manage a tree with nodes of varying degrees. It is similar to program NAry except it uses a forward star representation. If you examine program FStar's code, you will see how difficult it is to add and remove nodes. The following code shows how the program removes a node from the tree.

Figure 6.8 Adding a node to forward star.

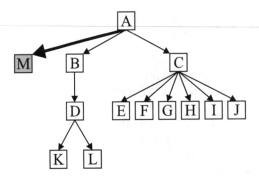

FirstLink:

Index	0	1	2	3	4	5	6	7	8	9	10	11	12	13
Label	A	B	C	D	E	F	G	H	I	J	K	L	M	
FirstLink	0	3	4	10	12	12	12	12	12	12	12	12	12	12

ToNode:

Index	0	1	2	3	4	5	6	7	8	9	10	11
ToNode	12	1	2	3	4	5	6	7	8	9	10	11

```
// Remove the selected node from the tree.
// The node must have no children.
procedure TFStarTree.RemoveSelected;
var
    i, first_link, last_link : Integer;
    parent_node, parent_link : Integer;
begin
    // Find the parent link.
    parent_node := Node^[Selected].Parent;
    first_link := Node^[parent_node].FirstLink;
    last_link := Node^[parent_node + 1].FirstLink - 1;
    for parent_link := first_link to last_link do
        if (ToNode^[parent_link] = Selected) then break;

    // If we found the parent link, remove it.
    if (parent_link <= last_link) then
    begin
        // Fill in the hole in ToNode.
        for i := parent_link to NumLinks - 1 do
            ToNode^[i] := ToNode^[i + 1];
        NumLinks := NumLinks - 1;
        // Don't bother to resize the ToNode array.

        // Update the nodes' FirstLink entries.
        for i := 1 to NumNodes do
            if (Node^[i].FirstLink > parent_link) then
                Node^[i].FirstLink := Node^[i].FirstLink - 1;
    end;

    // Remove the node itself by filling in the hole in
    // the Node array.
    for i := Selected to NumNodes - 1 do
        Node^[i] := Node^[i + 1];
    NumNodes := NumNodes - 1;

    // Update the ToNode entries.
    for i := 1 to NumLinks do
        if (ToNode^[i] > Selected) then
            ToNode^[i] := ToNode^[i] - 1;

    Selected := 0;
end;
```

This is much more complicated than the corresponding code used by program NAry to update a node with an array of child pointers.

```
// Remove a child from this node.
procedure TNAryNode.RemoveChild(target : TNAryNode);
var
    num, i : Integer;
begin
    // Find the child.
    for num := 1 to NumChildren do
    begin
        if (Children^[num] = target) then break;
    end;

    if (num > NumChildren) then
        raise EInvalidOperation.Create(
            'The target is not a child of this node.');

    // Free the child.
    Children^[num].Free;

    // Move the remaining children over to fill the hole.
    for i := num + 1 to NumChildren do
        Children^[i - 1] := Children^[i];
    Children^[NumChildren] := nil;
    NumChildren := NumChildren - 1;
end;
```

Complete Trees

A *complete* tree has as many nodes as it can hold at each level, except it may be missing some nodes on the bottom level. Any nodes present on the bottom level are pushed to the left. Each level in a ternary tree, for example, has exactly three children, except for the leaves and possibly one node on the level above the leaves. Figure 6.9 shows complete binary and ternary trees.

Figure 6.9 Complete trees.

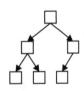

Complete binary tree   Complete ternary tree

Complete trees have a number of important properties. First, they are the shortest trees that can hold a given number of nodes. The binary tree in Figure 6.9, for example, is as short as any other binary tree that holds six nodes. There are other binary trees of height 3 with six nodes, but there are none of height less than 3.

Second, if a complete tree of degree D contains N nodes, it will have $O(\log_D(N))$ height and $O(N)$ leaf nodes. These facts are important because many algorithms traverse trees from the top to the bottom or vice versa. An algorithm that does this once has $O(\log(N))$ runtime.

A particularly useful property of complete trees is that they can be stored very compactly in arrays. If you number the nodes in the "natural" way, from top to bottom and left to right, you can place the tree entries in an array in this natural order. Figure 6.10 shows how to store a complete binary tree in an array.

The tree's root belongs in position 0. The children of node i belong in positions 2 * i + 1 and 2 * i + 2. For example, in Figure 6.10 the children of the node at position 1 (node B) are in positions 3 and 4 (nodes D and E).

It is easy to generalize this representation for complete trees of higher degree D. Again, the root node belongs in position 0. The children of node i belong in positions D * i + 1 through D * i + D. In a ternary tree, for instance, the children of a node at position 2 would be at positions 7, 8, and 9. Figure 6.11 shows a complete ternary tree and its array representation.

Accessing the children of a node using this array storage technique is fast and easy. This method is compact—it does not need extra storage for child collections or forward star sentinels. Saving and loading the tree from a file is a simple matter of reading and writing the tree's array. For these reasons, this is clearly the best tree representation for programs that store data in complete trees.

Tree Traversal

Visiting each node in a tree is called *traversing* the tree. There are several possible orders in which you might want to visit the nodes in a binary tree. The

Figure 6.10 Placing a complete binary tree in an array.

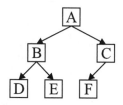

Index	0	1	2	3	4	5
Node	A	B	C	D	E	F

Figure 6.11 Placing a complete ternary tree in an array.

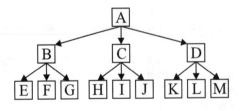

Index	0	1	2	3	4	5	6	7	8	9	10	11	12
ToNode	A	B	C	D	E	F	G	H	I	J	K	L	M

three simplest—preorder, inorder, and postorder—have straightforward recursive algorithms. When the algorithm is considering any given node it should do the following:

Preorder:

1. Visit the node.
2. Recursively traverse the left subtree in preorder.
3. Recursively traverse the right subtree in preorder.

Inorder:

1. Recursively traverse the left subtree in inorder.
2. Visit the node.
3. Recursively traverse the right subtree in inorder.

Postorder:

1. Recursively traverse the left subtree in postorder.
2. Recursively traverse the right subtree in postorder.
3. Visit the node.

All three of these are *depth first* traversals. The traversal begins by working its way deeply into the tree until it reaches the leaves. As the recursive procedure calls return, the algorithm works its way back up through the tree visiting paths that it skipped on the way down.

Depth first traversals are useful in algorithms that must visit a leaf early. For example, the branch and bound algorithm described in Chapter 8, "Decision Trees," visits a leaf node as soon as possible. It uses the results it finds at the leaf to reduce the size of the search it makes through the rest of the tree.

A fourth method of visiting the nodes in a tree is *breadth first* traversal. This method visits all the nodes at a given level of the tree before it visits any nodes on deeper levels. Algorithms that perform an exhaustive search of a tree often use breadth first traversals. The label setting shortest path algorithm described in

Chapter 12, "Network Algorithms," is a breadth first traversal of a shortest path tree within a network.

Figure 6.12 shows a small tree and the order in which the nodes are visited during preorder, inorder, postorder, and breadth first traversals.

For trees of degree greater than 2, it still makes sense to define preorder, postorder, and breadth first traversals. There is some ambiguity in defining inorder traversals because each node could be visited after one, two, or more of its children. In a ternary tree, for example, a node might be visited after its first child was visited or after its second child was visited.

Details for traversing a tree depend on how it is stored. To traverse a tree stored using arrays of child pointers, a program would use a slightly different algorithm than the one it would use to traverse a tree stored in forward star format.

Complete trees stored in arrays are particularly easy to traverse. The breadth first traversal, which requires extra work for other tree representations, is trivial for array-based representations because the nodes are stored in breadth first order. The following code shows the traversal algorithms for a complete binary tree.

```
type
    String10 = String[10];
    TStringArray = array[1..1000000] of String10;
    PStringArray = ^TStringArray;
var
    NumNodes  : Integer;
    NodeLabel : PStringArray; // Array of node labels.

    // Initialize the tree.
        :
```

Figure 6.12 Tree traversals.

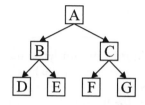

Preorder: A B D E C F G
Inorder: D B E A F C G
Postorder: D E B F G C A
Breadth first: A B C D E F G

```
procedure Preorder(node : Integer);
begin
    VisitNode(NodeLabel^[node]); // Visit the node.
    if (node * 2 + 1 <= NumNodes) then
        Preorder(node * 2 + 1);  // Visit child 1.
    if (node * 2 + 2 <= NumNodes) then
        Preorder(node * 2 + 2);  // Visit child 2.
end;

procedure Inorder(node : Integer);
begin
    if (node * 2 + 1 <= NumNodes) then
        Inorder(node * 2 + 1);   // Visit child 1.
    VisitNode(NodeLabel^[node]); // Visit the node.
    if (node * 2 + 2 <= NumNodes) then
        Inorder(node * 2 + 2);   // Visit child 2.
end;

procedure Postorder(node : Integer);
begin
    if (node * 2 + 1 <= NumNodes) then
        Postorder(node * 2 + 1); // Visit child 1.
    if (node * 2 + 2 <= NumNodes) then
        Postorder(node * 2 + 2); // Visit child 2.
    VisitNode(NodeLabel^[node]); // Visit the node.
end;

procedure BreadthFirst(node : Integer);
var
    i : Integer;
begin
    for i := 0 to NumNodes do
        VisitNode(NodeLabel^[i]);
end;
```

Example program Trav1 demonstrates preorder, inorder, postorder, and breadth first traversals for array-based complete binary trees. Enter the height of the tree you want to traverse, and click the Create Tree button to create a full binary tree. Then click the Preorder, Inorder, Postorder, or Breadth First buttons to see the tree's traversals. Figure 6.13 shows the program displaying the inorder traversal for a tree of depth 5.

The preorder and postorder traversals for trees stored in other representations are just as easy. The following code shows the preorder traversal procedure for a tree stored in forward star format.

Figure 6.13 Program Trav1 displaying a tree's inorder traversal.

```
procedure Preorder(node : Integer);
var
    link : Integer;
begin
    VisitNode(NodeLabel^[node]);
    for link := FirstLink^[node] to FirstLink^[node + 1] - 1 do
        Preorder(ToNode^[link]);
end;
```

As mentioned earlier, it is hard to define inorder traversals for trees of degree greater than 2. If you do decide what an inorder traversal means, however, you should not have much trouble implementing it. The following code shows an inorder traversal procedure that visits half of a node's children (rounding down), then visits the node itself, and then visits the remaining children.

```
procedure Inorder(node : Integer);
var
    mid_link, link : Integer;
begin
    // Find the middle child.
    mid_link := (FirstLink^[node + 1] - 1 + FirstLink^[node]) div 2;

    // Visit the first group of children.
    for link := FirstLink^[node] to mid_link do
        Inorder(ToNode^[link]);
```

```
// Visit the node.
VisitNode(NodeLabel^[node]);

// Visit the second group of children.
for link := mid_link + 1 to FirstLink^[node + 1] - 1 do
    Inorder(ToNode^[link]);
end;
```

For complete trees stored in an array, the nodes just happen to be stored in breadth first order. This makes breadth first traversals easy for this kind of tree. For other tree representations, breadth first traversals are a bit harder.

To traverse other kinds of trees, you can use a queue to store the nodes that must still be visited. Start by placing the root node in the queue. To visit a node, remove it from the front of the queue and add its children to the back. Repeat this process until the queue is empty. The following code shows a breadth first traversal procedure for a tree that stores child pointers in resizable arrays.

```
type
    PTrav2NodeArray = ^TTrav2NodeArray;
    TTrav2Node = class(TObject)
        // Code omitted...
            :
        public
            NumChildren : Integer;
            Children    : PTrav2NodeArray;
            // Code omitted...
                :
    end;
    TTrav2NodeArray = array [1..100000000] of TTrav2Node;

function TTrav2Node.BreadthFirstTraverse : String;
var
    i, oldest, next_spot : Integer;
    queue                : PTrav2NodeArray;
begin
    Result := '';

    // Make the queue array big enough to hold every
    // node in the tree.
    GetMem(queue, NumNodes * SizeOf(TTrav2Node));

    // Start with this node in the queue.
    queue^[1] := TTrav2Node.Create;
    queue^[1] := Self;
```

```
oldest := 1;
next_spot := 2;


// Repeatedly process the oldest item in the queue
// until the queue is empty.
while (oldest < next_spot) do
begin
    with queue^[oldest] do
    begin
        // Visit the oldest node.
        Result := Result + Id + ' ';


        // Add the node's children to the queue.
        for i := 1 to NumChildren do
        begin
            queue^[next_spot] := Children^[i];
            next_spot := next_spot + 1;
        end;
    end; // End with queue^[oldest]^ do...
    oldest := oldest + 1;
end;


    FreeMem(queue);
end;
```

Example program Trav2 demonstrates tree traversal for trees using resizable child arrays. The program is a combination of program NAry, which manages N-ary trees, and program Trav1, which demonstrates tree traversals.

Select a node and click the Add Child button to add a new child to the node. Select a node and click Remove to remove the node and its descendants. Click the Preorder, Inorder, Postorder, or Breadth First buttons to see the corresponding tree traversals. Figure 6.14 shows program Trav2 displaying a postorder traversal.

Sorted Trees

Binary trees are often a natural way to store and manipulate information in computer programs. Because many computer operations are binary, they map naturally onto binary trees. For example, you can map the binary relationship "less than" onto a binary tree. If you use the tree's internal nodes to mean "the left child is less than the right child," you can use a binary tree to build and store a sorted list. Figure 6.15 shows a binary tree holding a sorted list containing the numbers 1, 2, 4, 6, 7, 9.

Figure 6.14 Program Trav2 displaying a tree's postorder traversal.

```
Trav2                                                    _□×
File  Help
 Add Child    Remove        Preorder    Inorder   Postorder   Breadth First
                              ┌─────┐
                              │ Root│
              ┌──────────────────┴──────────────────────────┐
         ┌─────┐          ┌─────┐            ┌─────┐    ┌─────┐
         │  1  │          │  2  │            │  3  │    │  4  │
         ┌──┴──┐      ┌────┴─┬─────┐      ┌────┴───┐
      │ 16 │        │  5  │ │  6  │ │  7 │   │  8  │  │  9 │
    ┌──┴──┐      ┌───┴──┬──┐ └──┐           ┌──┴──┐
 │ 17 │ │ 18 │  │ 14 │ │ 15 │ │ 21 │      │ 10 │
      ┌──┴──┬──┬──┘                    ┌────┴─┬─────┐
   │ 19 │ │ 20 │ │ 22 │             │ 11 │ │ 12 │ │ 13 │
                ┌──┘
             │ 23 │



17 19 20 18 16 1 23 22 14 15 5 21 6 7 2 11 12 13 10 8 9 3 4 Root
```

Adding Items

The algorithm for inserting a new item into this kind of tree is simple. Begin at the root node. As you examine each node, compare that node's value to the value of the new item. If the new value is less than or equal to the value at the node, continue down the left branch of the tree. If the new value is greater than the node's value, continue down the right branch. When you reach the bottom of the tree, insert the item at that position.

To insert the value 8 in the tree shown in Figure 6.15, you begin at the root, which has value 4. Because 8 is greater than 4, you follow the right branch to node 9. Because 8 is less than 9, you then follow the left branch to node 7. Because 8 is greater than 7, you next try to follow the right branch again, but this node has no right child. This is where you insert the new item giving the tree shown in Figure 6.16.

Figure 6.15 The sorted list: 1, 2, 4, 6, 7, 9.

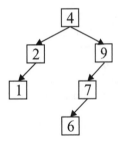

Figure 6.16 The sorted list: 1, 2, 4, 6, 7, 8, 9.

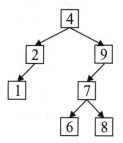

The following code adds a new value beneath a node in a sorted tree. The program begins the insertion at the root as in InsertItem(Root, new_value).

```
procedure InsertItem(var node : PSortNode; new_value : Integer);
begin
    if (node = nil) then
    begin
        // We have reached a leaf.
        // Insert the item here.
        GetMem(node, SizeOf(TSortNode));
        node^.Value := new_value;
    end else if (new_value <= node^.Value) then
    begin
        // Branch left.
        InsertItem(node^.LeftChild, new_value);
    end else begin
        // Branch right.
        InsertItem(node^.RightChild, new_value);
    end;
end;
```

When this procedure reaches the bottom of the tree, something fairly subtle occurs. This procedure's node parameter is declared with the var keyword. That means this procedure works with the same copy of node that the calling procedure uses. If the procedure modifies the value of the node parameter, the value is changed for the calling procedure as well.

When it recursively calls itself, procedure InsertItem passes itself a pointer to a child in the tree. For example, in the following statement the procedure passes a pointer to the node's right child as the node parameter. If the called procedure modifies the value of the node parameter, the child pointer is automatically updated in the calling procedure as well. This automatically adds the new node to the tree.

```
InsertItem(node^.RightChild, new_value);
```

Removing Items

Removing an item from a sorted tree is a bit trickier than inserting one. After an item is removed, the program may need to rearrange other nodes so the "less than" relationship still holds throughout the tree. There are several cases to consider.

First, if the removed node has no children, you can just remove it from the tree. Because the node has no children, the ordering of the remaining nodes is not changed.

Second, if the removed node has one child, you can replace it with its child. The ordering of the node's descendants stays the same since those nodes are also descendants of the child. Figure 6.17 shows a tree where node 4, which has only one child, is being removed.

If the removed node has two children, you cannot necessarily replace it with one of its children. If the node's children also have two children, there is no room for all the children at the removed node's location. The removed node has one extra child, and the child node you might like to replace it with has two children, so you would need to assign three children to the node in this location.

To solve this problem, you should replace the removed node with the right-most node to the left of it in the tree. In other words, move down the left branch out of the node being removed. Then move down right branches until you find a node with no right branch. That is the rightmost node to the left of the node you are removing. In the tree on the left in Figure 6.18, node 3 is the rightmost node to the left of node 4. You can replace node 4 with node 3 and preserve the tree's ordering.

One last detail remains if the replacement node has a left child. In that case, you can move this child into the position vacated by the replacement node and the tree will again be properly ordered. You know that the rightmost node does not have a right child; otherwise, it would not have been the rightmost node. That means you do not need to worry about the replacement node having two children.

Figure 6.19 shows this complicated situation. In this example, node 8 is being removed. The rightmost node to its left is node 7. Node 7 also has a child—node 5. To remove node 8 while preserving the tree's ordering, replace node 8 with node 7,

Figure 6.17 Removing a node with one child.

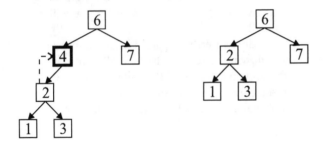

Figure 6.18 Removing a node with two children.

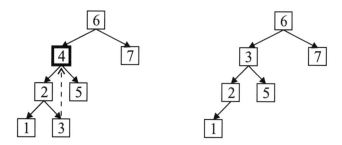

and node 7 with node 5. Notice that node 7 gets completely new children, while node 5 keeps its single child.

The following code removes a node from a sorted binary tree.

```
// Remove a value from below the indicated node.
procedure TSortTree.RemoveNode(var node : TSortNode;
    target_value : Integer);
var
    target : TSortNode;
begin
    // If we cannot find the item, say so.
    if (node = nil) then
    begin
        ShowMessage(Format('Item %d is not in the tree.',
            [target_value]));
        exit;
    end;
```

Figure 6.19 Removing a node when the replacement node has a child.

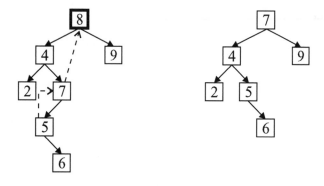

```
        if (target_value < node.Id) then
            // Continue down left subtree.
            RemoveNode(node.LeftChild, target_value)
        else if (target_value > node.Id) then
            // Continue down right subtree.
            RemoveNode(node.RightChild, target_value)
        else begin
            // This is the target.
            if (node.LeftChild = nil) then
            begin
                // If the target has no left child,
                // replace it with its right child.
                target := node;
                node := node.RightChild;
                target.RightChild := nil;
                target.Free;
            end else if (node.RightChild = nil) then
            begin
                // If the target has no right child,
                // replace it with its left child.
                target := node;
                node := node.LeftChild;
                target.LeftChild := nil;
                target.Free;
            end else begin
                // If the target has 2 children,
                // use ReplaceRightmost to replace the target
                // with the rightmost descendant to its left.
                ReplaceRightmost(node, node.LeftChild);
            end; // End replacing the target.
        end; // End if left ... else if right ... else ...
end;


// Replace the target node with the rightmost descendant
// to its left.
procedure TSortTree.ReplaceRightmost(var target, repl : TSortNode);
var
    old_repl, tmp : TSortNode;
begin
    if (repl.RightChild <> nil) Then
    begin
        // Move farther down to the right.
        ReplaceRightmost(target, repl.RightChild);
    end else begin
```

```
    // We've reached the bottom. Remember node repl.
    old_repl := repl;

    // Replace repl with its left child.
    repl := repl.LeftChild;

    // Replace the target with repl.
    old_repl.LeftChild := target.LeftChild;
    old_repl.RightChild := target.RightChild;
    tmp := target;
    target := old_repl;
    tmp.LeftChild := nil;
    tmp.RightChild := nil;
    tmp.Free;
  end;
end;
```

This algorithm uses the trick of passing parameters by reference into recursive procedures in two places. First, procedure RemoveNode uses this trick to make the target node's parent point to the replacement node. The following statement shows how procedure RemoveNode is invoked.

```
RemoveNode(node.LeftChild, target_value)
```

When the procedure finds the target node (node 8 in Figure 6.19), it receives the parent node's pointer to the target in the node parameter. By setting this parameter to the replacement node (node 7), DeleteItem sets the parent's child so it points to the new node.

The following statement shows how procedure ReplaceRightmost recursively calls itself.

```
ReplaceRightmost(target, repl.RightChild);
```

When this procedure finds the rightmost node to the left of the node being removed (node 7), the repl parameter holds the pointer from the parent to the rightmost node. When the procedure sets the value of repl to repl.LeftChild, it automatically connects the rightmost node's parent to the rightmost node's left child (node 5).

Example program TrSort uses these procedures to manage sorted binary trees. Enter an integer and click the Add button to add an item to the tree. Enter an integer and click Remove to remove that item from the tree. When you remove a node, the tree automatically rearranges itself to preserve the "less than" ordering.

Traversing Sorted Trees

A useful fact about sorted trees is that the inorder traversal visits the nodes in their sorted order. The inorder traversal of the tree shown in Figure 6.20, for instance, visits the nodes in the order 2, 4, 5, 6, 7, 8, 9.

Figure 6.20 Inorder traversal of a sorted tree: 2, 4, 5, 6, 7, 8, 9.

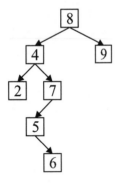

The fact that inorder traversals of sorted trees visit the items in sorted order leads to a simple sorting algorithm.

1.   Add the items to a sorted tree.

2.   Print the items using an inorder traversal.

This algorithm usually works quite well. If you add items to a tree in certain orders, however, the tree may become tall and thin. Figure 6.21 shows the sorted tree you get if you add items to it in the order 1, 6, 5, 2, 3, 4. Many other orders also produce tall, thin trees.

The taller a sorted tree becomes, the longer it takes to add new items at the bottom of the tree. In the worst case, after you add N items, the tree will have height O(N). The total time to insert all the items into the tree will be O(N²).

Figure 6.21 The tree obtained by adding items in the order 1, 6, 5, 2, 3, 4.

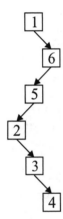

Because it takes O(N) time to traverse the tree, the total time needed to sort the numbers using the tree would be $O(N^2) + O(N) = O(N^2)$.

If the tree remains fairly short, it will have height $O(\log(N))$. In that case, it will take only $O(\log(N))$ steps to insert an item in the tree. To insert all N items in the tree would require $O(N * \log(N))$ steps. Then to sort the items using the tree would take time $O(N * \log(N)) + O(N) = O(N * \log(N))$.

This $O(N * \log(N))$ time is much better than $O(N^2)$. For example, building a tall, thin tree containing 1000 items would take about 1 million steps. Building a short tree of height $O(\log(N))$ would take only about 10,000 steps.

If the items are initially randomly arranged, the tree's shape will probably be somewhere between these two extremes. While the tree may have height slightly larger than $\log(N)$, it will not be too tall and thin, so the sorting algorithm will perform well.

Chapter 7, "Balanced Trees," describes ways you can rebalance trees so they do not grow tall and thin no matter how the items are added. Those methods are quite complicated, however, and they are really not worth applying to this tree-based sorting algorithm. Many of the sorting algorithms described in Chapter 9, "Sorting," provide better performance and are easier to implement.

Threaded Trees

Chapter 2, "Lists," explains how adding threads to a linked list makes listing the items in different orders easy. You can use the same idea to make visiting the nodes in a tree in different orders easy. For example, by placing threads in a binary tree's leaf nodes, you can make inorder and reverse inorder traversal easier. If the tree is a sorted tree, these are the nodes' sorted and reversed sorted orders.

To create the threads, store pointers to the nodes' inorder predecessors and successors in unused child pointers. If a node has an unused left child pointer, store a thread in that position indicating the node's predecessor in the inorder traversal. If a node has an unused right child pointer, store a thread in that position indicating the node's successor in the inorder traversal. Because the threads are symmetric, with left child threads pointing to predecessors and right child threads pointing to successors, this kind of tree is called a *symmetrically threaded tree*. Figure 6.22 shows a symmetrically threaded tree with the threads drawn in dashed lines.

Because the threads occupy the positions of child pointers in the tree, you need a way to tell the difference between thread pointers and normal child pointers. The easiest way to do this is to add new Boolean variables HasLeftChild and HasRightChild to the nodes, indicating whether they have left and right children.

To use the threads to find the predecessor of a node, examine the node's left child pointer. If the pointer is a thread, the thread indicates the node's predecessor. If the pointer has the value nil, this node is the first node in the tree so it has no predecessor. Otherwise, follow the pointer to the node's left child. Then follow the descendants' right child pointers until you reach a node that has a thread instead of

Figure 6.22 A symmetrically threaded tree.

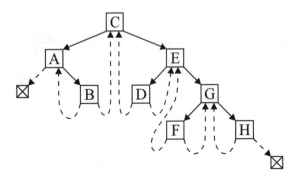

a right child. That node (not the one indicated by the thread) is the predecessor of the original node. This node is the rightmost node to the left of the original node in the tree. The following code shows how to find a node's predecessor in Delphi.

```
function Predecessor(node : PThreadedNode) : PThreadedNode;
var
    child : PThreadedNode;
begin
    if (node^.LeftChild = nil) then
        // This is the first node in the inorder traversal.
        Predecessor := nil;
    else if (node^.HasLeftChild) then
    begin
        // This is a node pointer.
        // Find the rightmost node to the left.
        child := node^.LeftChild;
        while (child^.HasRightChild) do
            child := child^.RightChild;
        Predecessor := child;
    end else
        // The thread points to the predecessor.
        Predecessor := node^.LeftChild;
end;
```

Using the threads to locate the successor of a node is similar. If the node's right child pointer is a thread, the thread indicates the node's successor. If the pointer has the value nil, this node is the last node in the tree so it has no successor. Otherwise, follow the pointer to the node's right child. Then follow left child pointers until you reach a node with a thread for a left child pointer. That node is the successor of the original node. This node is the leftmost node to the right of the original node in the tree.

It is also convenient to have functions that locate the first and last nodes in the tree. To find the first node, simply follow the left child pointers down from the root until you reach a node with left child nil. To find the last node, follow the right child pointers down from the root until you reach a node with right child nil.

```
function FirstNode : PThreadedNode;
begin
    Result := Root;
    while (Result^.LeftChild <> nil) do
        Result:= Result^.LeftChild;
end;


function LastNode : PThreadedNode;
begin
    Result := Root;
    while (Result^.RightChild <> nil) do
        Result:= Result^.RightChild;
end;
```

Using these functions, you can easily write procedures that display the nodes in the tree in their forward and backward orders.

```
procedure Inorder;
var
    node : PThreadedNode;
begin
    // Find the first node.
    node := FirstNode;

    // Traverse the list.
    while (node <> nil) do
    begin
        VisitNode(node^.Value);
        node := Successor(node);
    end;
end;


procedure ReverseInorder;
var
    node : PThreadedNode;
begin
    // Find the last node.
    node := LastNode;
```

```
    // Traverse the list.
    while (node <> nil) do
    begin
        VisitNode(node^.Value);
        node := Predecessor(node);
    end;
end;
```

The inorder printing procedure presented earlier in the chapter uses recursion. These new procedures use neither recursion nor the stack you might use to remove recursion.

Every child pointer in the tree contains either a link to a child or a thread to a predecessor or successor. Because each node has two child pointers, if there are N nodes in the tree there must be 2 * N links and threads. These traversal algorithms visit each link and thread in the tree once, so they require O(2 * N) = O(N) steps.

You can make these procedures a bit faster if you keep track of the indexes of the first and last nodes in the tree. Then you do not need to search for the first or last node before listing the nodes in order. Because these algorithms visit all N nodes in the tree, the runtime for the algorithms is still O(N), but they will be a little faster in practice.

Maintaining Threaded Trees

To maintain a threaded tree, you must be able to add nodes to and remove nodes from the tree while keeping the tree properly threaded.

Suppose you want to add a new node to the tree as the left child of node A. Because you are inserting the node in this position, the left child of node A must currently be unused as a child pointer, and therefore it contains a thread. That thread points to the predecessor of node A. Because the new node will be the left child of node A, it will become node A's predecessor. Node A will be the new node's successor. The node that was the predecessor of node A now becomes the predecessor of the new node. Figure 6.23 shows the tree in Figure 6.22 after the new node X has been added as the left child of node H.

If you are keeping track of the index of the first and last nodes in the tree, you should check at this point to see whether the new node is the new first node in the tree. If the predecessor thread of the new node has the value nil, then it is the new first node.

Using all these facts, it is easy to write a procedure to insert a new left child for a node. Inserting a right child is similar.

```
procedure AddLeftChild(parent, child : PThreadedNode);
begin
```

Figure 6.23 Threaded tree with node X added.

```
// The parent's predecessor becomes the new node's
// predecessor.
child^.LeftChild := parent^.LeftChild;
child^.HasLeftChild := False;

// Insert the node.
parent^.LeftChild := child;
parent^.HasLeftChild := True;

// The parent is the new node's successor.
child^.RightChild := parent;
child^.HasRightChild := False;

// See if the new node is the first node in the tree.
if (child^.LeftChild = nil) then FirstNode := child;
end;
```

Before you can remove a node from the threaded tree, you should remove its descendants. Once the node has no children, removing it is easy.

Suppose the target node being removed is the left child of its parent. The target's left pointer is a thread indicating its predecessor in the tree. When the target is removed, that predecessor becomes the predecessor of the parent node. To remove the target, simply set the parent node's left child pointer to the target's left child pointer.

The target's right child pointer is a thread indicating its successor in the tree. Because the target is the left child of its parent, and because the target has no children, that thread indicates the parent node, so you can simply ignore it. Figure 6.24 shows the tree in Figure 6.23 after the node F has been removed. The method for removing a right child is similar.

Figure 6.24 Threaded tree with node F removed.

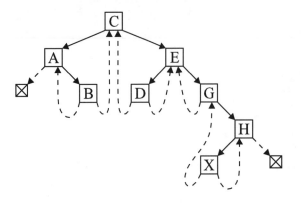

```
procedure RemoveLeftChild(parent : PThreadedNode);
var
    target : PThreadedNode;
begin
    target := parent^.LeftChild;
    parent^.LeftChild := target^.LeftChild;
end;
```

Quadtrees

A *quadtree* describes the spatial relationships between items within a physical area. For example, the area might be a map, and the items might be the locations of houses or businesses on the map.

Each node in a quadtree represents a part of the total area represented by the quadtree. Each nonleaf node has four children that represent the northwest, northeast, southeast, and southwest quadrants of the area represented by the node. A leaf node can store the items it contains in a linked list. The following code shows the key parts of the TQtreeNode class declaration.

```
type
    NorthOrSouth = (North, South);
    EastOrWest = (East, West);
    TPointArray = array[1..MAX_QTREE_NODES] of TPoint;
    PPointArray = ^TPointArray;
    TQtreeNode = class(TObject)
        private
        public
            Children : array [NorthOrSouth, EastOrWest] of
TQtreeNode;
```

```
Xmin, Xmax, Ymin, Ymax : Integer;
Pts                      : PPointArray; // The data
                                        // items.
NumPts                   : Integer;
        :
end;
```

To build a quadtree, place all the items in the root node. Then examine that node to see if it contains enough items to be worth subdividing. If it does, create four children for the node. Distribute the items among the four children according to the positions of the items within the four quadrants of the original area. Then recursively check the four children to see if they are worth subdividing. Continue subdividing the nodes until each leaf contains no more than some desired number of items.

Figure 6.25 shows a picture of several data items arranged in a quadtree. Each region has been subdivided until it contains no more than two items.

Quadtrees are useful for locating objects near specific locations. Suppose you have a program that draws a map with many locations on it. When the user clicks on the map, the program should find the location nearest to the point clicked. The program could search through the entire list of locations, checking each to see how close it is to the target point. If there are N locations, this is an O(N) algorithm.

A quadtree can make this operation much faster. Begin at the root node. Each time you examine a quadtree node, see which of the node's quadrants contains the point where the user clicked. Then move down the tree to the corresponding child node. If the user clicked in the upper-right corner of the node's area, you would descend into the northeast child. Continue down the tree until you locate the leaf node that contains the point where the user clicked.

The TQtreeNode's LocateLeaf function uses this method to find the leaf node that contains a given point. A program would invoke this function as in the_leaf := Root.LocateLeaf(X, Y).

Figure 6.25 A quadtree.

 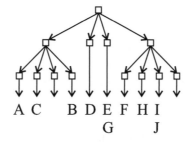

```
// See what leaf contains the point.
function TQtreeNode.LocateLeaf(X, Y : Integer) : TQtreeNode;
var
    xmid, ymid : Integer;
    ns          : NorthOrSouth;
    ew          : EastOrWest;
begin
    if (Children[North, West] = nil) then
    begin
        // This node has no children. It must be the node.
        Result := Self;
        exit;
    end;

    // Search the appropriate child.
    xmid := (Xmax + Xmin) div 2;
    ymid := (Ymax + Ymin) div 2;
    if (Y <= ymid) then
        ns := North
    else
        ns := South;
    if (X <= xmid) then
        ew := West
    else
        ew := East;

    Result := Children[ns, ew].LocateLeaf(X, Y);
end;
```

After deciding which leaf contains a point, examine the locations within that leaf to see which item is closest to the point. The NearPointInLeaf procedure does this.

```
// Return the index of the point closest to the given
// coordinates in this leaf.
procedure TQtreeNode.NearPointInLeaf(X, Y : Integer;
    var best_i, best_dist2 : Integer; var comp : Longint);
var
    i                : Longint;
    dist2, dx, dy : Integer;
begin
    best_dist2 := 32767;
    best_i := 0;

    for i := 1 to NumPts do
    begin
```

```
        dx := X - Pts^[i].X;
        dy := Y - Pts^[i].Y;
        dist2 := dx * dx + dy * dy;
        if (best_dist2 > dist2) then
        begin
            best_i := i;
            best_dist2 := dist2;
        end;
    end;
    comp := comp + NumPts;
end;
```

The item found by NearPointInLeaf is usually the item the user was trying to select. If the point is close to the boundary between two leaf nodes, however, an item in another leaf node might be closer to the point clicked.

Suppose D_{min} is the distance from the user's selected point to the closest location found so far. If D_{min} is less than the distance from the user's point to the edge of its leaf node, you are finished. The location is too far from the edge of the leaf for there to be a closer location in another leaf.

Otherwise, start back at the root node and move into the tree examining any quadtree nodes that are within distance D_{min} of the point clicked. If you find any items that are closer to the point, revise D_{min} and continue searching with the new value. When you finish checking the leaf nodes that are close to the point, you have found the correct item. Procedure CheckNearbyLeaves uses these methods to complete the search.

```
// Check nearby leaves to see if there is a better point.
procedure TQtreeNode.CheckNearbyLeaves(exclude : TQtreeNode;
    var best_leaf : TQtreeNode; X, Y : Integer;
    var best_i, best_dist2 : Integer; var comp : Longint);
var
    xmid, ymid, i, dist2, best_dist : Integer;
begin
    // If we are excluding this leaf, do nothing.
    if (exclude = Self) then exit;

    // If this is a leaf node, look for close nodes.
    if (Children[North, West] = nil) then
    begin
        NearPointInLeaf(X, Y, i, dist2, comp);
        if (best_dist2 > dist2) then
        begin
            best_dist2 := dist2;
            best_leaf := Self;
            best_i := i;
```

```
        end;
    end else begin
        // Examine children that lie within best_dist
        // of the point.
        xmid := (Xmax + Xmin) div 2;
        ymid := (Ymax + Ymin) div 2;
        best_dist := Round(Sqrt(best_dist2) + 0.5);
        if (X - best_dist <= xmid) then
        begin
            // The West children may be close enough.
            // See if the NorthWest child is close enough.
            if (Y - best_dist <= ymid) Then
                Children[North, West].CheckNearbyLeaves(
                    exclude, best_leaf, X, Y, best_i,
                    best_dist2, comp);

            // See if the SouthWest child is close enough.
            if (Y + best_dist > ymid) Then
                Children[South, West].CheckNearbyLeaves(
                    exclude, best_leaf, X, Y, best_i,
                    best_dist2, comp);
        end; // End the West children may be close enough.

        if (X + best_dist > xmid) then
        begin
            // The East children may be close enough.
            // See if the NorthEast child is close enough.
            if (Y - best_dist <= ymid) Then
                Children[North, East].CheckNearbyLeaves(
                    exclude, best_leaf, X, Y, best_i,
                    best_dist2, comp);

            // See if the SouthEast child is close enough.
            if (Y + best_dist > ymid) Then
                Children[South, East].CheckNearbyLeaves(
                    exclude, best_leaf, X, Y, best_i,
                    best_dist2, comp);
        end; // End the East children may be close enough.
    end; // End if a leaf ... else check children ...
end;
```

The FindPoint procedure uses the LocateLeaf, NearPointInLeaf, and CheckNearbyLeaves procedures provided by the QtreeNode class to quickly locate a point in a quadtree.

```
// Find the point closest to the given coordinates.
procedure TQtreeNode.FindPoint(var X, Y : Integer; var comp :
Longint);
var
    best_dist2, best_i     : Integer;
    leaf                   : TQtreeNode;
begin
    // See which leaf contains the point.
    leaf := LocateLeaf(X, Y);

    // Find the closest point within the leaf.
    comp := 0;
    leaf.NearPointInLeaf(X, Y, best_i, best_dist2, comp);

    // Check nearby leaves for closer points.
    CheckNearbyLeaves(leaf, leaf, X, Y, best_i, best_dist2, comp);

    X := leaf.Pts^[best_i].X;
    Y := leaf.Pts^[best_i].Y;
end;
```

Example program Qtree uses a quadtree. When the program begins, it asks how many data items it should create. It creates the items and draws them as points. Start with a small number of items (1000 or so) until you know how long it will take your computer to create the items.

Quadtrees are most interesting when the items are not evenly distributed, so this program selects the points using a *strange attractor* function from *chaos theory*. It selects the data points in a way that seems random, yet contains clusters that make the data interesting.

When you click on the form, program Qtree locates the item closest to the spot where you clicked. It highlights the item and displays the number of items it examined while locating the item.

Use the program's Options menu to tell the program whether it should use the quadtree. If you check the Use Quadtree option, the program displays the quadtree and uses it to locate items. If you do not check this option, the program does not display the quadtree and locates items by exhaustively searching them all.

The program examines far fewer items and is much faster when it uses the quadtree. If your computer is so fast that you do not notice this effect, run the program with 100,000 or so items. Even on a fast computer, you should notice the difference.

Figure 6.26 shows program Qtree displaying 100,000 items. The small white rectangle shows the selected item. The label in the upper left indicates the program examined only 25 of the 100,000 items before finding the one selected.

Figure 6.26 Program Qtree.

Modifying MAX_QTREE_NODES

An interesting experiment to perform with program Qtree is to modify the value of MAX_QTREE_NODES defined in the Declarations section of the QtreeNode class. This is the maximum number of items that will fit within a quadtree node before that node is subdivided. The program initially uses the value MAX_QTREE_NODES = 100. If you make this number small, like 10, each leaf node contains fewer data items, so the program will examine fewer items to locate the one closest to the spot you click. Locating items will be faster. On the other hand, the program will build far more quadtree nodes, so it will use a lot of memory.

Conversely, if you increase MAX_QTREE_NODES to 1000, the program will create fewer quadtree nodes. It will take a bit longer to locate items, but it will create a smaller quadtree that requires less memory.

This is an example of a time versus space trade-off. Using more quadtree nodes makes locating items faster, but takes more memory. In this example, a value for MAX_QTREE_NODES around 100 gives a reasonable balance between speed and memory usage. You may need to experiment with MAX_QTREE_NODES to find the right balance for other applications.

Octtrees

An *octtree* is similar to a quadtree except it divides a three-dimensional volume instead of a two-dimensional area. While quadtree nodes contain four children, octtree nodes contain eight children, representing the eight octants that make up a three-dimensional volume. These octants are in the northwest top, northwest bottom, northeast top, northeast bottom, and so forth.

Octtrees are useful for managing objects spatially in three dimensions. A robot, for example, might use an octtree to keep track of nearby objects. A ray tracing program can use an octtree to quickly determine whether a ray passes near an object before it begins the slow process of calculating the exact intersection between the two.

You can build octtrees using techniques similar to those used to build quadtrees.

Summary

There are many ways to represent trees. Complete trees stored in arrays use the most efficient and compact representation. Forward star allows fast tree traversal and requires little extra memory, but it is very hard to modify. It is commonly used in network algorithms, however, so it is important to understand. Resizable child arrays make tree modification easier, and linked child lists make modification easiest of all, though these are more difficult to store in files. After you analyze the types of operations you will perform most on a tree, you can select the representation that gives you the best trade-off between flexibility and ease of use.

BALANCED TREES

As a program works with an ordered tree, adding and removing nodes over time, the tree may become unbalanced. When that happens, algorithms that manipulate the tree become less efficient. If the tree becomes sufficiently unbalanced, it becomes little more than a complicated form of linked list, and the program using the tree may give very poor performance.

This chapter discusses techniques you can use to keep a tree balanced, even when items are added and removed over time. By keeping a tree balanced, you keep it efficient.

The chapter begins by describing what it means for a tree to be unbalanced and explaining how an unbalanced tree can ruin performance. Then it discusses AVL trees. In an AVL tree, the heights of the left and right subtrees at any node always differ by at most 1. By maintaining this property, you can keep the tree from becoming unbalanced.

Next, the chapter describes B-trees and B+trees. These trees keep all of their leaves at the same depth. By ensuring that the number of branches at each node is within certain limits, these trees keep themselves balanced. B-trees and B+trees are commonly used in database programming. The final example program in this chapter uses a B+tree to implement a simple yet powerful database.

Balance

As mentioned in Chapter 6, "Trees," the shape of a sorted tree depends on the order in which you add items to it. Figure 7.1 shows two different trees created by adding the same items to trees in different orders.

Tall, thin trees like the one on the left in Figure 7.1 can have up to $O(N)$ depth. Inserting or locating an item in such an unbalanced tree could take $O(N)$ steps. Even if new items are placed randomly within the tree, on the average they will wind up at depth $N / 2$, which is still $O(N)$.

Suppose you build a sorted binary tree containing 1000 nodes. If the tree is balanced, the height of the tree will be around $\log_2(1000)$, or about 10. Adding a new item to the tree will take only 10 steps. If the tree is tall and thin, it could

Figure 7.1 Trees built in different orders.

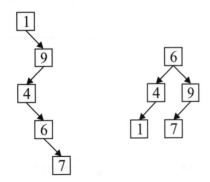

Order: 1 9 4 6 7   Order: 6 4 1 9 7

have height 1000. In this case, adding a new item at the bottom of the tree will take 1000 steps.

Now suppose you want to add 1000 more nodes to the tree. If the tree remains balanced, all 1000 nodes will fit on the next couple of levels of the tree. It will only take about 10 * 1000 = 10,000 steps to add the new items. If the tree continues to grow in an unbalanced fashion, each new item will make the tree grow taller. Adding the items will take around 1000 + 1001 +...+ 2000 = 1.5 million steps.

Although you cannot guarantee items will enter and leave a tree in a particular order, you can use techniques to keep a tree more or less balanced no matter how items are added and removed.

AVL Trees

AVL trees were named after the Russian mathematicians Adelson-Velskii and Landis, who invented them. At every node in an AVL tree, the heights of the left and right subtrees differ by at most 1. Figure 7.2 shows several AVL trees.

Even though an AVL tree may not be as short as a complete tree containing the same number of nodes, it still has depth O(log(N)). That means you can

Figure 7.2 AVL trees.

locate nodes within an AVL tree in time O(log(N)), which is relatively fast. It is not as obvious, but it is also possible to add or remove items from an AVL tree in O(log(N)) time while keeping the tree balanced.

Adding Nodes to an AVL Tree

Each time you add a node to an AVL tree, you must check to see if the AVL property is still satisfied. After adding a node, you can follow the node's ancestors back up toward the root, verifying that the subtrees at each ancestor have heights differing by at most 1. If you find a spot where this is not true, you can shuffle some of the nodes around to rebalance the subtrees, while still keeping the tree properly ordered.

The procedure that adds a new node to the tree recursively descends into the tree searching for the item's location. After inserting the new item, the recursive calls to the procedure return and backtrack up the tree. As each call returns, the procedure checks to see if the AVL property still holds at the higher level. This sort of backwards recursion, where the procedure performs an important action on the way out of a chain of recursive calls, is called *bottom-up* recursion.

As the procedure returns up the tree, it also checks to see if the height of the subtree it is examining has changed. If the procedure ever reaches a point where the height of its subtree has not changed, the heights of any subtrees farther up the tree cannot have changed either. In that case, the tree must once again be balanced, so the procedure can stop checking.

For example, the tree on the left in Figure 7.3 is a properly balanced AVL tree. If you add a new item E to the tree, you get the tree shown in the middle. You then begin searching upwards through the tree from the new node E. The tree is balanced at node E because the two subtrees at this node are both empty and have the same height: 0.

The tree is also balanced at node D. The left subtree at node D is empty, so it has height 0. The right subtree contains the single node E, so it has height 1. The heights of these subtrees differ by only 1, so the tree is balanced at node D.

The tree is not balanced at node C. The left subtree at node C has height 0, while the right subtree has height 2. You can rebalance the subtrees at this node as shown on the right in Figure 7.3. Here, node D has replaced node C. The subtree

Figure 7.3 Adding a node to an AVL tree.

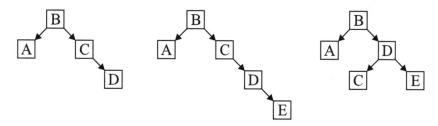

rooted at node D now contains nodes C, D, and E, and has height 2. Notice that the original subtree located at this position, which was rooted at node C, had height 2 before the new node was added. Because the height of the subtree has not changed, the tree is now balanced at all nodes above node D.

AVL Tree Rotations

When you add a node to an AVL tree, there are four ways the tree can become unbalanced, depending on where the node was added. Each of these requires a different rebalancing. The rebalancing techniques are called *right rotation, left rotation, left-right rotation,* and *right-left rotation.* They are abbreviated R, L, LR, and RL.

Suppose you add a new node to an AVL tree and the tree is now unbalanced at node X, as shown in Figure 7.4. Node X and its two children are shown explicitly. The other parts of the tree are indicated by triangles because you will not need to look at them closely.

The new node may have been placed in any of the four subtrees drawn as triangles below node X. When you place the new node in one of these triangles, you must use the corresponding rotation to rebalance the tree. Keep in mind that the new node may not unbalance the tree, so sometimes no rebalancing is needed.

Right Rotation

First, suppose you added a new node to the R subtree in Figure 7.4. In that case, you do not need to worry about the right two subtrees below node X, so you can group them together in a single triangle, as shown in Figure 7.5. The new node has been added to tree T_1, causing the subtree T_A rooted at node A to be at least two levels taller than subtree T_3.

Figure 7.4 The anatomy of an unbalanced AVL tree.

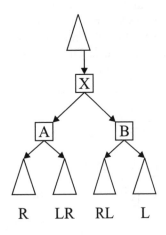

R   LR   RL   L

Figure 7.5 Adding a new node to the R subtree.

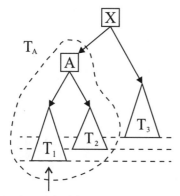

Node added here

In fact, because the tree was an AVL tree before you added the new node, T_A used to be at *most* one level taller than subtree T_3. You added only one node to the tree, so T_A must now be exactly two levels taller than subtree T_3.

You also know subtree T_1 is not more than one level taller than subtree T_2. Otherwise, node X would not be the lowest node in the tree with unbalanced subtrees. If T_1 were two levels taller than T_2, the tree would be unbalanced at node A.

You can rearrange the nodes using a right rotation, as shown in Figure 7.6. This is called a right rotation because the nodes A and X seem to have been rotated one position to the right.

Notice that this rotation preserves the "less than" ordering of the tree. An inorder traversal of either of these trees would visit the subtrees and nodes in the

---

Figure 7.6 Right rotation.

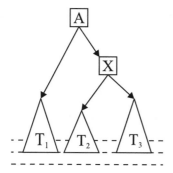

order T_1, A, T_2, X, T_3. Because the inorder traversals of both trees are the same, the orderings of the items within the trees are the same.

It is also important to note that the height of the subtree you are working with has remained the same. Before the new node was added, the height of the subtree was 2 plus the height of subtree T_2. After adding the node and applying the right rotation, the height of the subtree is still 2 plus the height of subtree T_2. Any parts of the tree that lie above node X must now be balanced, so you do not need to continue rebalancing the tree.

Left Rotation

A left rotation is similar to a right rotation. You use a left rotation to rebalance a tree when a new node is added to the L subtree shown in Figure 7.4. The AVL tree is shown before and after a left rotation in Figure 7.7.

Left-Right Rotation

When a node is added in the LR subtree shown in Figure 7.4, you must look one level deeper. Figure 7.8 shows the tree assuming the new node was added on the left side T_2 of the LR subtree. It could just as easily have been added to the right subtree T_3. In either case, the T_A and T_C subtrees still have the AVL property, but the T_X subtree does not.

Because the tree was an AVL tree before the node was added, T_A used to be at most one level taller than T_4. Only one node was added, so T_A has grown only one level taller. That means T_A must now be exactly two levels taller than T_4.

You also know that T_2 has height at most 1 greater than T_3. Otherwise, T_C would not be balanced, and node X would not be the lowest node in the tree with unbalanced subtrees.

Figure 7.7 Left rotation.

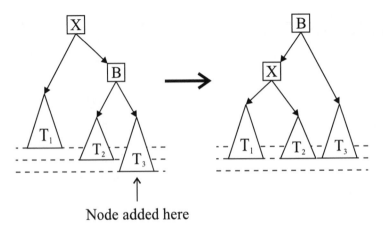

Node added here

Figure 7.8 Adding a new node to the LR subtree.

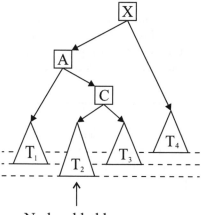

Node added here

Also, T_1 must reach the same depth as T_3. If it were shorter, T_A would be unbalanced, again contradicting the assumption that node X is the lowest node in the tree that has unbalanced subtrees. If T_1 reached a greater depth than T_3, then T_1 would reach a depth 2 greater than the depth reached by T_4. In that case, the tree would have been unbalanced before the new node was added.

All of this means that the bottoms of the trees are exactly as shown in Figure 7.8. Subtree T_2 reaches the greatest depth, T_1 and T_3 reach a depth one level above that, and T_4 reaches one level above T_1 and T_3.

Using these facts, you can rebalance the tree, as shown in Figure 7.9. This is called a left-right rotation because it looks as if nodes A and C were rotated one position to the left, and then nodes C and X were rotated one position to the right.

Figure 7.9 Left-right rotation.

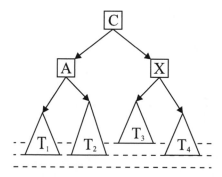

Like the other rotations, this rotation does not change the order of the items within the tree. The inorder traversal of the tree before and after the rotation visits the subtrees and nodes in the order: T_1, A, T_2, C, T_3, X, T_4.

The height of the subtree being rebalanced has also not changed. Before the new node was added, the height of the subtree was 2 plus the height of subtree T_1. After the tree is rebalanced, the height of the subtree is again 2 plus the height of subtree T_1. That means the rest of the tree is balanced, so you do not need to continue rebalancing other parts of the tree.

Right-Left Rotation

A right-left rotation is similar to a left-right rotation. Use a right-left rotation to rebalance the tree after adding a new node to the RL subtree in Figure 7.4. The AVL tree is shown before and after the right-left rotation in Figure 7.10.

Summary of Rotations

Figure 7.11 shows all the AVL tree rotations. Each preserves the tree's inorder traversal, and each leaves the height of the tree unchanged. After adding a new item and applying the appropriate rotation, the tree is once again balanced.

Adding Nodes in Delphi

Before considering how to remove AVL tree nodes, this section discusses some of the details of adding a node to an AVL tree in Delphi.

In addition to the usual LeftChild and RightChild fields, the TAVLNode class contains a Balance field that indicates which subtree at the node is taller. Balance takes the value LeftHeavy if the left subtree is taller, RightHeavy if the right subtree is taller, and Balanced if the two subtrees have the same height.

Figure 7.10 Right-left rotation.

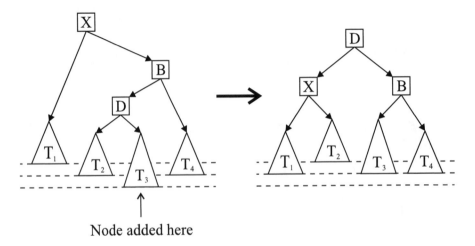

Node added here

Figure 7.11 Summary of AVL tree rotations.

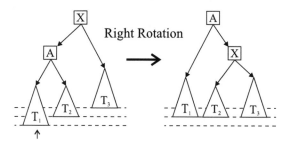

Right Rotation

Node added here

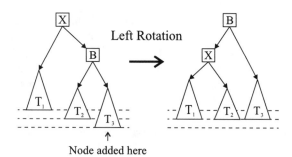

Left Rotation

Node added here

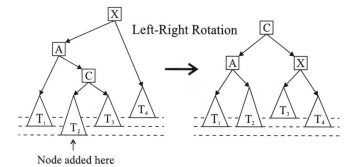

Left-Right Rotation

Node added here

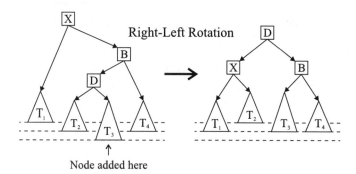

Right-Left Rotation

Node added here

```
type
    TBalance = (LeftHeavy, Balanced, RightHeavy);
    TAVLNode = class(TObject)
        private
        public
            Id                    : Integer;
            LeftChild, RightChild : TAVLNode;
            Balance               : TBalance;
            Position              : TPoint;
            // Code omitted...
                :
    end;
```

Procedure AddNode, shown shortly, recursively descends through the tree looking for the new item's location. When it reaches the bottom of the tree, the procedure creates the new node and adds it to the tree.

AddNode then uses bottom-up recursion to rebalance the tree. As the recursive calls return, the procedure travels back up the tree. Each time it returns, AddNode sets the parameter grew to be True if the subtree it is leaving has grown taller. In the instance of AddNode that made the recursive call, the procedure uses this parameter to determine whether the subtree it is examining is out of balance. If so, the procedure applies the correct rotation to rebalance the subtree.

For example, suppose the procedure is currently examining node X. Suppose it has just returned from visiting the right subtree beneath node X and that the parameter grew is True, indicating the right subtree grew taller. If the subtrees below node X previously had the same height, then the right subtree is now taller than the left. The tree is balanced at this point, but the subtree rooted at node X has also grown since its right subtree grew taller.

If the left subtree below node X was previously taller than the right, then the left and right subtrees are now the same height. The height of the subtree rooted at node X has not changed—it is still 1 plus the height of the left subtree. In this case, AddNode would reset variable grew to False, indicating that the tree is balanced.

Finally, if the right subtree below node X was previously taller than the left, the new node has unbalanced the tree at node X. AddNode invokes procedure RebalanceRightGrew to rebalance the tree. RebalanceRightGrew performs either a left or right-left rotation, depending on the exact situation.

Procedure AddNode follows a similar procedure if the new item was inserted into the left subtree. The following code shows procedures AddNode and RebalanceRightGrew. Procedure RebalanceLeftGrew is similar to RebalanceRightGrew.

```
procedure TAVLTree.AddNode(var parent : TAVLNode; new_id :
    Integer; var grew : Boolean);
begin
```

```
// If this is the bottom of the tree, create the new
// node and make parent point to it.
if (parent = nil) then
begin
    parent := TAVLNode.Create;
    parent.Id := new_id;
    parent.Balance := Balanced;
    grew := True;
    exit;
end;

// Continue down the appropriate subtree.
if (new_id <= parent.Id) then
begin
    // Insert the child in the left subtree.
    AddNode(parent.LeftChild, new_id, grew);

    // See if we need to rebalance.
    if (not grew) then exit;

    if (parent.Balance = RightHeavy) then
    begin
        // We were right heavy. The left subtree grew
        // so we are balanced and we did not grow.
        parent.Balance := Balanced;
        grew := False;
    end else if (parent.Balance = Balanced) then
    begin
        // We were balanced. The left subtree grew so
        // no we are left heavy. This subtree is still
        // balanced but it grew so we must continue
        // checking balance above.
        parent.Balance := LeftHeavy;
    end else begin
        // We were left heavy. The left subtree grew
        // so we are now left unbalanced. Perform the
        // appropriate rotation to rebalance.
        RebalanceLeftGrew(parent);
        grew := False;
    end; // End checking parent's balance.
end else begin
    // Insert the child in the right subtree.
    AddNode(parent.RightChild, new_id, grew);
```

```
    // See if we need to rebalance.
    if (not grew) then exit;

    if (parent.Balance = LeftHeavy) then
    begin
        // We were left heavy. The right subtree grew
        // so we are balanced and we did not grow.
        parent.Balance := Balanced;
        grew := False;
    end else if (parent.Balance = Balanced) then
    begin
        // We were balanced. The right subtree grew so
        // now we are right heavy. This subtree is still
        // balanced but it grew so we must continue
        // checking balance above.
        parent.Balance := RightHeavy;
    end else begin
        // We were right heavy. The right subtree grew
        // so we are now right unbalanced. Perform the
        // appropriate rotation to rebalance.
        RebalanceRightGrew(parent);
        grew := False;
    end; // End checking parent's balance.
    end; // End if (left subtree) ... else (right subtree) ...
end;

// Perform a left or right-left rotation to rebalance
// the tree at this node.
procedure TAVLTree.RebalanceRightGrew(var parent : TAVLNode);
var
    child, grandchild : TAVLNode;
begin
    child := parent.RightChild;

    if (child.Balance = RightHeavy) then
    begin
        // Left rotation.
        parent.RightChild := child.LeftChild;
        child.LeftChild := parent;
        parent.Balance := Balanced;
        parent := child;
    end else begin
        // Right-left rotation.
        grandchild := child.LeftChild;
```

```
        child.LeftChild := grandchild.RightChild;
        grandchild.RightChild := child;
        parent.RightChild := grandchild.LeftChild;
        grandchild.LeftChild := parent;
        if (grandchild.Balance = RightHeavy) then
            parent.Balance := LeftHeavy
        else
            parent.Balance := Balanced;
        if (grandchild.Balance = LeftHeavy) then
            child.Balance := RightHeavy
        else
            child.Balance := Balanced;
        parent := grandchild;
    end; // End if (R rotation) ... else (RL rotation) ...
    parent.Balance := Balanced;
end;
```

Removing Nodes from an AVL Tree

In Chapter 6, "Trees," you saw that it is harder to remove an item from a sorted tree than it is to insert one. If the removed node has one child, you can replace it with that child and still preserve the tree's ordering. If the node has two children, you must replace it with the rightmost node to the left in the tree. If that node has a left child, you must also replace it with its left child.

Because AVL trees are a type of sorted tree, you still need to perform these same steps. After you have finished, however, you must travel back up the tree to make sure it is still balanced. When you find a node where the AVL property does not hold, you must perform the appropriate rotations to rebalance the tree. While the rotations are the same ones used earlier for inserting a node in the tree, the cases you must look for are slightly different.

Left Rotation

Suppose you remove a node from the left subtree under node X. Suppose also that the right subtree is either evenly balanced or its right half has height 1 greater than its left half. Then the left rotation shown in Figure 7.12 will rebalance the tree at node X.

The bottom level of subtree T_2 in Figure 7.12 is shaded to indicate that the subtree T_B is either evenly balanced (T_2 and T_3 have the same height) or its right half is taller (T_3 is taller than T_2). In other words, the shaded level may or may not be part of subtree T_2.

If T_2 and T_3 have the same height, then the subtree T_X rooted at node X does not change in height when you remove the node. The height of T_X was and remains 2 plus the height of subtree T_2. Because the height does not change, the tree above this node is balanced.

Figure 7.12 Left rotation when removing a node.

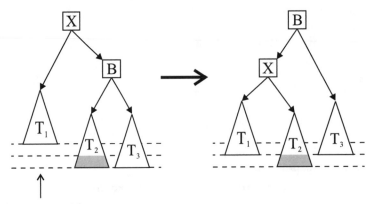

Node removed here

If T$_3$ is taller than T$_2$, subtree T$_X$ grows shorter by 1. In that case, the tree above node X may not be balanced, so you must continue up the tree checking to see if the AVL property holds for the ancestors of node X.

Right-Left Rotation

Suppose a node is taken from the left subtree under node X, but the left half of the right subtree is taller than the right half. Then you need to use a right-left rotation to rebalance the tree. Figure 7.13 shows this rotation.

Figure 7.13 Right-left rotation when removing a node.

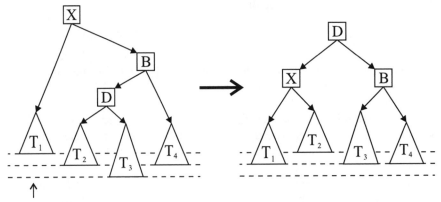

Node removed here

Whether subtree T_2 or T_3 is taller, the right-left rotation will rebalance the subtree T_X. The rotation will also reduce the height of T_X by 1. That means the tree above node X may not be balanced, so you must continue up the tree, checking to see if the AVL property holds for the ancestors of node X.

Other Rotations

The other rotations are similar to these. In these cases, the node being removed is in the right subtree below node X. All four of these rotations are the same as the rotations used to balance the tree after adding a node, with one exception.

When you add a new node to the tree, the first rotation you perform rebalances the subtree T_X without changing its height. That means the tree above T_X must still be balanced. When you use the rotations after removing a node from the tree, the rotation might reduce the height of the subtree T_X by 1. In that case, you cannot be sure the tree above node X is still balanced. You must continue up the tree, checking the AVL property at each node.

Removing Nodes in Delphi

Procedure RemoveFromNode removes items from the tree. It recursively descends through the tree looking for the item to be deleted. When it finds the target node, it removes the node. If the target has no children, the procedure is finished. If the node has a single child, it replaces the node with its child.

If the node has two children, RemoveFromNode calls procedure ReplaceRightmost to replace the target node with the rightmost node to the target's left. ReplaceRightmost performs its duty much as it does in Chapter 6, "Trees," where it removes items from a normal (nonbalanced) sorted tree. The main difference occurs when the procedure returns and recursively moves back up the tree. As it does so, ReplaceRightmost uses bottom-up recursion to make sure the tree is balanced at each node.

Each time a call returns, the calling instance of ReplaceRightmost invokes RebalanceRightShrunk to ensure that the tree is balanced at that point. Because ReplaceRightmost descended through the right branches, it always uses Rebalance-RightShrunk rather than RebalanceLeftShrunk to perform the rebalancing.

RemoveFromNode invoked the first call to ReplaceRightmost by sending it down the left branch beneath the node being removed. When that first call to ReplaceRightmost returns, RemoveFromNode uses RebalanceLeftShrunk to ensure the tree is balanced at that point.

After this, the recursive calls to RemoveFromNode return one at a time and work their way back up the tree. Like ReplaceRightmost, procedure RemoveFromNode uses bottom-up recursion to verify that the tree is balanced. As each call to RemoveFromNode returns, the calling procedure invokes RebalanceRightShrunk or RebalanceLeftShrunk, depending on which path it followed down into the tree.

RebalanceLeftShrunk is similar to RebalanceRightShrunk, so it is not shown in the following code.

```
// Remove a value from below the indicated node.
procedure TAVLTree.RemoveFromNode(var node : TAVLNode;
    target_id : Integer; var shrunk : Boolean);
var
    target : TAVLNode;
begin
    // If we are at the bottom of the tree, the target is
    // not here.
    if (node = nil) then
    begin
        ShowMessage(Format('Value %d is not in the tree.',
            [target_id]));
        shrunk := False;
        exit;
    end;

    if (target_id < node.Id) then
    begin
        // Search the left subtree.
        RemoveFromNode(node.LeftChild, target_id, shrunk);
        if (shrunk) then RebalanceLeftShrunk(node, shrunk);
    end else if (target_id > node.Id) then
    begin
        // Search the right subtree.
        RemoveFromNode(node.RightChild, target_id, shrunk);
        if (shrunk) then RebalanceRightShrunk(node, shrunk);
    end else begin
        // This is the target.
        target := node;
        if (node.RightChild = nil) then
        begin
            // node has no children or a left child only.
            node := node.LeftChild;
            shrunk := True;
        end else if (node.LeftChild = nil) then
        begin
            // node has a right child only.
            node := node.RightChild;
            shrunk := True;
        end else begin
            // node has two children.
            ReplaceRightmost(node, node.LeftChild, shrunk);
```

```
            if (shrunk) then RebalanceLeftShrunk(node, shrunk);
        end; // End replacing the target node in the tree.

            // Free the target node.
            target.LeftChild := nil;
            target.RightChild := nil;
            target.Free;
        end; // End (in left) ... (in right) ... (on target) ...
    end;


// Replace the target node with the rightmost descendant
// to its left.
procedure TAVLTree.ReplaceRightmost(var target, repl : TAVLNode;
    var shrunk : Boolean);
var
    old_repl : TAVLNode;
begin
    if (repl.RightChild = nil) then
    begin
        // repl is the node to replace target with.
        // Remember where the node is.
        old_repl := repl;

        // Replace repl with its left child.
        repl := repl.LeftChild;

        // Replace the target with old_repl.
        old_repl.LeftChild := target.LeftChild;
        old_repl.RightChild := target.RightChild;
        old_repl.Balance := target.Balance;
        target := old_repl;

        shrunk := True;
    end else begin
        // Look further down right child branches.
        ReplaceRightmost(target, repl.RightChild, shrunk);
        if (shrunk) then RebalanceRightShrunk(repl, shrunk);
    end;
end;


// Perform right or left-right rotations to rebalance
// after the right branch has shrunk.
procedure TAVLTree.RebalanceRightShrunk(var node : TAVLNode;
    var shrunk : Boolean);
```

```
var
    child, grandchild        : TAVLNode;
    child_bal, grandchild_bal : TBalance;
begin
    if (node.Balance = RightHeavy) then
    begin
        // It was right heavy. Now it is balanced.
        node.Balance := Balanced;
    end else if (node.Balance = Balanced) then
    begin
        // It was balanced. Now it is left heavy.
        node.Balance := LeftHeavy;
        shrunk := False;
    end else begin
        // It was left heavy. Now it is left unbalanced.
        child := node.LeftChild;
        child_bal := child.Balance;
        if (child_bal <> RightHeavy) then
        begin
            // Right rotation.
            node.LeftChild := child.RightChild;
            child.RightChild := node;
            if (child_bal = Balanced) then
            begin
                node.Balance := LeftHeavy;
                child.Balance := RightHeavy;
                shrunk := False;
            end else begin
                node.Balance := Balanced;
                child.Balance := Balanced;
            end;
            node := child;
        end else begin
            // Left-right rotation.
            grandchild := child.RightChild;
            grandchild_bal := grandchild.Balance;
            child.RightChild := grandchild.LeftChild;
            grandchild.LeftChild := child;
            node.LeftChild := grandchild.RightChild;
            grandchild.RightChild := node;
            if (grandchild_bal = LeftHeavy) then
                node.Balance := RightHeavy
            else
                node.Balance := Balanced;
```

```
        if (grandchild_bal = RightHeavy) then
            child.Balance := LeftHeavy
        else
            child.Balance := Balanced;
        node := grandchild;
        grandchild.Balance := Balanced;
    end; // End (R rotation) ... else (LR rotation) ...
  end; // End if balanced/left heavy/left unbalanced
end;
```

Example program AVL manipulates an AVL tree. Enter a value, and click the Add button to add an item to the tree. Enter a value, and click Remove to delete that item from the tree. Figure 7.14 shows program AVL.

B-trees

B-trees (pronounced *bee trees*) are a different form of balanced tree, one that is a bit more intuitive than AVL trees. Each node in a B-tree can hold several data keys and several pointers to child nodes. Because each node holds several items, the nodes are often called *buckets*.

Between each pair of adjacent child pointers in a node is a key you can use to determine which branch to follow when inserting or looking for an item. For example, in the tree shown in Figure 7.15, the root node contains two keys: G and R. To locate an item with value that comes before G, you look down the first branch. To find a value between G and R, you look down the second branch. To locate an item that comes after R, you look down the third branch.

A B-tree of *order* K has these properties:

- Each node holds at most 2 * K keys.

- Each node, except possibly the root, holds at least K keys.

- An internal node containing M keys has M + 1 children.

- All leaves are at the same level in the tree.

Figure 7.14 Program AVL.

Figure 7.15 A B-tree.

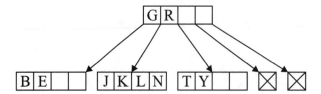

The B-tree in Figure 7.15 has order 2. Each node can hold up to four keys. Each node, except possibly the root, must hold at least two keys. For convenience, B-tree nodes usually can hold an even number of keys, so the order is a whole number.

Requiring that each node in a B-tree of order K contains between K and 2 * K keys keeps the tree balanced. Because each node must hold at least K keys, it must have at least K + 1 children so the tree cannot grow too tall and thin. A B-tree containing N nodes can have height at most $O(\log_{K+1}(N))$. This means searching the tree will be an $O(\log(N))$ operation. Although it is not obvious, inserting and removing items from a B-tree are also $O(\log(N))$ operations.

B-tree Performance

B-trees are particularly useful in large database applications. If the order of a B-tree is reasonably large, you will be able to locate any item in the tree after examining only a few nodes. For example, a B-tree of order 10 containing 1 million records can be at most $\log_{11}(1,000,000)$, or about six levels tall. You would need to examine at most six nodes before finding a particular item.

A balanced binary tree containing the same 1 million items would have height $\log_2(1,000,000)$, or about 20. These nodes, however, contain only one key value. To find an item in a binary tree, you would examine 20 nodes and 20 values. To find an item in a B-tree, you might need to examine 5 nodes and 100 keys.

The B-tree will be faster if it is easy to examine keys, but relatively hard to examine nodes. For example, if the database is stored on a hard disk, reading data from the disk will be slow. Once the data is in memory, examining it is quite fast.

Disk drives read data in large chunks, and it takes no longer to read an entire chunk of data than it takes to read a single byte. If a B-tree's nodes are not too large, it takes no longer to read a B-tree node from a disk than it takes to read a binary tree node. In that case, searching 5 nodes in a B-tree will require 5 slow disk accesses plus up to 100 fast memory accesses. Searching 20 nodes in a binary tree will require 20 slow disk accesses plus 20 fast memory accesses. The binary search is slower because the time spent on 15 extra disk accesses is much greater than the time saved by avoiding 80 memory accesses. Disk access issues are discussed more thoroughly later in this chapter.

Inserting Items in a B-tree

To insert a new item into a B-tree, locate the leaf node in which the new item should be placed. If that node contains fewer than 2 * K keys, there is room to add the new item to that node. Add the new item in its correct position so the items inside the node are in their proper order.

If the node already contains 2 * K items, there is no room for the new item. To make room, break the node into two new nodes. Counting the new item, there are 2 * K + 1 items to distribute between the two new nodes. Place K items in each node, keeping them in their proper order. Move the middle item up to the nodes' parent.

For example, suppose you want to insert the item Q into the B-tree shown in Figure 7.15. This new item belongs in the second leaf node, which is already full. To split the node, divide the items J, K, N, P, and Q between the two new nodes. Place the items J and K in the left node. Place P and Q in the right node. Then move the middle item, N, up to the nodes' parent. Figure 7.16 shows the new tree.

Dividing a node in two is called a *bucket split*. When a bucket split occurs, the parent node gains a new key and a new pointer. If the parent is already full, adding the new key and pointer will cause it to split as well. That, in turn, will require a new entry in the original node's grandparent. That may cause another bucket split and so on up the tree. In the worst case, inserting an item causes a chain reaction that rises up the tree until the root node splits.

When a root split occurs, the B-tree grows taller. That is the only way a B-tree grows taller. This gives B-trees the strange property of always growing from the leaves toward the root.

Removing Items from a B-tree

In theory, removing an item from a B-tree is as simple as adding an item. In practice, the details are pretty complicated.

If the item being removed is not in a leaf node, you must replace it with another item so the tree maintains a proper ordering of the items. This is much like the case of removing an item from a sorted tree or from an AVL tree, and you can handle it similarly. Replace the item with the rightmost item to its left in the tree. This rightmost item will always be in a leaf node. After you have replaced

Figure 7.16 B-tree after adding item Q.

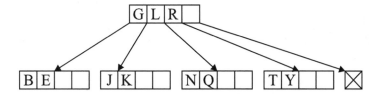

the item, you can treat the removal as if you had simply removed its replacement in the leaf node.

To remove an item from a leaf node, first slide the other items to the left if necessary to fill in the hole left behind. Remember that each node in a B-tree of order K must hold between K and 2 * K items. After you remove an item from a leaf node, the leaf may contain only K – 1 items.

In that case, you can try to borrow some items from one of the leaf's sibling nodes. You can then redistribute the items in the two nodes so they each have at least K items. In Figure 7.17, an item has been removed from the leftmost leaf in the tree, leaving that node with only one item. Redistributing items between the node and its right sibling gives both nodes at least two keys. Notice how the middle item J is moved up into the parent node.

When you try to rebalance nodes in this way, you may find the sibling node contains only K items. Between the target node and its sibling, there are only 2 * K – 1 items, so there are not enough for the two nodes to share. In that case, all the items in both nodes can fit within a single node, so you can merge them. Remove the key that separates the two nodes from their parent. Place that item and the 2 * K – 1 items in the two nodes in the merged node. This process of merging two nodes is called a *bucket merge* or *bucket join*. Figure 7.18 shows how to merge two nodes.

When you merge two nodes, you remove a key from the nodes' parent. The parent may then hold only K – 1 items. In that case, you must rebalance or merge it with one of its siblings. That, in turn, may cause the grandparent node to contain K – 1 items, and the whole process will start over again. In the worst case, the deletion will cause a chain reaction of bucket merges that reaches all the way to the root.

If you remove the last item from the root node, merge the root's two remaining children into a new root and shorten the tree by one level. The only way a B-tree grows shorter is when the children of the root node merge to form a new root.

Example program Btree allows you to manipulate a B-tree. Enter a text value and click the Add button to add an item to the tree. Enter a value and click

Figure 7.17 Rebalancing after removing an item.

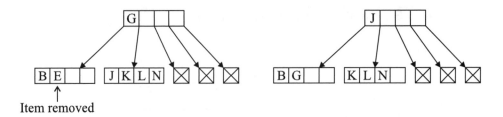

Item removed

Figure 7.18 Merging after removing an item.

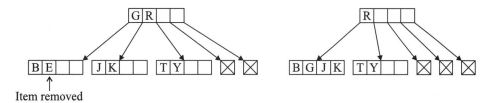

Remove to remove an item from the tree. Figure 7.19 shows program Btree managing an order 2 B-tree.

B-tree Variations

There are several variations of B-trees, only a few of which are described here. *Top-down B-trees* manage the B-tree structure already described in a different way. By splitting full nodes whenever they are encountered, this variation is able to use more intuitive top-down recursion instead of bottom-up recursion when adding items. It also reduces the chances of having long cascades of bucket splits later.

The second variation is the *B+tree* (pronounced *bee plus tree*). B+trees store only data keys in internal nodes and store data records in leaf nodes. This allows B+trees to store more items in each bucket so they are shorter than corresponding B-trees.

Figure 7.19 Program Btree.

Top-Down B-trees

The procedure that adds a new item to a B-tree first searches recursively through the tree to find the bucket where the item belongs. When it tries to insert the new item, the procedure may need to split the bucket and move one of the node's items up to its parent.

As the procedure returns from its recursive calls, the calling procedure checks to see if the parent node must also split. If so, an item is passed up to its parent. Each time the procedure returns from a recursive call, the calling procedure must see if it should split the next ancestor node. Because these bucket splits occur as the procedure is leaving its recursive procedure calls, this is bottom-up recursion. B-trees managed in this way are sometimes called *bottom-up B-trees*.

An alternative strategy is to split any full nodes encountered on the way down. As the procedure searches for a bucket to hold the new item, it splits any node it encounters that is already full. Each time it splits a node, it passes an item up to the parent. Because the procedure has already split every full node it encountered on the way down, there is always room for the new item in the parent node.

When the procedure reaches the leaf that should hold the item, the parent node is guaranteed to have room. If the program must split the leaf node, there is always room to pass the middle item up to the parent. Because this system works from the top down, this sort of B-tree is called a *top-down B-tree*.

This method causes bucket splits to occur sooner than they are absolutely necessary. A top-down B-tree splits a full node even if its child nodes contain lots of unused space. By splitting nodes early, the top-down method causes the tree to hold more empty space than a bottom-up B-tree. On the other hand, by performing node splits early, this method reduces the chances of creating a long cascade of bucket splits.

Unfortunately, there is no top-down version for node merging. As the node removal procedure descends down the tree, it cannot merge nodes that are half empty as it encounters them. It cannot know at that time whether two children of a node will be merged and an item removed from their parent. Because it cannot know if the parent will lose an item, it cannot tell if the parent should be merged with one of its siblings.

B+trees

B-trees are often used to store large records. A typical B-tree might hold employee records, each occupying several kilobytes of memory. The B-tree would arrange the records according to some key field such as employee name or ID number. In that case, rearranging data items could be relatively slow. To merge two buckets, a program must move many records, each of which is quite large. Similarly, to split a bucket, the program must move many large records.

To avoid moving large amounts of data, the program can store only record keys in the B-tree's internal nodes. The nodes also contain pointers to the actual data records stored elsewhere. Now when the program rearranges buckets, it needs to move only the record keys and pointers, not the entire records themselves. This type of B-tree is called a *B+tree*.

Keeping the items in the B+tree nodes small also allows the program to store more keys in each node. With the same node size, the program can increase the order of the tree and make it shorter.

For example, suppose you have an order 2 B-tree so each node has three to five children. To hold 1 million records, this tree would need to have height between $\log_5(1,000,000)$ and $\log_3(1,000,000)$, or between 9 and 13. To locate an item in this tree, a program might need to perform as many as 13 disk accesses.

Now suppose you store the same 1 million records in a B+tree using nodes of roughly the same size in bytes. Because a B+tree stores only keys in its nodes, this tree may be able to hold the keys for up to 20 records in each node. In that case, the tree would have between 11 and 21 children per node, so it would have height between $\log_{21}(1,000,000)$ and $\log_{11}(1,000,000)$, or between 5 and 6. To locate an item, the program would need to perform only six disk accesses to find the item's key, plus one additional disk access to retrieve the item itself.

Storing only pointers to the data within B+tree nodes also makes it easier to associate multiple keys with a set of records. In an employee record system, one B+tree could use last names as keys while another could use Social Security numbers. Both trees would contain pointers to the actual data records stored outside the trees.

Improving B-trees

This section discusses two techniques for improving the performance of B-trees and B+trees. The first technique allows you to rearrange items within a node and its siblings to avoid splitting a bucket. The second allows you to load or reload your data to add unused entries to the tree. This reduces the chances of bucket splits occurring later.

Rebalancing to Avoid Bucket Splits

When you add an item to a bucket that is full, the bucket splits. You can avoid the bucket split if you rebalance the node with one of its siblings. For example, adding a new item Q to the B-tree shown on the left in Figure 7.20 normally causes a bucket split. You can avoid this by rebalancing the node containing J, K, L, and N with its left sibling containing B and E. This gives the tree shown on the right in Figure 7.20.

This sort of rebalancing has a couple of advantages. By rebalancing the nodes, you have increased the usage of the buckets. There are now fewer unused tree entries, so you have decreased the amount of wasted memory. More importantly, if you do not split the bucket you do not need to move an item up to the bucket's parent. That prevents a time-consuming cascade of bucket splits.

Figure 7.20 Rebalancing to avoid a bucket split.

On the other hand, reducing the number of unused entries in the tree decreases the amount of wasted space, but it increases the chances of bucket splits in the future. Because there is less empty space, nodes are more likely to be full when a new node is added.

Initial Loading

Suppose you have a small customer database that contains 10 customer records. You could load the records into a B-tree so they filled each bucket completely, as shown in Figure 7.21. This tree contains little wasted space, but adding a new item to the tree immediately causes a bucket split. In fact, because every node is full, it will cause a cascade of bucket splits, reaching all the way to the root.

Instead of loading the tree densely, you could add some extra empty entries to each node, as shown in Figure 7.22. While this makes the tree a bit larger, it lets you add new items to the tree without immediately causing a long chain of bucket splits. After you use the tree for a while, the amount of free space might decrease to the point where bucket splits are likely. You can then rebuild the tree to add more empty space.

B-trees in real applications usually have larger orders than the trees shown here. Initially loading the tree with a small amount of empty space greatly reduces the need for rebalancing and bucket splits. For example, you might give 10 percent empty space to a B-tree of order 10 so each node has room for two new items. You could work with this tree for quite a while before causing any long chains of bucket splits.

This is an example of a space versus time trade-off. Adding empty space to the nodes makes the tree larger, but reduces the chances of bucket splits.

Figure 7.21 Loading a B-tree densely.

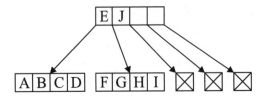

Figure 7.22 Loading a B-tree loosely.

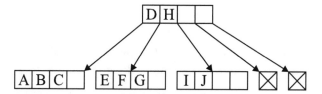

Disk Access Issues

B-trees and B+trees are particularly well suited for large database applications. A typical B+tree might hold hundreds of thousands or even millions of records. In that case, only a small fraction of the tree would fit in memory at any one time. Each time a program accesses a node, it will need to retrieve it from a hard disk. This section describes three issues that are particularly important when the data is stored on a hard disk: *pointer faking*, *bucket size*, and *root caching*.

Pointer Faking

Objects and pointers make building a tree in memory easy, but they are not useful for storing a tree on a hard disk. You cannot create a pointer to part of a file.

Instead, you can use *pointer faking* techniques to replace pointers with record numbers. Instead of using a pointer to point to a node, you use the node's record number in the file. For example, suppose a B+tree of order 12 uses 80-byte keys. You could declare the node data structure using the following code:

```
const
    ORDER = 12;
    KEYS_PER_NODE = 2 * ORDER;

type
    String80 = String[80];
    TBtreeNode = record
        Key   : array [1..KEYS_PER_NODE] of String80; // Keys.
        Child : array [0..KEYS_PER_NODE] of Longint;  // Child
                                                      // pointers.
    end;
```

The Child array entries indicate the record number of the child nodes within the file.

You open the B+tree data file for random access using records that matched the BtreeNode structure.

```
AssignFile(IdxFile, file_name);
Reset(IdxFile);
```

Once the file is open, you can fetch a particular record using the Seek and Read commands.

```
Seek(IdxFile, node_number);
Read(IdxFile, node_record);
```

To make managing B+trees easier, you can store the B+tree nodes and the data records in separate files and use the same disk pointer faking techniques to manage each separately.

When a program no longer needs to use a record in a file, it cannot simply clear all of the references to that record's index. If it did, it would no longer be able to use that record, but the record would still take up space in the file.

The program must keep track of unused records so it can find and reuse them later. One easy way to do this is to keep a linked list of the unused records. When a record is no longer needed, it is added to the list. When the program needs a new record, it removes one from the list. If the program needs a new item and the list is empty, the program expands the file.

Selecting a Bucket Size

Disk drives read data in natural chunks. Most disk drives read data in blocks of 512 or 1024 bytes, or some other number of bytes that is a power of 2. It takes the disk no longer to read one of these blocks than it takes it to read a single byte.

You can take advantage of this fact by making buckets some multiple of the size your disk reads naturally. Then pack as many records or keys as possible into that size. For example, suppose you decide to make your buckets roughly 2048 bytes in size. If you are building a B+tree with 80-byte keys, you would be able to pack up to 24 keys plus their 25 pointers (assuming 4-byte long integer pointers) into each bucket. You could then create an order 12 B+tree with buckets declared by the following code:

```
const
    ORDER = 12;
    KEYS_PER_NODE = 2 * ORDER;

type
    String80 = String[80];
    TBtreeNode = record
        Key   : array [1..KEYS_PER_NODE] of String80; // Keys.
        Child : array [0..KEYS_PER_NODE] of Longint;  // Child
                                                       // pointers.
    end;
```

Node Caching

Every search through a B+tree starts at the root node. You can make searching faster if you always keep the root node loaded in memory. When you search for an item, you perform one less disk access. You still need to write the root node to disk any time it changes; otherwise, if the program crashes after there has been a change, the B+tree will not be up to date.

You can also cache other B+tree nodes in memory. If you can keep all the children of the root node in memory, you will not need to read them from disk either. For a B+tree of order K, the root node will have between 1 and 2 * K keys and therefore will have between 2 and 2 * K + 1 children. That means you will have to cache up to 2 * K + 1 nodes.

A program can also cache nodes while traversing a B+tree. In a preorder traversal, for example, the program visits a node and then recursively visits its children. The program descends into one child. When it returns, it descends into the next. Each time it returns, the program must look at the parent node again to find the child to visit next. By caching the parent in memory, the program avoids the need to read it from disk again.

Recursion allows a program to automatically keep the nodes in memory without using a complicated caching scheme. Each call to the recursive traversal algorithm declares a local variable to hold the node while it is needed. When the recursive call returns, Delphi automatically frees this variable. The following code shows how you might implement this traversal algorithm in Delphi.

```
procedure Preorder(node_number : Longint);
var
    i    : Integer;
    node : BtreeNode;
begin
    // Cache the node.
    Seek(IdxFile, node_number);
    Read(IdxFile, node);

    // Visit this node.
    VisitNode(node_number);

    // Visit the children;
    for i := 0 to KEYS_PER_NODE do
    begin
        if (node.Child[i] < 0) then break;  // There's no such
                                            // child.
        Preorder(node.Child[i]);
    end;
end;
```

A B+tree Database

Example program Bplus manages a B+tree database using two data files: Custs.dat contains customer data records, and Custs.idx holds the B+tree nodes.

Enter data in the Customer Record area, and click the Add button to add a new item to the database. Enter a first name and a last name in the top part of the form and click Find to locate the corresponding record.

Figure 7.23 shows the program after finding the record for Rod Stephens. The Accesses label in the Search area indicates the program needed only three disk accesses to find the record. The statistics at the bottom indicate that the data was found in record number 2002. The B+tree has height 3, holds 3004 data records, and contains 262 buckets.

When you add a record or find an old one, program Bplus selects that record. If you click the Remove button, the program removes the record from the database.

If you select the Display menu's Internal Nodes command, the program shows you the internal nodes in the tree. It displays the keys for each node indented to show the tree's internal structure.

The Display menu's Complete Tree command makes the program show the complete structure of the tree. Customer data is shown inside pointed brackets.

Index file records contain 41-byte keys. Each key is a customer's last name padded to 20 characters, followed by a comma, followed by the customer's first name padded to 20 characters.

Program Bplus reads data in roughly 1024-byte chunks. Assuming K keys per bucket, each bucket holds K keys of length 41 bytes, K + 1 child pointers of length 4 bytes, and the 2-byte integer NumKeys. This total size should be as large as possible while still fitting within 1024 bytes.

Figure 7.23 Program Bplus.

Solving the equation 41 * K + 4 * (K + 1) + 2 <= 1024 for K, you get K <= 22.62, so K should be 22. In this case, the B+tree should have order 11 so it contains 22 keys per bucket. Each bucket occupies 41 * 22 + 4 * (22 + 1) + 2 = 996 bytes.

```
const
    KEY_SIZE = 41;
    ORDER = 11;
    KEYS_PER_NODE = 2 * ORDER;
```

To make managing the two data files easier, program Bplus uses two variant record types to represent the records in each file.

The TBucket data type represents a record in the B+tree index file Custs.idx. The first record in Custs.idx contains header information that describes the B+tree. This includes the number of buckets used in Custs.dat, the number of data records used in Custs.dat, the first record in each file's garbage list, and so forth.

The other records in the Custs.idx file store record keys and indexes. The variable NumKeys tells how many keys are actually used in the record.

```
TBucket = record
    case IsHeader : Boolean of
        True : ( // Header information.
            NumBuckets        : Longint;  // # buckets in Custs.idx.
            NumRecords        : Longint;  // # records in Custs.dat.
            Root              : Longint;  // Root index in
                                          // Custs.idx.
            NextTreeRecord    : Longint;  // Next unused in
                                          // Custs.idx.
            NextCustRecord    : Longint;  // Next unused in
                                          // Custs.dat.
            FirstTreeGarbage  : Longint;  // First garbage in
                                          // Custs.idx.
            FirstCustGarbage  : Longint;  // First garbage in
                                          // Custs.dat.
            Height            : Integer;  // Height of tree.
        );
        False : ( // A bucket containing keys.
            // # keys in use in this bucket.
            NumKeys : Integer;

            // Key = Last Name, First Name.
            Key     : array [1..KEYS_PER_NODE] of String[KEY_SIZE];

            // Indexes of child buckets.
            Child   : array [0..KEYS_PER_NODE] of Longint;
        );
end; // End TBucket record definition.
```

The TCustomer data type represents a record in the B+tree data file Custs.dat. This variant record is a little simpler than the TBucket data type. Each record is either on the file's garbage linked list or it contains customer data. Garbage list entries just contain the index of the next record in the garbage linked list. Customer data entries contain customer data.

```
TCustomer = record
    case IsGarbage : Boolean of
        True : ( // It's on the garbage list.
            NextGarbage : Longint; // Index of next garbage record.
        );
        False : ( // It's a real customer record.
            LastName   : String[20];
            FirstName  : String[20];
            Address    : String[40];
            City       : String[20];
            State      : String[2];
            Zip        : String[10];
            Phone      : String[12];
        );
    end; // End TCustomer record definition.
```

When program Bplus begins, it prompts you for a data directory. It then opens the B+tree data files Custs.dat and Custs.idx in that directory. If the files do not exist, the program creates them. Otherwise, it reads the tree's header information from Custs.idx. It then reads the B+tree's root node and caches it in memory.

When the program descends into the tree to insert or delete an item, it caches the nodes it visits. As it recursively returns back up the tree, it may need these nodes again if there has been a bucket split, merge, or other node rearrangement. Because the program caches the nodes on the way down, they are available on the way back up.

Large bucket sizes make B+trees efficient, but it makes them harder to test manually. To make an order 11 B+tree grow to height 2, you would have to add 23 items to the database. To make it grow to height 3, you would need to add more than 250 additional items.

To make program Bplus easier to test, you might want to change the B+tree's order to 2. In file BplusC.pas, comment out the line that sets the order to 11 and uncomment the line that makes the order 2.

```
// ORDER = 11;
ORDER = 2;
```

The Bplus program's Data menu contains a Create Data command you can use to create many data records quickly. Enter the number of records you want to create and the number the program should use to build the first item. The program then creates the records and inserts them into the B+tree. For example, if you tell the program to create 100 records starting from the value 200, the program creates entries for 200, 201, ... , 299 similar to this one:

```
FirstName:   First_200
LastName:    Last_200
Address:     Addr_200
City:        City_200
```

You can use these entries to experiment with a reasonably large B+tree.

Summary

Balanced trees allow a program to manipulate data efficiently. High-order B+trees are particularly useful for storing large databases on hard drives or other relatively slow storage devices. You can even use multiple B+trees to provide different indexes into the same large set of data.

Chapter 11, "Hashing," describes an alternative to balanced trees. Hashing allows even faster access to data under some circumstances, though it does not allow a program to perform such operations as listing records sequentially.

Decision Trees

Many difficult real-world problems can be modeled using *decision trees*. Each node in the tree represents one step in the solution to the problem. Each branch in the tree represents a decision that leads to a more complete solution. Leaf nodes represent a complete solution. The goal is to find the best path through the tree from the root to a leaf while satisfying certain constraints. Exactly what the constraints are and what the "best" path means depend on the problem.

Decision trees are usually enormous. A decision tree for selecting a move in tic-tac-toe contains more than half a million nodes. Tic-tac-toe is a simple game, and many real-world problems are much more complicated. The corresponding decision trees may contain more nodes than there are atoms in the universe.

This chapter examines techniques you can use to search these huge trees. First, it examines *game trees*. Using tic-tac-toe as an example, it discusses ways to search game trees to find the best possible move.

The sections that follow describe ways to search more general decision trees. For the smallest trees, you can use *exhaustive searching* to examine every possible solution. For larger trees, *branch and bound* techniques allow you to find the best possible solution without searching the entire tree.

For even larger trees, you must use a *heuristic*. The solution you find may not be the absolute best possible solution, but it should be good enough to be useful. Using heuristics, you can search practically any tree.

Finally, this chapter discusses several very difficult problems that you can try to solve using branch and bound and heuristic techniques. Many of these problems have important applications, and finding good solutions is critical.

Searching Game Trees

A strategy board game like chess, checkers, or tic-tac-toe can be modeled using a *game tree*. Each branch out of a node corresponds to a different move by one of the players. If a player has 30 possible moves at some point in the game, that node in the game tree will have 30 branches.

For example, in tic-tac-toe the root node corresponds to the initial, empty board position. The first player can place an X in any of the nine squares on the board. Corresponding to each of those nine moves is a branch leaving the root node. The nine nodes below these branches correspond to the nine different board positions where player X has chosen a square.

Once X has moved, O can pick any of the remaining eight squares. Corresponding to each of these moves is a branch leading out of the node representing the current board position. Figure 8.1 shows a small part of the tic-tac-toe game tree.

As you can see from Figure 8.1, the tic-tac-toe game tree grows extremely quickly. If the tree continued to grow like this, with each node in the tree having one less branch than its parent, the complete tree would have $9 * 8 * 7 ... * 1 = 362,880$ leaves. There would be 362,880 paths through the tree corresponding to 362,880 possible games.

Actually, many of the possible nodes are missing from the tic-tac-toe game tree because they are forbidden by the rules of the game. In the first three moves, if X selects the upper-left, upper-center, and upper-right squares, X wins and the game ends. The node representing this board position has no children because the game has ended. This game is shown in Figure 8.2.

Removing all the impossible nodes leaves about a quarter million leaf nodes. This is still a pretty big tree, and searching it exhaustively still takes some time. For more complicated games like checkers, chess, or go, the game trees are enormous. If each player had only 16 options during each move in a chess game, the

Figure 8.1 Part of the tic-tac-toe game tree.

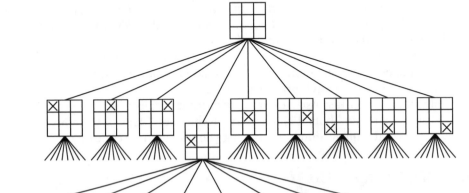

Figure 8.2 A game that ends early.

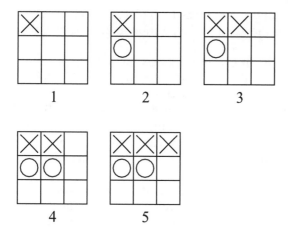

game tree would have more than 1 trillion nodes after each player had moved only five times. Some of the later sections in this chapter explain searching these enormous game trees further. The next section deals only with the relatively simple example of tic-tac-toe.

Minimax Searching

To begin searching a game tree, you need to be able to determine the value of a board position. In tic-tac-toe, X places a high value on board positions with three Xs in a row because X wins those games. The O player places a low value on those board positions because player O loses those games.

For each player, you can assign one of four values to a particular board position. The value 4 means the board position will result in a win for this player. A value of 3 means it is not clear from the current board position who will eventually win. The value 2 means the board position will result in a draw (cat's game). Finally, the value 1 means the board position will give victory to the other player.

To search the game tree exhaustively, you can use a *minimax* strategy. Here you try to *minimize* the *maximum* value your opponent can get from the current board position. You can do this by determining the maximum value the opponent can achieve for each of your possible moves. You then take the move that gives your opponent the smallest value.

Procedure BoardValue shown later computes the value of a board position. This procedure examines each possible move. For each move, it recursively calls itself to see what the opponent's value for the new board position would be. It then selects the move that gives the opponent the smallest of those values.

To determine the value of a board position, BoardValue recursively calls itself until one of three things happens. First, it might find a position in which a player has won. In that case, it sets the value of the board position to 4, indicating that the player who just moved has won.

Second, BoardValue might find a position in which no player can move. The game is a draw so the procedure sets the value of the position to 2, indicating that the game is a tie.

Finally, the procedure might reach a predetermined maximum depth of recursion. If it exceeds its allowed depth, BoardValue assigns the board position the value 3, indicating that it cannot tell who will win. The maximum depth of recursion stops the program from taking too long while searching the game tree. This is particularly important for more complicated games, such as chess, in which the program could search the game tree practically forever. The maximum depth can also set the program's skill level. The deeper into the tree the program can look, the better its moves will be.

Figure 8.3 shows a tic-tac-toe game tree near the end of a game. It is X's turn, and X has three possible moves. To select the best move for X, BoardValue recursively examines each of the three possible moves X can make. The first and third moves (the left and right branches in the tree) result in wins for player O, so those moves have value 4 for player O. The second possible move results in a draw, which has value 2 for player O. BoardValue picks the second move because it gives player O the smallest board value.

Figure 8.3 The bottom of a game tree.

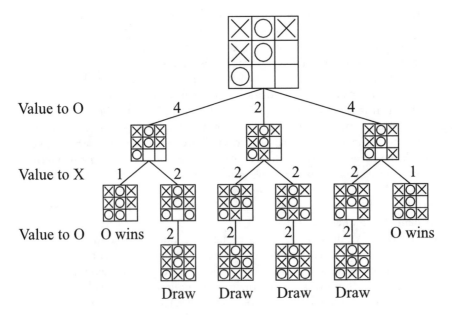

```
procedure TTicTacForm.BoardValue(var best_move : Integer;
    var best_value : TBoardValue; player1, player2 : TPlayer;
    depth : Integer);
var
    good_value, enemy_value : TBoardValue;
    i, good_i, enemy_i      : Integer;
    player                  : TPlayer;
begin
    // If we are in too deep, we know nothing.
    if (depth >= SkillLevel) then begin
        best_value := bvUnknown;
        exit;
    end;

    // If this board is finished, we know how we would do.
    player := Winner;

    if (player <> plNone) then
    begin
        // Convert the value for the winner pl into the
        // value for player player1.
        if (player = player1) then
            best_value := bvWin
        else if (player = player2) then
            best_value := bvLose
        else
            best_value := bvDraw;
        exit;
    end;

    // Try all the legal moves.
    good_i := -1;
    good_value := bvTooBig; // Bigger than is possible.
    for i := 1 to NUM_SQUARES do
    begin
        // If the move is legal, try it.
        if (Board[i] = plNone) then
        begin
            // See what value this would give the opponent.
            // Make the move.
            Board[i] := player1;
            BoardValue(enemy_i, enemy_value, player2, player1, depth
    + 1);
```

```
        // Unmake the move.
        Board[i] := plNone;

        // See if this is lower than the previous best
        // move for the opponent.
        if (enemy_value < good_value) then
        begin
            good_i := i;
            good_value := enemy_value;
            // If the opponent will lose, things can't
            // get better for us so take this move.
            if (good_value <= bvLose) then break;
        end;
    end; // End if (Board[i] := None) then ...
end; // End for i := 1 to NUM_SQUARES do.

// Translate the opponent's value into ours.
if (good_value = bvWin) then
    // Opponent wins, we lose.
    best_value := bvLose
else if (enemy_value = bvLose) then
    // Opponent loses, we win.
    best_value := bvWin
Else
    // DRAW and UNKNOWN are the same for both players.
    best_value := good_value;
best_move := good_i;
end;
```

Example program TicTac uses procedure BoardValue to run a tic-tac-toe program. The bulk of the program manages interaction with the user. It draws the board, lets the user pick squares, sets options, and so forth. Commands in the Options menu allow you to play either X or O and to set the program's skill level (maximum depth of recursion).

Improving Game Tree Searching

If the only tool you had for searching game trees was minimax, searching large trees would be pretty hard. A game like chess is so complicated that a program could not hope to search more than a few levels of the tree. Fortunately, there are several tricks you can use for searching large game trees.

Precomputed Initial Moves and Responses

First, the program can store some initial moves chosen by game experts. You might decide that the tic-tac-toe program should take the center square if it moves first. That determines the first branch in the game tree so the program can ignore any paths that do not take this first branch. For tic-tac-toe, this reduces the size of the tree by a factor of 1 / 9.

In fact, the program does not need to search the tree until its opponent has also made a move. Then both the computer and its opponent have selected branches, so the tree remaining is much smaller. It contains fewer than 7! = 5040 paths. By precomputing only one move, you reduce the size of the game tree from around a quarter million paths to fewer than 5040.

Similarly, you can save responses to initial moves if the opponent moves first. The user has nine choices for a first move so you need to store nine responses. Now the program does not need to search the game tree until the opponent moves, the computer moves, and the opponent moves again. At that point, the game tree holds fewer than 6! = 720 paths. By storing nine moves, you reduce the size of the game tree enormously. This is an example of a space versus time trade-off. Using extra memory to store a few moves greatly reduces the time needed to search the game tree. Example program TicTac uses 10 precomputed moves: one for moving first and nine for responding if the opponent moves first.

Commercial chess programs also begin with stored moves and responses commonly used by chess experts. These programs can make their first few moves extremely quickly. Once the game progresses beyond the stored responses, the program must search the game tree, so moves take much longer.

Recognizing Important Patterns

Another way to improve game tree searches is to look for important patterns. When the program identifies one of these patterns, it can take specific action or it can alter the way in which it searches the tree.

During a chess game, players often arrange the pieces to protect each other. If the opponent captures a piece, the player can capture one of the opponent's pieces. Often that capture allows the opponent to capture another piece, and so forth. Sometimes the series of exchanges can involve quite a few pieces.

Some programs look for possible sequences of trades. If the program recognizes a trade, it temporarily breaks its limits on how far down the tree it can search so it can examine the sequence of trades to its end. This allows the computer to decide whether the exchange will be profitable. If the exchange takes place, the number of pieces remaining is also reduced, so searching the game tree becomes easier in the future.

Some chess programs also look for patterns such as castling moves, moves that threaten more than one of the opponent's pieces at the same time, moves that threaten the opponent's king or queen, and so forth.

Heuristics

In games more complicated than tic-tac-toe, it is almost never possible to search even a tiny fraction of the game tree. In these cases, you must use some sort of *heuristic* (pronounced *you-riss-tik*). A heuristic is an algorithm or rule of thumb that is likely, but not guaranteed, to produce a good result.

A common heuristic in chess is, "When ahead, trade mercilessly." If your opponent has lost more valuable pieces than you have, and if all else is equal, you should exchange pieces whenever possible as long as you do not lose on the deal. For example, if you can capture a knight but you will lose a knight in exchange, you should do so. By reducing the number of pieces remaining, you make the decision tree smaller and you make your relative strength advantage greater. This strategy does not guarantee that you will win the game, but it does improve your chances.

Another heuristic used in many strategy games is to assign different values to different parts of the board. In chess, the squares nearest the center of the board are most valuable because pieces in those positions can attack a large part of the board. When the BoardValue procedure calculates the value of a board position, it can give greater weight to pieces that hold these key squares.

Searching Other Decision Trees

Some of the techniques used to search game trees do not apply to more general decision trees. Many of these trees do not include a concept of players alternating moves, so minimax and precomputed moves make no sense. The following sections explain techniques you can use to search these other kinds of decision trees.

Branch and Bound

Branch and bound is a technique for pruning a decision tree so you do not need to consider all of the tree's branches. The general strategy is to keep track of bounds on the solutions discovered so far and on the solutions that are still possible. If you ever reach a point where the best solution so far is better than the best solution possible below a node, you can ignore all the paths below that node.

For example, suppose you have $100 million to spend and you can spend it on several possible investments. Each has a different cost and a different expected return. You must decide how to spend the money to get the greatest possible profit.

This sort of problem is called a *knapsack* problem. You have several items (investments) that you want to fit into a knapsack with a fixed size ($100 million). Each of the items has some cost (money) and a value (also money). You must find a selection of items that fits in the knapsack and gives the greatest possible total value.

You can model this problem using a decision tree. Each node in the tree represents a combination of items placed in the knapsack. Each branch represents the decision to put an item in the knapsack or to leave the item out. The left branch at the first node corresponds to spending money on the first investment. The right branch represents not paying for the first investment. Figure 8.4 shows a decision tree for four possible investments.

The decision tree for this problem is a complete binary tree of depth equal to the number of investments. Each leaf node corresponds to a complete selection of investments.

The size of this tree grows very quickly as the number of investments increases. For 10 possible investments, the tree holds $2^{10} = 1024$ leaf nodes. For 20 investments, the tree holds more than 1 million leaves. Searching every node in this tree is possible, but you do not have to add too many more investment choices to make the tree unreasonably large.

To use branch and bound, use an array to keep track of the items in the best solution you have found so far. Initialize the array so it does not contain any items. Use a variable to keep track of the value of this solution. Initially, this should be some small value so the first real solution considered will be an improvement.

While you search the decision tree, if you ever reach a point where the solution you are examining has no chance of improving enough to beat the current best solution, you can stop searching down that path in the tree. Also, if you ever reach a point where the selections cost more than $100 million, you can stop searching.

As a concrete example, suppose you can make any of the investments shown in Table 8.1. Figure 8.4 shows the corresponding decision tree. Some of these investment packages violate the problem's constraints. The leftmost path, for example, forces you to spend $178 million on all four choices.

Suppose you have started searching the tree shown in Figure 8.4. You have found that you could spend $97 million on options A and B for a profit of $23 million. This corresponds to the fourth leaf node from the left in Figure 8.4.

As you continue searching the tree, you come to the second node labeled C in Figure 8.4. This corresponds to investment packages that include option A, do not include option B, and may or may not include options C and D. At this

Figure 8.4 An investment decision tree.

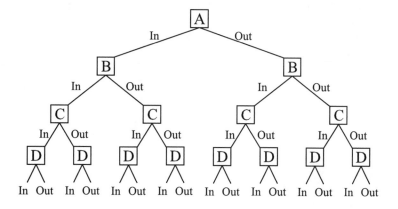

Table 8.1 Possible Investments

Investment	Cost ($ millions)	Profit ($ millions)
A	45	10
B	52	13
C	46	8
D	35	4

point, the package already costs $45 million for option A and produces a profit of $10 million.

The only remaining options are C and D. Together, they can improve the solution by $12 million. The current solution has a value of $10 million, so the best possible solution below this node is worth at most $22 million. This is smaller than the $23 million solution you already found, so you do not need to continue down this path.

As the program moves through the tree, it does not need to continuously check to see if the partial solution it is considering is better than the best solution so far. If a partial solution is an improvement, the rightmost leaf node below that partial solution is also an improvement. That leaf represents the same combination of items as the partial solution with all other items excluded. This means the program needs to check for improved solutions only when it reaches a leaf node.

In fact, any leaf node the program reaches is always an improved solution. If it were not, it would have been trimmed from the tree when the program considered the node's parent. At that point, moving to the leaf would reduce the total value of the unassigned items to zero. If the value of the solution is not already larger than the best solution so far, the lower bound test stops the program from continuing to the leaf. Using this fact, the program can update the best solution whenever it reaches a leaf node.

The following code uses the upper and lower bound tests to implement the branch and bound algorithm.

```
type
  TItem = record
    Cost   : Integer;
    Profit : Integer;
  end;
  TItemArray = array [1..1000000] of TItem;
  PItemArray = ^TItemArray;

  TBoolArray = array [1..1000000] of Boolean;
```

```
    PBoolArray = ^TBoolArray;

TBandBForm = class(TForm)
     // Code omitted...
   private
     NumItems          : Integer;
     Items             : PItemArray;
     AllowedCost       : Integer;

     // Search variables.
     NodesVisited      : Longint;
     UnassignedProfit  : Integer;     // Total of unassigned profits.
     BestSolution      : PBoolArray;  // True for items in best
                                      // solution.
     BestCost          : Integer;
     BestProfit        : Integer;
     TestSolution      : PBoolArray;  // True for items in test
                                      // solution.
     TestCost          : Integer;     // Cost of test solution.
     TestProfit        : Integer;     // Profit of test solution.

// Initialize test values and start an exhaustive or
// branch and bound search.
procedure TBandBForm.Search(b_and_b : Boolean);
var
     i : Integer;
begin
     NodesVisited := 0;
     BestProfit := 0;
     BestCost := 0;
     TestProfit := 0;
     TestCost := 0;
     UnassignedProfit := 0;
     for i := 1 to NumItems do
         UnassignedProfit := UnassignedProfit +
             Items[i].Profit;

     // Start the search with the first item.
     if (b_and_b) then
         BranchAndBound(1)
     else
         ExhaustiveSearch(1);
end;
```

```
// Perform a branch and bound search starting with
// the indicated item.
procedure TBandBForm.BranchAndBound(item_num : Integer);
var
    i : Integer;
begin
    NodesVisited := NodesVisited + 1;

    // If this is a leaf node, it must be a better
    // solution than we have so far or it would have been
    // cut off earlier in the search.
    if (item_num > NumItems) then
    begin
        // Save the improved solution.
        for i := 1 to NumItems do
            BestSolution[i] := TestSolution[i];
        BestProfit := TestProfit;
        BestCost := TestCost;
        exit;
    end;

    // Otherwise descend down the child branches. First
    // try including this item making sure it fits within
    // the cost bound.
    if (TestCost + Items[item_num].Cost <= AllowedCost) then
    begin
        // Add the item to the test solution.
        TestSolution[item_num] := True;
        TestCost := TestCost + Items[item_num].Cost;
        TestProfit := TestProfit + Items[item_num].Profit;
        UnassignedProfit := UnassignedProfit - Items[item_num].Profit;

        // Recursively see what the result might be.
        BranchAndBound(item_num + 1);

        // Remove the item from the test solution.
        TestSolution[item_num] := False;
        TestCost := TestCost - Items[item_num].Cost;
        TestProfit := TestProfit - Items[item_num].Profit;
        UnassignedProfit := UnassignedProfit + Items[item_num].Profit;
    end;

    // Try excluding the item. See if the remaining items
    // have enough profit to make a path down this branch
    // reach our lower bound.
```

```
        UnassignedProfit := UnassignedProfit - Items[item_num].Profit;
        if (TestProfit + UnassignedProfit > BestProfit) then
            BranchAndBound(item_num + 1);
        UnassignedProfit := UnassignedProfit + Items[item_num].Profit;
end;
```

Example program BandB uses exhaustive search and branch and bound to solve the knapsack problem. Enter minimum and maximum costs and values you want assigned to the items, and the number of items you want created. Then click the Make Data button to make the program generate the items.

Next use the option buttons at the bottom of the form to select either exhaustive search or branch and bound. When you click Go, the program uses the method you selected to find the best solution. The program displays the solution along with the number of nodes in the complete decision tree and the number of nodes the program actually visited.

Figure 8.5 shows program BandB after solving a 20-item knapsack problem. In this case, branch and bound found the best solution after visiting only 999 of the tree's more than 2 million nodes. Try small examples before you let the program run an exhaustive search on 20 items. A 90-megahertz Pentium can take 30 seconds or more to exhaustively search for a solution to the 20-item knapsack problem.

Branch and bound searches visit far fewer nodes than exhaustive searches. The decision tree for a 20-item knapsack problem contains 2,097,151 nodes. While exhaustive search always visits them all, branch and bound may visit only 1000 or so.

Figure 8.5 Program BandB.

The number of nodes branch and bound visits depends on the exact data values. If the item costs are large, only a few items at a time will fit in a valid solution. Once several items are placed in the test solution, the remaining items are too expensive to consider, so much of the tree will be trimmed away.

On the other hand, if the items have small costs, many will fit in a valid solution, so the program must explore many valid combinations. Table 8.2 shows the number of nodes program BandB visited in a series of tests using different item costs. The program randomly generated 20 items, and the total allowed cost of the solution was 100.

Heuristics

Sometimes even branch and bound algorithms cannot search a decision tree completely. The decision tree for a 65-item knapsack problem holds more than $7 * 10^{19}$ nodes. If branch and bound visited only a tenth of 1 percent of those nodes, and if your computer could examine 1 million nodes per second, it would take you more than 2 million years to solve the problem. In problems where branch and bound is not fast enough, you can use a heuristic.

If the quality of the solution is not critical, the answer given by a heuristic may be good enough to be useful. In some cases, you may not know the input data with perfect accuracy. Then a good heuristic solution may be as valid as the theoretically best solution.

The previous example uses branch and bound to select investment combinations. Investments are risky, however, and exact results are often not known ahead of time. You may not know the exact profit or even cost of some of the investments. In that case, an effective heuristic solution may be just as reliable as the best solution you can calculate exactly.

This section discusses heuristics that are useful for many difficult problems. Example program Heur demonstrates each of the heuristics. It also allows you to

Table 8.2 Nodes Visited by Exhaustive and Branch and Bound Searches

Average Item Cost	Exhaustive Search	Branch and Bound
60	2,097,151	203
50	2,097,151	520
40	2,097,151	1322
30	2,097,151	4269
20	2,097,151	13,286
10	2,097,151	40,589

compare the heuristics to exhaustive search and branch and bound. Enter information in the Parameters area to tell the program how to generate the test data. Select the algorithms you want to test and click the Go button. The program displays the total cost and profit of the best solution found by each of the methods selected. It also ranks the solutions and displays the time required by each algorithm. Be sure to use branch and bound only on relatively small problems and exhaustive search only on the tiniest problems.

Figure 8.6 shows program Heur after solving a 30-item knapsack problem. In this test, none of the heuristics found the best solution possible, though several found solutions that were quite good.

Hill Climbing

A *hill climbing* heuristic makes changes to the current solution to move as far as possible towards the goal. This process is called hill climbing because it is like a lost hiker at night searching for the top of a mountain. Even if it is too dark to see far, the hiker can try to reach the mountain top by always moving uphill.

Of course, there is a chance the hiker will become stuck on top of a smaller hill and not make it all the way to the peak. This sort of problem can also occur when using hill climbing heuristics. The algorithm may find a solution that seems good locally, but is not the best solution possible.

In the knapsack problem, the goal is to pick a set of items with total cost no more than an allowed limit and with a large total profit. A hill climbing heuristic for this problem would select the item that gives the largest profit at each step. That moves the solution closer to the goal of selecting a large profit.

Figure 8.6 Program Heur.

The program starts by adding the item with the largest profit to the solution. It then adds the item with the next largest profit that still fits within the remaining cost allowance. It continues adding the item with the next largest profit until no more items fit within the allowance.

For the investments shown in Table 8.3, the program first selects option A because it has the largest profit at $9 million. Next, the program picks option C because it has the next largest profit at $8 million. At this point, $93 million of the $100 million allowance is spent, and the program cannot afford any other options. The solution produced by the heuristic includes items A and C, has a cost of $93 million, and gives a profit of $17 million.

The hill climbing heuristic fills the knapsack very quickly. If the items are initially sorted in order of decreasing profit, this is an O(N) algorithm. The program simply moves through the list adding each item if there is room. Even if the list is not sorted, this is only an $O(N^2)$ algorithm. This is much better than the $O(2^N)$ steps required for an exhaustive search of every node in the tree. For 20 items, this heuristic uses around 400 steps, compared with a few thousand for branch and bound and more than 2 million for an exhaustive search.

```
// Search the tree using a hill climbing heuristic.
procedure THeurForm.HillClimbing(node : Integer);
var
    i, j, big_value, big_j : Integer;
begin
    // Repeatedly pass through the list looking for the
    // remaining item with the largest profit that fits
    // within the cost bounds.
    for i := 1 to NumItems do
    begin
        big_value := 0;
        big_j := -1;
        for j := 1 to NumItems do
```

Table 8.3 Possible Investments

Investment	Cost	Return	Profit
A	63	72	9
B	35	42	7
C	30	38	8
D	27	34	7
E	23	26	3

```
        // Make sure it is not already in the solution.
        if ((not BestSolution[j]) and
            (big_value < Items[j].Profit) and
            (BestCost + Items[j].Cost <= AllowedCost))
        then begin
            big_value := Items[j].Profit;
            big_j := j;
        end;

    // Stop when no more items fit.
    if (big_j < 0) then break;

    // Add the selected item to the solution.
    BestCost := BestCost + Items[big_j].Cost;
    BestSolution[big_j] := True;
    BestProfit := BestProfit + Items[big_j].Profit;
    end; // End for i := 1 to NumItems do...
end;
```

Least-Cost

A strategy that, in a sense, is the opposite of hill climbing is *least-cost*. Instead of moving the solution as far as possible toward the goal at each step, you move the cost of the solution as little as possible toward the constraint. In the knapsack example, you add the item with the lowest cost to the solution.

This strategy will fit as many items as possible into the solution. If all items have roughly the same profit, this will be a good solution. If an expensive option has a large profit, this strategy may miss the option and not produce the best possible result.

For the investments shown in Table 8.3, a least-cost strategy starts by adding option E to the solution at a cost of $23 million. Next, it selects D at $27 million and then C at $30 million. At this point, the algorithm has spent $80 million of the $100 million allowance, and it cannot afford any other investments.

This solution has a cost of $80 million and gives a profit of $18 million. This is $1 million better than the hill climbing heuristic's solution, but least-cost does not always do better than hill climbing. Which gives the better solution depends on the exact data values.

The program structure for the least-cost heuristic is almost identical to that of the hill climbing heuristic. The only difference is in selecting the next item to add to the test solution. The least-cost heuristic chooses the item that has the lowest cost instead of the item with the largest profit. Because the two methods are so similar, they have the same runtime. If the items are properly sorted, both algorithms each run in $O(N)$ time. Even with the items arranged randomly, both can run in $O(N^2)$ time.

Because the Delphi code for the two heuristics is so similar, only the lines where the new item is selected are shown here.

```
if ((not BestSolution[j]) and
    (small_cost > Items[j].Cost) and
    (BestCost + Items[j].Cost <= AllowedCost))
then begin
    small_cost := Items[j].Cost;
    small_j := j;
end;
```

Balanced Profit

The hill climbing strategy does not take into account the cost of the items being added to the solution. It selects items with large profits even if they also have large costs. The least-cost strategy does not take into account the profit returned by an item. It selects items with small costs even if they have small profits.

A *balanced profit* heuristic compares both the profit and cost of the items to decide which items to select. At each step, the heuristic selects the item with the largest profit-to-cost ratio.

Table 8.4 shows the same data as Table 8.3 with an additional profit/cost column. The balanced profit strategy first picks option C because it has the highest ratio at 0.27. Next it adds D to the solution with a ratio of 0.26 and B with a ratio of 0.20. At this point, the heuristic has spent $92 million of the $100 million and can fit no more items in the solution.

This solution has a cost of $92 million and gives a profit of $22 million. This is $4 million better than the least-cost solution and $5 million better than the hill climbing solution. In this case, it is also the best possible solution and would be found by either exhaustive search or branch and bound. However, balanced profit is still a heuristic so it does not always find the best possible solution. It often finds better solutions than hill climbing and least-cost, but not always.

Table 8.4 Possible Investments with Profit/Cost Ratio

Investment	Cost	Return	Profit	Profit/Cost
A	63	72	9	0.14
B	35	42	7	0.20
C	30	38	8	0.27
D	27	34	7	0.26
E	23	26	3	0.13

In structure, the balanced profit heuristic is almost identical to the hill climbing and least-cost heuristics. The only difference is in the way the heuristic selects the next item to add to the solution.

```
test_ratio := Items[j].Profit / Items[j].Cost;
if ((not BestSolution[j]) and
    (good_ratio < test_ratio) and
    (BestCost + Items[j].Cost <= AllowedCost))
then begin
    good_ratio := test_ratio;
    good_j := j;
end;
```

Random Searching

A *random search* is exactly what it sounds like. At each step, the algorithm adds a randomly chosen item that fits within the cost bounds. This kind of search is also called a *Monte Carlo search* or a *Monte Carlo simulation*.

Because a randomly selected solution is unlikely to give the best possible solution, you must repeat the search many times to get a reasonable result. Even though it may seem that the odds of finding a good solution are small, this method sometimes produces surprisingly good results. Depending on the data values and the number of random solutions examined, this heuristic often does better than hill climbing or least-cost.

Random searching also has the advantage of being easy to understand and implement. Sometimes it is hard to decide how to create hill climbing, least-cost, or balanced profit heuristics for a problem. It is always easy to generate solutions at random. Even for extremely complicated problems, random search provides an easy heuristic.

The RandomSearch procedure in program Heur uses function AddToSolution to add a random item to the solution. This function returns the value True if it can find an item that fits within the cost allowance and False otherwise. RandomSearch calls AddToSolution until no more items fit within the allowance.

```
// Add a random item to the test solution. Return True if
// successful, False if no more items will fit.
function THeurForm.AddToSolution : Boolean;
var
    num_left, j, selection : Integer;
begin
    // See how many items remain that will fit within
    // the cost bound.
    num_left := 0;
    for j := 1 to NumItems do
        if ((not TestSolution[j]) and
```

```
            (TestCost + Items[j].Cost <= AllowedCost)) then
                num_left := num_left + 1;

    // Stop when no items fit.
    Result := (num_left > 0);
    if (not Result) then exit;

    // Pick one of the items that fit at random.
    selection := Random(num_left - 1) + 1;

    // Find the chosen item.
    for j := 1 to NumItems do
        if ((not TestSolution[j]) and
            (TestCost + Items[j].Cost <= AllowedCost)) then
        begin
            selection := selection - 1;
            if (selection < 1) then break;
        end;

    TestProfit := TestProfit + Items[j].Profit;
    TestCost := TestCost + Items[j].Cost;
    TestSolution[j] := True;
end;


// Search the tree using a random heuristic.
procedure THeurForm.RandomSearch(node : Integer);
var
    num_trials, trial, i : Integer;
begin
    // Make several trials and keep the best.
    num_trials := NumItems;
    for trial := 1 to num_trials do
    begin
        // Make random selections until no more items fit.
        while (AddToSolution) do ;

        // See if this solution is an improvement.
        if (TestProfit > BestProfit) then
        begin
            BestProfit := TestProfit;
            BestCost := TestCost;
            for i := 1 to NumItems do
                BestSolution[i] := TestSolution[i];
        end;
```

```
        // Reset the test solution for the next trial.
        TestProfit := 0;
        TestCost := 0;
        for i := 1 to NumItems do
            TestSolution[i] := False;
    end; // End for trial := 1 to num_trials do...
end;
```

Incremental Improvement

Another strategy is to start with a random solution and then make *incremental improvements*. Starting with a randomly generated solution, the program makes a random change. If the new solution is an improvement, the program makes the change permanent and continues testing other random changes. If the change does not improve the solution, the program discards it and tries again.

It is particularly easy to generate random changes for the knapsack problem. Given a test solution, the program simply picks one or more items in the solution at random and removes them. It then randomly adds items back into the solution until no more fit. If the removed items have a large cost, the program may be able to add several new items to the solution.

Like a random search, this heuristic is easy to understand and implement. It may be hard to design hill climbing, least-cost, and balanced profit heuristics for a difficult problem, but it is usually easy to write an incremental improvement heuristic.

When to Stop

There are several good ways to decide when to stop making random changes. First, you can perform a fixed number of changes. For an N-item problem, you might make N or N^2 random changes before stopping.

In program Heur, the MakeChangesFixed procedure uses this approach. It makes a certain number of random changes to a number of different trial solutions.

```
// Switch k items at a time to improve the test solution.
// Run num_trials trials making num_changes changes
// during each.
procedure THeurForm.MakeChangesFixed(k, num_trials, num_changes :
Integer);
var
    trial, change, i, removal : Integer;
begin
    for trial := 1 to num_trials do
    begin
        // Find a random test solution to start from.
        while (AddtoSolution) do ;
```

```
// Start with this as the trial solution.
TrialProfit := TestProfit;
TrialCost := TestCost;
for i := 1 to NumItems do
    TrialSolution[i] := TestSolution[i];

for change := 1 to num_changes do
begin
        // Remove k random items.
    for removal := 1 to k do
        RemoveFromSolution;

        // Add back as many random items as will fit.
    while (AddtoSolution) do ;

        // If this improves the trial, save it.
        // Otherwise reset the trial to its
        // previous value.
    if (TestProfit > TrialProfit) then
    begin
            // Save the improvement.
        TrialProfit := TestProfit;
        TrialCost := TestCost;
        for i := 1 to NumItems do
            TrialSolution[i] := TestSolution[i];
    end else begin
            // Reset the trial.
        TestProfit := TrialProfit;
        TestCost := TrialCost;
        for i := 1 to NumItems do
            TestSolution[i] := TrialSolution[i];
    end;
end; // End for change := 1 to num_changes do...

    // If this trial is better than the best solution
    // so far, save it.
if (TrialProfit > BestProfit) then
begin
    BestProfit := TrialProfit;
    BestCost := TrialCost;
    for i := 1 to NumItems do
        BestSolution[i] := TrialSolution[i];
end;
```

```
        // Reset the test solution for the next trial.
        TestProfit := 0;
        TestCost  := 0;
        for i := 1 to NumItems do
            TestSolution[i] := False;
    end; // End for trial := 1 to num_trials do...
end;


// Remove a random item from the test solution.
procedure THeurForm.RemoveFromSolution;
var
    num, j, selection : Integer;
begin
    // See how many items are in the solution.
    num := 0;
    for j := 1 to NumItems do
        if (TestSolution[j]) then
            num := num + 1;
    if (num < 1) then exit;


    // Pick one at random.
    selection := Random(num) + 1;


    // Find the randomly chosen item.
    for j := 1 to NumItems do
        if (TestSolution[j]) then
        begin
            selection := selection - 1;
            if (selection < 1) then break;
        end;


    // Remove the item from the solution.
    TestProfit := TestProfit - Items[j].Profit;
    TestCost := TestCost - Items[j].Cost;
    TestSolution[j] := False;
end;
```

Program Heur uses procedure MakeChangesFixed in two ways. The Fixed 1 heuristic uses MakeChangesFixed to perform N trials. During each trial, it tries to improve the test solution by replacing a single item in the test solution. It repeats this replacement 2 * N times.

The Fixed 2 heuristic uses MakeChangesFixed to perform a single trial. During the trial, it tries to improve the test solution by replacing two items in the test solution. It repeats this replacement 10 * N times looking for a good solution.

```
// Search the tree using an incremental improvement
// heuristic that makes N trials of 2 * N one item changes.
procedure THeurform.Fixed1(node : Integer);
begin
    MakeChangesFixed(1, NumItems, 2 * NumItems);
end;
```

```
// Search the tree using an incremental improvement
// heuristic that makes 1 trial of 10 * N two item changes.
procedure THeurform.Fixed2(node : Integer);
begin
    MakeChangesFixed(2, 1, 10 * NumItems);
end;
```

Another strategy is to make changes until there is no improvement for several consecutive changes. For an N-item problem, the program could make changes until it saw no improvement for N changes in a row.

In program Heur, the MakeChangesNoChange procedure follows this strategy. It runs trials until a certain number of consecutive trials generate no improvement. For each trial, it makes random changes to the trial solution until it finds no improvement in a certain number of random changes in a row.

```
// Switch k items at a time to improve the test solution.
// Repeat trials until we have max_bad_trials runs in a
// row with no improvement.
//
// During each trial, try random changes until we try
// max_non_changes in a row with no improvement.
procedure THeurform.MakeChangesNoChange(k, max_bad_trials,
    max_non_changes : Integer);
var
    i, removal   : Integer;
    bad_trials   : Integer; // # consecutive ineffective trials.
    non_changes  : Integer; // # consecutive ineffective-changes.
begin
    // Repeat trials until we have max_bad_trials
    // runs in a row without an improvement.
    bad_trials := 0;
    repeat
        // Find a random test solution to start from.
        while (AddtoSolution) do ;

        // Start with this as the trial solution.
        TrialProfit := TestProfit;
        TrialCost := TestCost;
```

```
for i := 1 to NumItems do
    TrialSolution[i] := TestSolution[i];

// Repeat until we try max_non_changes in a row
// with no improvement.
non_changes := 0;
while (non_changes < max_non_changes) do
begin
    // Remove k random items.
    for removal := 1 to k do
        RemoveFromSolution;

    // Add back as many random items as will fit.
    while (AddtoSolution) do ;

    // If this improves the trial, save it.
    // Otherwise reset the trial to its
    // previous value.
    if (TestProfit > TrialProfit) then
    begin
        // Save the improvement.
        TrialProfit := TestProfit;
        TrialCost := TestCost;
        for i := 1 to NumItems do
            TrialSolution[i] := TestSolution[i];
        non_changes := 0; // This was a good change.
    end else begin
        // Reset the trial.
        TestProfit := TrialProfit;
        TestCost := TrialCost;
        for i := 1 to NumItems do
            TestSolution[i] := TrialSolution[i];
        non_changes := non_changes + 1; // Bad change.
    end;
end; // End while trying changes.

// If this trial is better than the best solution
// so far, save it.
if (TrialProfit > BestProfit) then
begin
    BestProfit := TrialProfit;
    BestCost := TrialCost;
    for i := 1 to NumItems do
        BestSolution[i] := TrialSolution[i];
```

```
            bad_trials := 0; // This was a good trial.
        end else
            bad_trials := bad_trials + 1; // Bad trial.

        // Reset the test solution for the next trial.
        TestProfit := 0;
        TestCost := 0;
        for i := 1 to NumItems do
            TestSolution[i] := False;
    until (bad_trials >= max_bad_trials);
end;
```

Program Heur uses procedure MakeChangeNoChange in two ways. The No Changes 1 heuristic makes trials until N in a row show no improvement. During each trial, it randomly replaces one item until it finds no improvement in N consecutive replacements.

The No Changes 2 heuristic makes a single trial. During the trial, it randomly replaces two items until it finds no improvement in N consecutive replacements.

```
procedure THeurform.NoChange1(node : Integer);
begin
    MakeChangesNoChange(1, NumItems, NumItems);
end;


procedure THeurform.NoChange2(node : Integer);
begin
    MakeChangesNoChange(2, 0, NumItems);
end;
```

Local Optima

If a program randomly replaces a single item in a test solution, it may find a solution that it cannot improve, but that is also not the best possible solution. For example, consider the investments shown in Table 8.5.

Suppose the algorithm randomly selects items A and B for its initial solution. This solution has a cost of $90 million and a profit of $17 million.

If the program removes either A or B, the solution will still have a cost large enough that the program can add only one new item to the solution. Because items A and B have the largest profits, replacing them with one of the other items will decrease the total profit. Randomly removing one item from this solution will never result in an improvement.

The best solution contains items C, D, and E. It has a total cost of $98 million and a total profit of $18 million. To find this solution, the algorithm would need to remove both items A and B from the solution at the same time and then add new items.

Table 8.5 Possible Investments

Investment	Cost	Return	Profit
A	47	56	9
B	43	51	8
C	35	40	5
D	32	39	7
E	31	37	6

This kind of solution where small changes cannot improve the solution is called a *local optimum*. There are two ways to stop a program from becoming stuck in a local optimum so it can search for the *global optimum*.

First, you can modify the program so that it removes more than one item when it makes its random changes. If the program removes two random items, it can find the correct solution to this example. For larger problems, however, removing two items may not be enough. The program may need to remove three, four, or even more items at a time.

An easier alternative is to run more trials starting with different initial solutions. Some of the starting solutions may lead to local optima, but one should allow the program to reach a global optimum.

Example program Heur demonstrates four incremental improvement strategies. Method Fixed 1 makes N trials. During each trial, it selects a random solution and tries to improve the solution 2 * N times by randomly replacing a single item.

Method Fixed 2 makes only one trial. It selects a random solution and tries to improve the solution 10 * N times by randomly replacing two items.

Heuristic No Changes 1 runs trials until it finds no improvements in N successive trials. During each, the program selects a random solution and then tries to improve it by randomly replacing one item until it finds no improvement during N consecutive changes.

Heuristic No Changes 2 runs a single trial. It selects a random solution and tries to improve it by randomly replacing two items until it finds no improvement during N successive changes.

The names and descriptions of the heuristics are summarized in Table 8.6.

Simulated Annealing

The method of *simulated annealing* was inspired by thermodynamics. When a metal is annealed, it is heated to a high temperature. While the metal is hot, the molecules in the metal move rapidly in relation to each other. If the metal cools slowly, the molecules start to line up to form crystals. These crystals are the minimum energy arrangements of the molecules they contain.

Table 8.6 Incremental Improvement Strategies

Name	# Trials	# Changes	Items Removed per Change
Fixed 1	N	2 * N	1
Fixed 2	1	10 * N	2
No Changes 1	No improvement in N trials	No improvement in N changes	1
No Changes 2	1	No improvement in N changes	2

As the metal slowly cools, different crystals that are adjacent to each other merge. The molecules in one crystal temporarily leave their minimum energy arrangement to line up with the molecules in the other crystal. The new, larger crystal will have lower energy than the sum of the energies of the two smaller crystals. If the metal cools slowly enough, the crystals become huge. The final arrangement of molecules represents a very low energy state, and the metal is quite hard.

Starting from a high energy state, the molecules eventually reach a very low energy state. On the way to the final solution, they pass through many local minimums in energy. Every combination of crystals represents a local minimum. Only by temporarily raising the energy of the system can the crystals combine so the molecules fall into an even lower energy state.

Simulated annealing uses an analogous method to find the best solution to a problem. As the program works its way toward a solution, it may become stuck in a local optimum. To prevent this, the program occasionally makes a random change to the solution even though the change does not immediately improve the result. This may allow the program to break free of a local optimum and find a better solution later. If the change does not lead to a better solution, the program will probably undo the change in a short time anyway.

To prevent the program from making these modifications forever, the algorithm changes the probability of making random changes over time. The probability of making one of these changes is given by $P = 1 / Exp(E / (k * T))$. Here, E is the amount of energy being added to the system, k is a constant chosen to fit the problem, and T is a temperature variable.

Initially, T should be fairly large so $P = 1 / Exp(E / (k * T))$ is reasonably large. Otherwise, random changes will never occur. Over time, the value of T should slowly shrink so the probability of random changes grows smaller. Once the simulation has reached the point where it cannot find any more changes that give an improvement, and T is small enough that random changes are rare, the algorithm can stop.

For a knapsack problem, the energy E is the amount by which the profit of the solution is decreased by the change. For instance, if you remove an item that has profit $10 million and replace it with an item having profit $7 million, the energy added to the system is 3.

Notice that if E is large, the probability $P = 1 / Exp(E / (k * T))$ is small. This makes the chances of a large change occurring smaller than the chances of a small change occurring.

The simulated annealing algorithm in program Heur sets the constant k to 1. It initially sets T to 0.75 times the difference between the largest and smallest profits of the possible investment choices. Each time the program introduces a certain number of random changes, it multiplies T by 0.8 to make it smaller.

```
// Switch k items at a time to improve the test solution.
// When this gives an improvement, save the change.
// Otherwise save the change anyway with some probability.
// After max_slips saves anyway, decrease t.
// After max_unchanged unsaved changes, stop.
procedure THeurform.AnnealTrial(k, max_unchanged, max_slips : Integer);
const
    TFACTOR = 0.8;
var
    i, removal, num_unchanged, num_slips : Integer;
    max_profit, min_profit              : Integer;
    save_changes, slipped               : Boolean;
    t                                   : Single;
begin
    // Find the largest and smallest profits.
    max_profit := Items[1].Profit;
    min_profit := max_profit;
    for i := 2 to NumItems do
    begin
        if (max_profit <  Items[i].Profit) then
            max_profit := Items[i].Profit;
        if (min_profit >  Items[i].Profit) then
            min_profit := Items[i].Profit;
    end;

    // Initialize t.
    t := 0.75 * (max_profit - min_profit);

    // Find a random test solution to start from.
    while (AddtoSolution) do ;

    // Start with this as the best solution.
    BestProfit := TestProfit;
```

```
BestCost := TestCost;
for i := 1 to NumItems do
    BestSolution[i] := TestSolution[i];


// Repeat until we try max_unchanged in a row
// with no improvement.
num_slips := 0;
num_unchanged := 0;
while (num_unchanged < max_unchanged) do
begin
    // Remove k random items.
    for removal := 1 to k do
        RemoveFromSolution;


    // Add back as many random items as will fit.
    while (AddtoSolution) do ;


    // See if this is an improvement.
    if (TestProfit > BestProfit) then
    begin
        save_changes := True;
        slipped := False;
    end else if (TestProfit = BestProfit) then
    begin
        // The probability equation would give 1.
        save_changes := False;
        slipped := False;
    end else begin
        // See if we should save the change anyway.
        save_changes := (Random <
            Exp((TestProfit - BestProfit) / t));
        slipped := save_changes;
    end;


    // See if we should save the solution.
    if (save_changes) then
    begin
        // Save the new solution.
        BestProfit := TestProfit;
        BestCost := TestCost;
        for i := 1 to NumItems do
            BestSolution[i] := TestSolution[i];
        num_unchanged := 0; // We saved a change.
    end else begin
```

```
        // Restore the previous solution.
        TestProfit := BestProfit;
        TestCost := BestCost;
        for i := 1 to NumItems do
            TestSolution[i] := BestSolution[i];
        num_unchanged := num_unchanged + 1;
    end;


    // See if we slipped (made an unimproving save).
    if (slipped) then
    begin
        num_slips := num_slips + 1;
        if (num_slips > max_slips) then
        begin
            num_slips := 0;
            t := t * TFACTOR;
            num_unchanged := 0;
        end;
    end;
    end; // Try again.
end;
```

Comparing Heuristics

Different heuristics behave differently for different problems. For the knapsack problem, the balanced profit heuristic does quite well considering how simple it is. Incremental improvement strategies usually do comparably, but they take much longer for large problems. For problems other than the knapsack problem, the best heuristic may be one of the others or it may be a heuristic not discussed here.

Heuristics are much faster than exhaustive or branch and bound searching. Some heuristics, like hill climbing, least-cost, and balanced profit, are extremely fast because they consider only one possible solution. These algorithms are so fast that it makes sense to run them all and take the best solution found by any of them. This still does not guarantee you will find the best solution possible, but it gives you some confidence that the solution is fairly good.

Other Hard Problems

Many problems other than the knapsack problem are extremely difficult to solve. Some have no known polynomial time solutions. In other words, there are no algorithms for solving these problems that run in $O(N^C)$ time for any constant C, not even $O(N^{1000})$.

The following sections briefly describe a few of these problems. They also explain in general terms why each problem is difficult and how large the most straightforward decision tree for the problem might be. You may want to test the branch and bound and heuristic techniques on a few of them.

Satisfiability (SAT)

Given a logical statement like (A And Not B) Or C, is there an assignment of True and False values to the variables A, B, and C that makes the statement true? In this example, it is easy to see that the statement is true if A = True, B = False, and C = False. For more complicated statements involving hundreds of variables, it can be hard to tell whether there is a way to make the statement true.

Using a method similar to the one used to solve the knapsack problem, you can build a satisfiability decision tree. Each branch in the tree represents a decision to set a variable to either True or False. For example, the left branch leaving the root corresponds to setting the first variable's value to True.

If there are N variables in the logical statement, the decision tree is a binary tree of height N + 1. This tree has 2^N leaf nodes, each representing a different assignment of the values True and False to the variables.

In the knapsack problem you can use branch and bound to avoid searching much of the tree. An assignment of values for the satisfiability problem, however, either makes the statement true or false. It does not give you a partial solution you can use to trim paths out of the tree.

You also cannot use heuristics to find approximate solutions for the satisfiability problem. Any assignment of values produced by a heuristic will make the statement either true or false. There is no such thing as an approximate solution in logic.

With weakened branch and bound techniques and no useful heuristics, the satisfiability problem is generally quite difficult to solve. You can solve only extremely small satisfiability problems.

The Partition Problem

Given a collection of items with values $X_1, X_2, ..., X_N$, is there a way to divide the items into two groups so the total value of the items in each group is the same? For example, if the items have values 3, 4, 5, and 6, you can divide them into the groups {3, 6} and {4, 5}, both having total value 9.

To model this problem as a tree, let the branches correspond to placing an item in one of the two groups. The left branch out of the root node corresponds to placing the first item in the first group. The right branch corresponds to placing the first item in the second group.

If there are N items, the decision tree is a binary tree of height N + 1. It contains 2^N leaf nodes and 2^{N+1} nodes altogether. Each leaf node corresponds to a complete assignment of the items into the two groups.

Branch and bound techniques do work with this problem. As you examine partial solutions in the tree, keep track of the amount by which the two groups of items differ. If you ever reach a branch where placing all of the remaining items in the smaller group cannot make that group at least as big as the larger, you do not need to continue down that branch of the tree.

As is the case for the satisfiability problem, you cannot generate approximate solutions for the partition problem. An assignment of items will create two groups that either do or do not have the same total values. This means that heuristics like the ones used for the knapsack problem will not help you find an even partition.

The partition problem can be generalized to: Given a collection of items with values X_1, X_2,..., X_N, in what way should they be divided into two groups so the total values of the groups are as close as possible?

This problem is more difficult than the partition problem to solve exactly. After all, if there were an easy way to solve this problem, you could use that method to solve the partition problem. You would simply find the groups that are closest in total value and see if their values are equal.

You can use a branch and bound technique similar to the one used in the partition problem to avoid searching the entire tree. You can also use heuristics to provide approximate solutions. One method would be to examine the items in decreasing order of value, placing the next item in the smaller of the two groups. It would also be easy to use random search, incremental improvement, or simulated annealing to find approximate solutions to this version of the problem.

The Hamiltonian Path Problem (HAM)

Given a network, a *Hamiltonian path* is a path that visits every node in the network exactly once and then returns to its starting point. Figure 8.7 shows a small network with a Hamiltonian path drawn in bold.

The Hamiltonian path problem is this: Given a network, does the network contain a Hamiltonian path?

Because a Hamiltonian path visits every node in the network, you do not need to decide which nodes to visit. You only need to determine the order in which they should be visited to produce a Hamiltonian path.

To model this problem as a tree, let branches correspond to selecting the node to visit next. The root node has N branches corresponding to starting the path at

Figure 8.7 A Hamiltonian path.

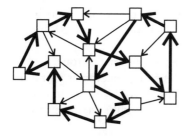

each of the N nodes. The nodes beneath the root each have N – 1 branches, one for each of the remaining N – 1 nodes that you could visit next. Nodes in the next level of the tree have N – 2 branches, and so forth. The bottom of the tree contains N! leaf nodes corresponding to the N! possible orderings of the nodes. The tree holds a total of O(N!) nodes.

Every leaf corresponds to a Hamiltonian path, but some of the leaves may not be reachable for every network. If two nodes in the network are not connected, the branches in the tree that correspond to moving from one node to the other will be missing. That reduces the number of paths through the tree and thus the number of leaf nodes.

As is the case for the satisfiability and partition problems, you cannot generate partial or approximate solutions for Hamiltonian paths. Either a path is Hamiltonian or it is not. This means branch and bound techniques and heuristics will not help you locate a Hamiltonian path. To make matters worse, the Hamiltonian path decision tree contains O(N!) nodes. This is far more than the $O(2^N)$ nodes contained in the satisfiability and partition decision trees. For example, 2^{20} is roughly $1 * 10^6$, while 20! is about $2.4 * 10^{18}$—more than a million million times as large. Because this tree is so large, you will be able to search it for only the smallest Hamiltonian path problems.

The Traveling Salesman Problem (TSP)

The traveling salesman problem is closely related to the Hamiltonian path problem. The traveling salesman problem asks: What is the shortest Hamiltonian path through a network?

This problem has a similar relationship to the Hamiltonian path problem as the generalized partition problem has to the partition problem. The first problem asks if a solution exists. The second asks what the best approximate solution is. If there were an easy solution to the second problem, you could use it to find a solution to the first problem.

Typically, the traveling salesman problem arises only for networks that contain many Hamiltonian paths. In a common example, a salesman must visit several customer locations using the shortest possible route. In a normal street network, there are paths between any two points in the network, so any ordering of the customer locations gives a Hamiltonian path. The problem is to find the shortest.

Like the Hamiltonian path problem, the decision tree for this problem contains O(N!) nodes. Like the generalized partition problem, you can use branch and bound techniques to trim the tree and make finding a solution possible for problems of modest size.

There are also several good incremental improvement heuristics for the traveling salesman problem. The *2-opt* improvement strategy examines pairs of links within the path. The program checks whether there would be an improvement if the links were removed and replaced with two new links that keep the path connected. Figure 8.8 shows how the path would change if links X_1 and X_2 were replaced with links Y_1 and Y_2. Similar improvement strategies consider replacing three or even more links at one time.

Typically, you would repeat this sort of improvement many times or until you had tried swapping all of the possible pairs of links in the path. Once you had improved the path as much as you could, you would save the results and start over again with a different randomly chosen initial path. By trying many different initial paths, you would have a good chance of finding a reasonably short path.

The Firehouse Problem

Given a network, a number F, and a distance D, is there a way to place F firehouses on nodes in the network in such a way that no node in the network is more than distance D away from the nearest firehouse?

You can model this problem with a decision tree in which each branch determines where in the network a particular firehouse will be located. The root node will have N branches corresponding to placing the first firehouse at one of the network's N nodes. Nodes at the next level of the tree will have N – 1 branches corresponding to placing the second firehouse at each of the remaining N – 1 nodes. If there are F firehouses, this tree will have height F and will contain $O(N^F)$ nodes. It will have N * (N – 1) *...* (N – F) leaf nodes corresponding to the possible locations where you could place the firehouses.

Like the satisfiability, partitioning, and Hamiltonian path problems, this problem asks a yes or no question. That means you cannot use partial or approximate solutions while examining the decision tree.

You may be able to use some sort of branch and bound technique if you can decide early on that certain firehouse placements will not lead to good solutions. For example, you gain nothing by placing a new firehouse between two other closely spaced firehouses. If all of the nodes within distance D of the new firehouse are already within distance D of another firehouse, you should place the new firehouse somewhere else. Making this sort of calculation is quite time consuming, however, so the firehouse problem is still very difficult to solve.

Figure 8.8 Improving a Hamiltonian path using 2-opt.

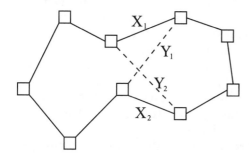

Just as the partitioning and Hamiltonian path problems have generalizations, so does the firehouse problem. The generalized question is: Given a network and a number F, at what nodes should you place F firehouses so the greatest distance between any node and a firehouse is minimized?

As is the case in the other generalized problems, you can use branch and bound techniques and heuristics to find partial and approximate solutions to this problem. That makes examining the decision tree a bit easier. While the decision tree is still enormous, you can at least find approximate solutions, even if they may not be the best solutions possible.

Summary of Hard Problems

While reading the previous sections, you may have noticed that many of these problems come in pairs. The first version of a problem asks, "Is there a solution of a certain quality to this problem?" The second, more general question asks, "What is the best solution to this problem?"

Both of the related problems use the same decision trees. In the first problem, you examine the decision tree until you find any solution. Because these problems do not have partial or approximate solutions, you generally cannot use branch and bound or heuristics to greatly reduce your work. Usually only a few paths through the decision tree lead to a solution, so these problems are very hard to solve.

While solving the more generalized version of the problem, you can often use partial solutions to apply branch and bound techniques. This does not make it easier to find a solution to the problem, so it will not help in solving the more specialized problem. For example, it is harder to find the shortest Hamiltonian path through a network than it is to find any Hamiltonian path through the same network.

On the other hand, these questions usually apply to different data. You generally ask if a network has a Hamiltonian path when the network is very sparse and it is hard to tell if there is such a path. You ask for the shortest Hamiltonian path when the network is dense and there are many such paths. In that case, it is easy to find partial solutions, and branch and bound techniques may simplify the problem greatly.

Summary

You can use decision trees to model many difficult problems. Finding the best solution to the problem corresponds to finding the best path through the tree. Unfortunately, for many interesting problems the decision trees are huge, so you can search them exhaustively for only the smallest problems.

Branch and bound techniques allow you to prune many of the branches from some decision trees. This lets you solve much larger problems exactly.

For the largest problems, however, even branch and bound cannot help. In those cases, you must use heuristics to generate approximate solutions. Using techniques such as random search and incremental improvement, you may be able to find a good solution, though you may never know if it is the best solution possible.

SORTING

Sorting is one of the most heavily studied topics in computer algorithms for several reasons. First, sorting is a common task in many computer applications. Almost any list of data is more meaningful when it is sorted in some way. Frequently, data must be sorted in several different ways.

Second, many sorting algorithms make interesting programming examples. They demonstrate important techniques such as partial ordering, recursion, merging of lists, and storing binary trees in an array.

Each sorting algorithm has different advantages and disadvantages. The performance of different algorithms depends on the data's type, number, initial arrangement, size, and values. It is important to understand several algorithms so you can pick the one that best fits a particular situation.

Finally, sorting is one of the few problems with exact theoretical performance bounds. It can be shown that any sorting algorithm that uses comparisons must take at least $O(N * \log(N))$ time. Several algorithms actually achieve this time, so you know they are optimal in the sense of Big O notation. There are even a few algorithms that use methods other than comparisons to achieve times faster than $O(N * \log(N))$.

General Considerations

This chapter describes several sorting algorithms that behave differently under different circumstances. For example, bubblesort is faster than quicksort when the items being sorted are already mostly in sorted order, but it is slower if the items are arranged randomly.

The peculiarities of each algorithm are described in the section that discusses the algorithm. Before discussing the specific algorithms, this chapter begins by discussing some issues that affect all sorting algorithms.

Sorting Pointers

As a program sorts data items, it rearranges them in some kind of data structure. Depending on what the items are, this may be fast or slow. Moving an integer to a new position in an array is fast. Moving a user-defined data structure to a new position might be much slower. If the data structure is an employee record containing thousands of bytes of data, copying one data item to another may take quite some time.

It is much easier to sort pointers to the actual data. Copying a pointer from one part of an array to another is quick and easy.

To sort an array of objects in a particular order, create an array of pointers to the objects. Then sort the pointers using the values in the corresponding data records. For example, suppose you want to sort employee records defined by the following structure:

```
type
    TEmployee = record
        ID         : Integer;
        LastName   : String[40];
        FirstName  : String[40];
        // Lots more stuff.
            :
    end;
    PEmployee = ^TEmployee;


// Allocate the records.
var
    EmployeeData : array [1..10000] of TEmployee;
```

To sort the employees by ID number, create an array of pointers to the employee data.

```
var
    IdIndex : array [1..10000] of PEmployee;
```

Initialize the array so the first entry points to the first data record, the second points to the second data record, and so forth.

```
for i := 1 to 10000 do IdIndex[i] := @EmployeeData[i];
```

Next, sort the index array by ID. When you finish, the index entries point to the employee data records in sorted order. For example, the first data record in the sorted list is ^IdIndex[1].

To sort the data in more than one order, create multiple index arrays and manage them separately. In this example, you might keep a separate index array ordering employees by last name. This is similar to the way threads can order lists in multiple ways, as described in Chapter 2, "Lists." When you add or remove a record, you must update each of the index arrays separately.

Keep in mind that index arrays take up extra memory. If you create an array for every field in the data records, you will use a lot of memory.

Key Combination and Compression

Sometimes a program can store and operate on a list's keys in a combined or compressed form. To sort a list of employees by their first and last names, a program could *combine* the two name fields by concatenating them into one key. This would make comparisons simpler and faster. Notice the differences between the following two code fragments that compare two employee records.

```
// Using separate keys:
if ((emp1^.LastName > emp2^.LastName) or
    ((emp1^.LastName = emp2^.LastName) and
        (emp1^.FirstName > emp2^.FirstName))) then
    DoSomething;
```

```
// Using a combined key:
if (emp1^.CombinedName > emp2^.CombinedName) then
    DoSomething;
```

You can also sometimes *compress* keys. Compressed keys take up less space, making data arrays smaller. This allows you to sort larger lists without running out of memory, makes moving items within the list faster, and often makes comparing the items faster as well.

One method for compressing strings is to encode them as integers or some other numeric data type. Numeric data types take up less space than strings, and the computer can compare two numeric values much more quickly than it can compare two strings. Of course, normal string operations do not work on numeric encodings, so you will need to translate to and from the encoding whenever you modify a value.

For example, suppose you want to encode strings consisting of uppercase letters. You can think of each character in the string as a base 27 digit. You need to use base 27 because you need to represent 26 letters plus one extra digit that represents the end of a word. Without an end-of-word marker, the encoding of AA would come after the encoding of B because AA has two digits but B has only one.

The base 27 encoding of a three-character string is 27^2 * (first letter $-$ A + 1) + 27 * (second letter $-$ A + 1) + (third letter $-$ A + 1). If the string has fewer than three characters, use 0 instead of (the letter $-$ A + 1). For example, the encoding of FOX is:

27^2 * (F $-$ A + 1) + 27 * (O $-$ A + 1) + (X $-$ A + 1) = 4803

The encoding of NO is:

27^2 * (N $-$ A + 1) + 27 * (O $-$ A + 1) + (0) = 10,611

Notice that 10,611 is greater than 4803. This makes sense because NO > FOX.

Using similar techniques, you can encode strings of 6 uppercase letters in a long integer and strings with 10 letters in a double. The following two procedures convert strings into doubles and back.

```
const
    STRING_BASE = 27;
    ASC_A = 65; // ASCII code for "A."


// Convert a string into a double encoding.
//
// full_len gives the full length of the string. For
// example, "AX" as a three character string would have
// full_len = 3.
function TEncodeForm.StringToDbl(txt : String; full_len : Integer)
    : Double;
var
    len, i : Integer;
    ch     : Char;
begin
    len := Length(txt);
    if (len > full_len) then len := full_len;

    Result := 0.0;
    for i := 1 to len do
    begin
        ch := txt[i];
        Result := Result * STRING_BASE +
            Ord(ch) - ASC_A + 1;
    end;

    for i := len + 1 to full_len do
        Result := Result * STRING_BASE;
end;


// Turn a double string encoding back into a string.
function TEncodeForm.DblToString(value : Double) : String;
var
    ch        : Integer;
    new_value : Double;
begin
    Result := '';
    while (value > 0) do
    begin
        new_value := Round(value / STRING_BASE);
```

```
        ch := Round(value - new_value * STRING_BASE);
        if (ch <> 0) then
            Result := Chr(ch + ASC_A - 1) + Result;
        value := new_value;
    end;
end;
```

Example program Encode allows you to create a list of random strings and sort them using numeric encodings. The program uses all the encodings possible so you can compare the results. For example, if you tell the program to create strings of length 10, the program sorts the list using string and double encodings.

Table 9.1 shows the times required by program Encode to sort 2000 strings of different lengths on a 133-megahertz Pentium. Notice that the results are similar for each type of encoding. It takes about the same amount of time to sort 2000 doubles, whether they represent 3-letter strings or 10-letter strings.

You can also encode strings containing characters other than capital letters. You could encode a string allowing uppercase letters and digits using a string base of 37 instead of 27. A maps to 1, B to 2, ... , Z to 26, 0 to 27, ... , and 9 to 36. The string AH7 would be encoded as $37^2 * 1 + 37 * 8 + 35 = 1700$.

With a larger string base, the longest string you could encode in an integer, long, or double data type is shorter. With a base of 37, you can encode 2 characters in an integer, 5 characters in a long, and you can still encode 10 characters in a double.

Example Programs

To make comparing different sorting algorithms easy, example program Sort demonstrates most of the algorithms described in this chapter. Sort allows you to specify the number of items to sort, the maximum value of the items, and whether the list should begin sorted, sorted backwards, or randomly arranged. The program creates a list of random long integers and sorts it using the algorithm you select. Be sure to start with small lists until you know how long your computer will take. This is particularly important for the slower algorithms insertionsort, linked list insertionsort, selectionsort, and bubblesort.

Table 9.1 Times to Sort 2000 Strings Using Different Encodings

String Length	3	6	10	20
String	4.81	4.92	5.08	5.24
Double	0.23	0.26	0.26	
Longint	0.05	0.05		
Integer	0.05			

Selectionsort

Selectionsort is a simple O(N²) algorithm. The idea is to search the list for the smallest item and then swap that item with the one at the top of the list. Next find the smallest remaining item, and swap it with the second item. Continue swapping items until every item has been swapped to its final sorted position.

```
procedure TSortForm.Selectionsort(list : PLongintArray;
    min, max : Longint);
var
    i, j, best_value, best_j : Longint;
begin
    for i := min to max - 1 do
    begin
        // Find the smallest remaining item.
        best_value := list^[i];
        best_j := i;
        for j := i + 1 to max do
            if (list^[j] < best_value) then
            begin
                best_value := list^[j];
                best_j := j;
            end;

        // Swap it into position.
        list^[best_j] := list^[i];
        list^[i] := best_value;
    end;
end;
```

While looking for the ith smallest item, the algorithm must examine each of the N – i items that have not yet been swapped to their final positions. The algorithm takes time N + (N – 1) + (N – 2) +...+ 1, or O(N²) time.

Selectionsort performs quite well on random and sorted lists, but it does slightly worse when the list starts sorted backwards. While it is looking for the smallest item in the list, selectionsort executes these lines of code:

```
if (list^[j] < best_value) then
begin
    best_value := list^[j];
    best_j := j;
end;
```

If the list begins in reverse sorted order, the condition list^[j] < best_value is true much of the time. During the first pass through the list, for example, it will be true for every item because each item is smaller than the one before. The algorithm must execute the lines of code within the if statement many times, and that slows the algorithm down slightly.

This is not the fastest algorithm described in this chapter, but it is extremely simple. Not only does that make it easy to implement and debug, it also makes selectionsort fast for small problems. Many of the other algorithms are so complicated they are slower at sorting very small lists.

Unsorting

Some programs need to perform the opposite of sorting. Given a list of items, the program needs to arrange them randomly. Randomizing a list is simple using an algorithm somewhat similar to selectionsort.

For each position in the list, the algorithm randomly selects an item to go in that position. It considers only the items that have not yet been placed in a previously considered position. It then swaps the selected item with the item that is currently in the position.

```
// Randomize an array.
procedure RandomizeList(list : PIntArray; min, max : Integer);
var
    i, range, pos, tmp : Integer;
begin
    range := max - min + 1;
    for i := min to max - 1 do
    begin
        pos := min + Trunc(Random(range));
        tmp := list^[pos];
        list^[pos] := list^[i];
        list^[i] := tmp;
    end;
end;
```

Because this algorithm fills each position in the array once, it is an O(N) algorithm.

It is not too hard to show that the probability of any given item ending up in any position is 1 / N. Because any item could end up in any position with equal probability, the algorithm generates a truly random arrangement of the items.

This result depends on the fact that the random number generator is a good source of randomness. Delphi's Random function works reasonably well under most circumstances. You should be certain that your program uses the Randomize statement at some point to initialize Random. Otherwise, Random will produce the same sequence of "random" values every time you run the program.

Note that it does not matter to the algorithm how the items are initially arranged. If you have a program that must repeatedly randomize a list of items, it need not sort the items first.

Example program Unsort uses this algorithm to randomize a sorted list. Enter the number of items you want randomized, and click the Go button. The program displays the original sorted list of numbers and the randomized version.

Insertionsort

Insertionsort is another O(N²) algorithm. The idea is to build a new, sorted list by considering each item in the original list in turn. As the algorithm considers each item, it looks through the growing sorted list to see where the new item belongs. It then inserts the new item into its correct position in the list.

```
procedure TSortForm.Insertionsort(list : PLongintArray;
    min, max : Longint);
var
    i, j, k, max_sorted, next_num : Longint;
begin
    max_sorted := min - 1;
    for i := min to max do
    begin
        // This is the number we are inserting.
        next_num := list^[i];

        // See where it belongs in the list.
        for j := min to max_sorted do
            if (list^[j] >= next_num) then break;

        // Bump the bigger sorted numbers down to make
        // room for the new number.
        for k := max_sorted downto j do
            list^[k + 1] := list^[k];

        // Insert the new number.
        list^[j] := next_num;

        // Increment the count of the sorted items.
        max_sorted := max_sorted + 1;
    end;
end;
```

For each item in the original list, the algorithm might have to examine all the items that have been sorted. This will happen, for example, if the items were in sorted order in the original list. In that case, the algorithm places each new item at the end of the growing sorted list.

The total number of steps executed will be 1 + 2 + 3 +...+ (N − 1), which is O(N²). This is not very efficient compared to the theoretical O(N * log(N)) possible for algorithms that sort by comparisons. In fact, this algorithm is not even as fast as other O(N²) algorithms like selectionsort.

Insertionsort spends a great deal of time searching for the new item's correct position. Chapter 10, "Searching," describes several algorithms for searching sorted lists. Using the interpolation search algorithm described in Chapter 10 to determine where items belong makes insertionsort considerably faster. Chapter 10 describes interpolation search in detail, so it is not explained here.

Insertion with Linked Lists

You can use a variation of insertionsort to sort items stored in a linked list instead of an array. The algorithm searches through the growing linked list for the position where the new item belongs. It then uses linked list operations to insert the new item.

```
procedure TSortForm.LLInsertionsort(var top : PCell);
var
    new_top, cell, after_me, nxt : PCell;
    new_value                    : Longint;
begin
    // Make the new list with a bottom sentinel.
    New(new_top);
    New(new_top^.NextCell);
    new_top^.NextCell^.Value := INFINITY;
    new_top^.NextCell^.NextCell := nil;

    cell := top^.NextCell;
    while (cell <> nil) do
    begin
        top^.NextCell := cell^.NextCell;
        new_value := cell^.Value;

        // See where the new item belongs.
        after_me := new_top;
        nxt := after_me^.NextCell;
        while (nxt^.Value < new_value) do
        begin
            after_me := nxt;
            nxt := after_me^.NextCell;
        end;

        // Insert the cell into the new list.
        after_me^.NextCell := cell;
        cell^.NextCell := nxt;
```

```
        // Examine the next cell in the old list.
        cell := top^.NextCell;
    end;

        // Free the old list top.
        Dispose(top);
        top := new_top;
end;
```

As the algorithm considers each item, it might have to compare the item to every item in the sorted list. This makes the algorithm $O(N^2)$ in this worst case.

The best case for this algorithm occurs when the original list starts sorted in reverse order. Then each new item considered is smaller than the one before, so the algorithm places it at the beginning of the sorted list. The algorithm needs to compare the item to only one other, so in the best case, the algorithm has $O(N)$ time.

In the average case, the algorithm will have to search about half way through the sorted list to find an item's correct location. The algorithm executes roughly $1 + 1 + 2 + 2 +...+ N / 2$, or $O(N^2)$ steps.

The array-based insertionsort is much faster than the linked list version. The linked list version is better only if your program already stores the items in a linked list.

Insertion with linked lists has the advantage of moving only object pointers instead of complete data records. If the items are large data structures, it may be quicker to move pointers rather than to recopy whole records whenever an item must be moved.

Bubblesort

Bubblesort is an algorithm designed to sort lists that are already in mostly sorted order. If the list begins completely sorted, the algorithm runs in $O(N)$ time and is extremely fast. If some of the items are out of order, the algorithm runs more slowly. When the items start in random order, the algorithm runs in $O(N^2)$ time. For that reason, it is extremely important to be certain the items are mostly in sorted order before using bubblesort.

Bubblesort scans through the list until it finds two adjacent items that are out of order. It swaps them and continues. The algorithm repeats this process until no more items are out of order.

In the example shown in Figure 9.1, the algorithm first finds that items 6 and 3 are out of order so it swaps them. During the next pass, the algorithm notices that items 5 and 3 are out of order so it swaps them. In the next pass, it swaps items 4 and 3. After one more pass through the array, the algorithm finds that there are no more items out of order so it stops.

Figure 9.1 Bubbling an item up.

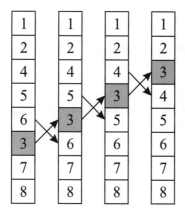

During bubblesort passes, you can follow an item that begins below its final position in the array, like item 3 in Figure 9.1. During each pass, the item moves one position closer to its final correct position. The item moves toward the top of the array like a bubble moving toward the top of a glass of water. This bubbling effect is what gives bubblesort its name.

You can make several refinements to this algorithm. First, if you watch an item that begins above rather than below its correct position, you see a picture very different from Figure 9.1. In Figure 9.2, the algorithm first notices that item 6 and item 3 are out of order so it swaps them. The algorithm then continues its pass through the array and notices that items 6 and 4 are out of order so it swaps

Figure 9.2 Bubbling an item down.

them, too. The algorithm next swaps items 6 and 5, and item 6 is in its final correct position.

During downward passes through the array, items that need to move up move only one position. Items that need to move down, however, move many positions. You can use this fact to make the first refinement to the bubblesort algorithm. If you alternate downward and upward passes through the array, items will be able to move quickly both upward and downward.

During downward passes, the largest item that is out of order will be moved into its final position. During upward passes, the smallest item that is out of order will be moved into its final position. If there are M items out of order in the list, the algorithm will need at most M passes upward and downward through the array to put all the items in order. If there are N items in the list, the algorithm will need N steps per pass through the list. That makes the total runtime for this algorithm $O(M * N)$.

If the list is initially randomly arranged, a large fraction of the items will be out of order. The number M will be on the order of N, so the runtime $O(M * N)$ becomes $O(N^2)$.

The next refinement is to hold items in a temporary variable while they undergo multiple swaps. In the example shown in Figure 9.2, item 6 is swapped three times in a row. Instead of performing three separate swaps, the program can hold the value 6 in a temporary variable until it finds the item's new location. This can save the algorithm many steps when items are being moved long distances through the array.

One last refinement is in bounding the passes through the array. After a pass through the array, the last items swapped mark the last part of the array that could be out of order. In a downward pass, for example, the largest item that was out of order is moved to its final position. Since no larger items will need to be moved later, the algorithm can start its next upward pass at this position. It can also end downward passes here.

Similarly, when the algorithm makes an upward pass through the list, it can adjust the position in the list where it starts the next downward pass and ends future upward passes.

The Delphi implementation of bubblesort uses variables min and max to indicate the first and last items in the list that might be out of order. As the algorithm makes passes through the list, it updates these variables to indicate where the last swaps took place.

```
procedure TSortForm.Bubblesort(list : PLongintArray; min, max :
Longint);
var
    i, j, tmp, last_swap : Longint;
begin
    // Repeat until we are done.
    while (min < max) do
```

```
begin
    // Bubble up.
    last_swap := min - 1;
    // For i := min + 1 To max.
    i := min + 1;
    while (i <= max) do
    begin
        // Find a "bubble."
        if (list^[i - 1] > list^[i]) then
        begin
            // See where to drop the bubble.
            tmp := list^[i - 1];
            j := i;
            repeat
                list^[j - 1] := list^[j];
                j := j + 1;
                if (j > max) then break;
            until (list^[j] >= tmp);
            list^[j - 1] := tmp;
            last_swap := j - 1;
            i := j + 1;
        end else
            i := i + 1;
    end; // End bubbling up.
    // Update max.
    max := last_swap - 1;

    // Bubble down.
    last_swap := max + 1;
    // For i := max - 1 To min Step -1.
    i := max - 1;
    while (i >= min) do
    begin
        // Find a "bubble."
        if (list^[i + 1] < list^[i]) then
        begin
            // See where to drop the bubble.
            tmp := list^[i + 1];
            j := i;
            repeat
                list^[j + 1] := list^[j];
                j := j - 1;
                if (j < min) then break;
            until (list^[j] <= tmp);
```

```
                list^[j + 1] := tmp;
                last_swap := j + 1;
                i := j - 1;
            end else
                i := i - 1;
        end; // End bubbling up.
        // Update min.
        min := last_swap + 1;
    end; // End downward and upward passes.
end;
```

To properly test bubblesort using program Sort, check the Sorted box in the Initial Ordering area. Enter a number of items in the # Unsorted field. When you click the Make List button, the program creates a list. It sorts the items if you have selected the Sorted option, and sorts the list in reverse order if you selected the Reversed option. It then randomly changes some values to give the list some unsorted items. For example, if you enter 10 in the # Unsorted field, the program randomly regenerates 10 items so they will probably be out of order.

Table 9.2 shows the times required by a 133-megahertz Pentium to bubble-sort 20,000 items where the original list was sorted in varying degrees. The table shows that bubblesort performs well only when the list begins mostly sorted. The quicksort algorithm described later in this chapter can sort the same list of 20,000 items in about 0.05 seconds when the list is initially randomly arranged. Bubblesort can beat this time only when the list is almost completely sorted.

Despite the fact that bubblesort is slower than many other algorithms, it still has uses. Bubblesort is often fastest if the list begins in almost sorted order. If a program manages a list that is initially sorted and is modified incrementally, bubblesort may be the best choice.

Quicksort

Quicksort is a recursive algorithm that uses a divide-and-conquer technique. Although the list of items to be sorted is at least a certain minimum size, quicksort divides it into two sublists. It then recursively calls itself to sort the two sublists.

The initial version of quicksort discussed here is quite simple. If the algorithm is called with a sublist containing zero or one item, the sublist is already sorted so the procedure ends. Otherwise, the procedure picks an item in the list to use as a

Table 9.2 Times to Bubblesort 20,000 Items

% Sorted	50	60	70	80	90	95	96	97	98	99	99.5
Time (seconds)	2.78	2.21	1.91	1.18	0.62	0.32	0.26	0.20	0.14	0.07	0.04

dividing point to break the list into two smaller sublists. It moves items that are smaller than the dividing item into the first sublist. It places the other items in the second sublist. It then recursively calls itself to sort the two sublists.

```
procedure TSortForm.Quicksort(list : PLongintArray; min, max :
Longint);
var
    med_value, hi, lo : Longint;
begin
    // If the list has 0 or 1 elements, we're done.
    if (min >= max) then exit;

    // Pick the dividing value.
    med_value := list^[min];
    lo = min
    hi = max

    repeat // Repeat infinitely.
        // Look down from hi for a value < med_value.
        while (list^[hi] >= med_value) do
        begin
            hi := hi - 1;
            if (hi <= lo) then break;
        end;
        if (hi <= lo) then
        begin
            list^[lo] := med_value;
            break;
        end;

        // Swap the lo and hi values.
        list^[lo] := list^[hi];

        // Look up from lo for a value >:= med_value.
        lo := lo + 1;
        while (list^[lo] < med_value) do
        begin
            lo := lo + 1;
            if (lo >= hi) then break;
        end;
        if (lo >= hi) then
        begin
            lo := hi;
            list^[hi] := med_value;
```

```
            break;
        end;

        // Swap the lo and hi values.
        list^[hi] := list^[lo];
    until (False);

    // Sort the two sublists.
    Quicksort(list, min, lo - 1);
    Quicksort(list, lo + 1, max);
end;
```

There are a couple of important points worth mentioning about this version of the algorithm. First, the dividing item med_value is not included in either sublist. That means the two sublists together contain one less item than the original list. Because the total number of items considered grows smaller, the algorithm must eventually finish.

This algorithm uses the first item in its list as the dividing item. Ideally, this value will belong somewhere in the middle of the list, so the two sublists will be of about equal size. If the items are initially in sorted order, however, the first item is the smallest item present. The algorithm will place no items in the first sublist and all of the items in the second sublist. The algorithm would take a path of execution like the one shown in Figure 9.3.

In this case, each call to the procedure requires O(N) steps to move all the items into the second sublist. Because the algorithm must recursively call itself a total of N − 1 times, the runtime is O(N²), which is no improvement on the algorithms already examined. Even worse is the fact that the recursion is N − 1 levels

Figure 9.3 Quicksort on a sorted list.

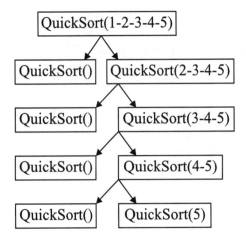

deep. For large lists, the great depth of recursion may exhaust the stack and crash the program.

There are many ways the program might select the dividing item. It could use the item currently in the middle of the list. This item would probably be a good choice, but the program might be unlucky and the item could be one of the largest or smallest. That would make one sublist much larger than the other and, if there were many unlucky choices, would give $O(N^2)$ performance and deep recursion.

Another strategy is to look through the list, compute the median of the values, and use that as the dividing value. This would work well, but it would require a lot of additional effort. An $O(N)$ pass through the list will not change the total theoretical runtime, but it will hurt the overall performance.

A third strategy used by some is to look at the first, last, and middle items and pick whichever value is between the other two. This method has the advantage of being quick because you need to look at only three items. The item selected is guaranteed not to be the absolute largest or smallest item in the list, and it will probably be somewhere near the middle.

A final strategy, and the one used by the Sort program, is to select the dividing item from the list randomly. The item selected will probably be a good choice. Even if it is not, the next time the algorithm divides the list it will probably make a better choice. The chance of the algorithm making a bad choice every time is extremely small.

An interesting fact about this method is that it turns "a small chance of bad runtime always" into "always a small chance of bad runtime." This rather confusing statement is explained in the following paragraphs.

With the earlier methods of selecting a dividing point, there is a small chance that the list will be arranged in a way that will produce $O(N^2)$ runtime. While the odds of the list starting in such a bad arrangement are very small, if you did encounter such an arrangement, you would definitely experience $O(N^2)$ runtime no matter what. That is what "a small chance of bad runtime always" means.

By selecting the dividing point randomly, the initial arrangement of the items makes no difference to the performance of the algorithm. There is a small chance of selecting a bad item, but the odds of selecting a bad item every time are extremely small. That is what "always a small chance of bad runtime" means. No matter how the list is initially arranged, there is a very small chance that the algorithm will give $O(N^2)$ performance.

There is still one situation that gives all of these methods trouble. If there are very few distinct values in the list, the algorithm places many identical values in the same sublist each time it is called. If every item in the list has the value 1, for instance, the algorithm follows the sequence of execution shown in Figure 9.4. This sequence causes $O(N^2)$ performance and deep recursion.

The same sort of behavior occurs if there are many duplicates of more than one value. If a list of 10,000 items contains only values between 1 and 10, the algorithm quickly divides the list into sublists that each contain only one value.

Figure 9.4 Quicksort on a list of 1s.

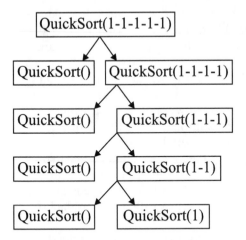

The easiest way to handle this problem is to ignore it. If you know the data values do not have such an unusual distribution, there is no problem. If the data does cover only a small number of values, you should consider a different sorting algorithm. Countingsort and bucketsort, described later in this chapter, are extremely fast at sorting lists where the range of the data values is small.

You can make one final improvement to quicksort. Like many of the other more complicated algorithms described in this chapter, quicksort is not the fastest algorithm for sorting very small lists. Due to its simplicity, selectionsort is faster at sorting a dozen or so items.

You can improve the performance of quicksort by stopping recursion before the sublists are empty and using selectionsort to finish the job. Table 9.3 shows times required by a 133-megahertz Pentium to quicksort 1 million items, stopping the recursion after the sublists reached a certain size. In this test, the best cutoff value was 15 items.

The following code shows the revised quicksort algorithm:

```
procedure TSortForm.Quicksort(list : PLongintArray; min, max :
Longint);
var
    med_value, hi, lo, i : Longint;
```

Table 9.3 Times to Quicksort 1 Million Items

Cutoff	1	5	10	15	20	25	30
Time (seconds)	2.62	2.31	2.17	2.09	2.15	2.17	2.25

```
begin
    // If the list has no more than CutOff elements,
    // finish it off with Selectionsort.
    if (max - min < CutOff) then
    begin
        Selectionsort(list, min, max);
        exit;
    end;

    // Pick the dividing value.
    i := min + Trunc(Random(max - min + 1));
    med_value := list^[i];

    // Swap it to the front.
    list^[i] := list^[min];

    lo := min;
    hi := max;
    repeat // Repeat infinitely.
        // Look down from hi for a value < med_value.
        while (list^[hi] >= med_value) do
        begin
            hi := hi - 1;
            if (hi <= lo) then break;
        end;
        if (hi <= lo) then
        begin
            list^[lo] := med_value;
            break;
        end;

        // Swap the lo and hi values.
        list^[lo] := list^[hi];

        // Look up from lo for a value >:= med_value.
        lo := lo + 1;
        while (list^[lo] < med_value) do
        begin
            lo := lo + 1;
            if (lo >= hi) then break;
        end;
        if (lo >= hi) then
        begin
            lo := hi;
```

```
        list^[hi] := med_value;
        break;
    end;

    // Swap the lo and hi values.
    list^[hi] := list^[lo];
until (False);

// Sort the two sublists.
Quicksort(list, min, lo - 1);
Quicksort(list, lo + 1, max);
end;
```

Because it provides good performance under most circumstances, quicksort is the sorting algorithm of choice for many programmers.

Mergesort

Like quicksort, mergesort is a recursive algorithm. Also like quicksort, it divides the list to be sorted into two sublists and recursively sorts the sublists.

Mergesort divides its list in the middle to form two sublists of equal size. It then recursively sorts the sublists and merges the results to form the completely sorted list.

Although the merging step is easy to understand, it is also the most interesting part of the algorithm. The sublists are merged into a scratch array, and the result is copied back into the original list. Creating a scratch array can be a drawback, particularly if the list of items is large. If the scratch array is too big, it may cause the algorithm to page and may slow performance greatly. The scratch array also forces the algorithm to spend a lot of time copying items back and forth between the arrays.

As is the case with quicksort, you can make mergesort faster by stopping the recursion when sublists reach a certain minimum size. The algorithm can then use selectionsort to finish the job.

```
procedure TSortForm.Mergesort(list, scratch : PLongintArray;
    min, max : Longint);
var
    middle, i1, i2, i3 : Longint;
begin
    // If the list has no more than CutOff elements,
    // finish it off with Selectionsort.
    if (max - min < CutOff) then
    begin
        Selectionsort(list, min, max);
```

```
            exit;
    end;


    // Recursively sort the sublists.
    middle := max div 2 + min div 2;
    Mergesort(list, scratch, min, middle);
    Mergesort(list, scratch, middle + 1, max);


    // Merge the sorted lists.
    i1 := min;          // Index in list 1.
    i2 := middle + 1;   // Index in list 2.
    i3 := min;          // Index in merged list.
    while ((i1 <= middle) and (i2 <= max)) do
    begin
        if (list^[i1] <= list^[i2]) then
        begin
            scratch^[i3] := list^[i1];
            i1 := i1 + 1;
        end else begin
            scratch^[i3] := list^[i2];
            i2 := i2 + 1;
        end;
        i3 := i3 + 1;
    end;


    // Empty out whichever list is not already empty.
    while (i1 <= middle) do
    begin
        scratch^[i3] := list^[i1];
        i1 := i1 + 1;
        i3 := i3 + 1;
    end;
    while (i2 <= max) do
    begin
        scratch^[i3] := list^[i2];
        i2 := i2 + 1;
        i3 := i3 + 1;
    end;


    // Move the merged list back into list.
    for i3 := min to max do
        list^[i3] := scratch^[i3];
end;
```

Mergesort is generally slightly slower than quicksort. In one test on a 133-megahertz Pentium, mergesort required 4.72 seconds to sort 1 million items with values between 1 and 10 million. Quicksort needed only 2.75 seconds.

Mergesort has the advantage that its times remain the same for different data distributions and initial arrangements. Quicksort gives $O(N^2)$ performance and enters deep recursion if there are many duplicated values in the list. If the list is large, quicksort may exhaust the stack and crash. Because mergesort always divides the list into equal parts, it never enters deep recursion. For an N-item list, mergesort reaches only $\log(N)$ depth of recursion.

In another test using 1 million items with values between 1 and 1000, mergesort took 4.67 seconds, roughly the same time it took to sort items with values between 1 and 10 million. Quicksort needed 16.12 seconds. With item values between 1 and 100, mergesort took 4.75 seconds while quicksort took 194.18 seconds.

Heapsort

Heapsort uses a special data structure called a *heap* to organize the items in a list. Heaps are also interesting in their own right and are useful for implementing priority queues.

This section begins by describing heaps and explaining how you can implement them in Delphi. It then shows how to use a heap to build an efficient priority queue. With the tools developed to manage heaps and priority queues, implementing heapsort is easy.

Heaps

A heap is a complete binary tree in which each node is at least as large as its two children. This does not say anything about the relationship between the two children.

Figure 9.5 A heap.

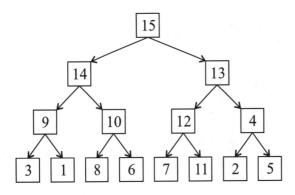

While both must be smaller than their parent, either may be larger than the other. Figure 9.5 shows a small heap.

Because each node is at least as large as the two nodes below it, the root node is always the largest node in the heap. This makes heaps a good data structure for implementing priority queues. Whenever you need the highest priority item in the queue, it is sitting at the top of the heap.

Because a heap is a complete binary tree, you can use techniques covered in Chapter 6, "Trees," to store the heap in an array. Place the root node at array position 1. Place the children of node i in positions 2 * i and 2 * i + 1. Figure 9.6 shows the heap in Figure 9.5 stored in an array.

To see how to build a heap, notice that a heap is made of smaller subheaps. The subtree starting at any node in a heap is also a heap. For example, in the heap shown in Figure 9.7, the subtree rooted at node 13 is a heap.

Using this fact, you can build a heap from the bottom up. First, place the items in a tree, as shown in Figure 9.8. Then make heaps out of the little three node subtrees at the bottom. Because there are only three nodes in these trees, this is simple. Compare the top node with its two child nodes. If either of the children is larger, swap it with the node on top. If both children are larger, swap the parent with the bigger child. Repeat this step until all of the three node subtrees at the bottom of the tree are heaps, as shown in Figure 9.9.

Now join little heaps to form larger heaps. In Figure 9.9, join the small heaps with tops 15 and 5 plus item 7 to form a larger heap. To join the two smaller heaps, compare the new top item 7 with each of its children. If one of the children is bigger than this item, swap the item with the larger child. In this case, 15 is larger than 7 and 4, so you should swap node 15 with node 7.

Because the right subtree starting with node 4 is not modified, that subtree is still a heap. The left subtree, however, has changed. To determine whether it is still a heap, compare its new top 7 to its children 13 and 12. Because 13 is larger than 7 and 12, you should swap the 7 and 13 nodes.

If the subtree was taller, you would continue pushing the 7 node down into the subtree. Eventually, you would either hit the bottom of the tree, or you would reach a point where the 7 node was larger than both of its children. Figure 9.10 shows the tree after this subtree has been turned into a heap.

Continue joining heaps to form larger heaps until you have combined all the items into one large heap, like the one in Figure 9.5.

Figure 9.6 Array representation of a heap.

Index	1	2	3	4	5	6	7	8	9	10	11	12	13	14	15
Value	15	14	13	9	10	12	4	3	1	8	6	7	11	2	5

Figure 9.7 A heap is made up of subheaps.

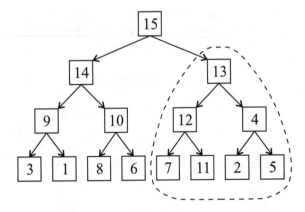

Figure 9.8 An unsorted list in a complete tree.

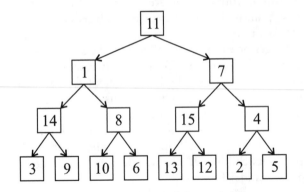

Figure 9.9 Two-level subtrees are heaps.

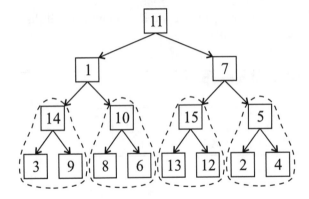

Figure 9.10 Combining subheaps into larger heaps.

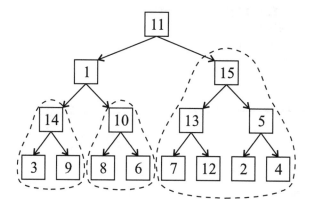

The following code pushes the item in position Queue[parent] down through a heap. If the subtrees below Queue[parent] are heaps, the procedure merges the subheaps to form a larger heap.

```
type
    QueueEntry = record
        value    : String[10];
        priority : Integer;
    end;

// Push an item down through the heap
// until it can go no farther.
procedure HeapPushDown(parent : Integer);
var
    child, top_priority : Integer;
    top_value           : String;
begin
    top_priority := Queue[parent].priority;
    top_value := Queue[parent].value;
    repeat // Repeat infinitely.
        child := 2 * parent;
        if (child > NumItems) then
            break // Done. Past end of heap.
        else begin
            // Make child the higher priority child.
            if (child < NumItems) then
                if (Queue[child + 1].priority > Queue[child].priority)
                    then
                        child := child + 1;
```

```
            if (Queue[child].priority > top_priority) then
            begin
                    // A child has higher priority.
                    // Swap the parent and child.
                Queue[parent] := Queue[child];
                    // Push down beneath that child.
                parent := child;
            end else
                    // The parent has higher priority. We're done.
                break;
        end;
    until (False);
    Queue[parent].priority := top_priority;
    Queue[parent].value := top_value;
end;
```

The complete algorithm for using HeapPushDown to create a heap out of a tree of items is remarkably simple.

```
procedure BuildHeap;
var
    i : Integer;
begin
    for i := (max + min) div 2 downto min do
        HeapPushDown(i);
end;
```

Priority Queues

It is easy to manage a priority queue using the BuildHeap and HeapPushDown procedures. If you use a heap as a priority queue, the item with the highest priority is always at the top. Finding the highest priority item is easy. When you remove this item, however, the rootless tree that remains is not a heap.

To turn the rootless tree back into a heap, take the last item (the rightmost item on the bottom level) and place it at the top of the heap. Then use the HeapPushDown procedure to push the new root node item down into the tree until the tree is once again a heap. At this point, the priority queue is ready to output the next highest priority item.

```
// Remove highest priority last from the queue.
function Pop : String;
begin
    Result := Queue[1].value;

    // Move the last item to the top of the queue.
```

```
Queue[1] := Queue[NumItems];
NumItems := NumItems - 1;

// Push the item down until we have a heap again.
HeapPushDown(1);
end;
```

To add a new item to the priority queue, enlarge the heap to make room for the new item. Place the new item in the empty position at the end of the array. The resulting tree may no longer be a heap.

To make the tree a heap again, compare the new item with its parent. If the new item is bigger, swap the two. You already know that the parent's other child is smaller than the parent, so you do not need to compare the new item to the other child. If the new item is larger than the parent, it is also larger than the other child.

Continue comparing the new item to its parent and moving it up through the tree until you find a parent that is already larger than the new item. At that point, the tree is once again a heap, and the priority queue is ready for business.

```
// Push the last item up toward the root.
procedure HeapPushUp;
var
     child, parent    : Integer;
     bottom_priority : Integer;
     bottom_value    : String;
begin
     bottom_priority := Queue[NumItems].priority;
     bottom_value := Queue[NumItems].value;
     child := NumItems;
     repeat // Repeat infinitely.
         parent := child div 2;
         if (parent < 1) then break;
         if (Queue[parent].priority < bottom_priority) then
         begin
             Queue[child] := Queue[parent];
             child := parent;
         end else
             break;
     until (False);
     Queue[child].priority := bottom_priority;
     Queue[child].value := bottom_value;
end;
```

The Push procedure adds a new item to the tree and uses procedure HeapPushUp to rebuild the heap.

```
// Add an item to the queue.
procedure Push(new_value : String; priority : Integer);
begin
    NumItems := NumItems + 1;
    Queue[NumItems].value := new_value;
    Queue[NumItems].priority := priority;
    HeapPushUp;
end;
```

Heap Analysis

When you first turn the list of items into a heap, you do so by building a lot of smaller heaps. For every internal node in the tree, you build a smaller heap rooted at that node. If the tree contains N items, there are O(N) internal nodes in the tree, so you end up building O(N) heaps.

As you build each heap, you might need to push the top item down the heap, possibly until it reaches a leaf node. The tallest heaps you build have height O(log(N)). Because you build O(N) heaps and the tallest requires at most O(log(N)) steps to build, you can build all of the heaps in O(N * log(N)) time.

In fact, it does not take even that much time to build the heaps. Only a few of the heaps have height O(log(N)). Most are much shorter. Only one heap actually has height equal to log(N), and half have height only 2. If you add up all the steps needed to build all the heaps, you actually need at most O(N) steps.

To see why this is true, suppose the tree contains N nodes. Let H be the height of the tree. This is a complete binary tree, so H = log(N).

Now suppose you are building larger and larger heaps. You build a heap of height i for each internal node that is H − i levels from the root of the tree. There are 2^{H-i} such nodes, so in total you build 2^{H-i} heaps of height i.

To build these heaps, you might need to push the top item down until it reaches a leaf. It takes up to i steps to push the item down through a heap of height i. To build 2^{H-i} heaps in at most i steps each, the total number of steps spent building heaps of height i is i * 2^{H-i}.

Adding together all the steps spent building heaps of different sizes, you get $1 * 2^{H-1} + 2 * 2^{H-2} + 3 * 2^{H-3} + ... + (H-1) * 2^1$. Dividing out a factor of 2^H gives $2^H * (1/2 + 2/2^2 + 3/2^3 + ... + (H-1)/2^{H-1})$.

It can be shown that $(1/2 + 2/2^2 + 3/2^3 + ... + (H-1)/2^{H-1})$ is less than 2. Then the number of steps spent building all the heaps is less than $2^H * 2$. Because H is the height of the tree and equals log(N), the total number of steps is less than $2^{log(N)} * 2 = N * 2$. That means it takes only O(N) steps to initially build a heap.

To remove an item from a priority queue, you move the last item to the top of the tree. You then push the item down until it reaches its final position and the tree is again a heap. Because the tree has height log(N), this process can take, at most, log(N) steps. That means you can remove an item from a heap-based priority queue in O(log(N)) steps.

When you add a new item to the heap, you place it at the bottom of the tree and push it toward the top until it comes to rest. Because the tree has height log(N), this can take, at most, log(N) steps. That means you can add a new item to a heap-based priority queue in O(log(N)) steps.

Another way to manage a priority queue is to use a sorted list. Using quick-sort you can build the initial queue in O(N * log(N)) time. When you remove or add an item, you can use bubblesort to put the list back in order in O(N) time.

These times are fast but not as fast as those given by a heap. Inserting or removing an item from a sorted list priority queue of 1 million items requires about 1 million steps. Inserting or removing an item from a comparable heap-based priority queue takes only 20 steps.

Example program HeapQ uses a heap to manage a priority queue. Enter a string and a priority and click the Push button to add the new item to the queue. Click the Pop button to remove the highest priority item from the queue.

The Heapsort Algorithm

Using the algorithms already described for manipulating heaps, the heapsort algorithm is straightforward. The idea is to build a priority queue and then remove each item from the queue one at a time in order.

To remove an item, the algorithm swaps it with the last item in the heap. This places the newly removed item in its proper final position at the end of the array. The algorithm then reduces its count of the number of items in the heap so it does not consider the last position again.

After swapping the largest item with the last item, the array is no longer a heap because the new top item may be smaller than its children. The algorithm uses the HeapPushDown procedure to push the new item to its proper position. The algorithm continues swapping items and rebuilding the heap until there are no items left in the heap.

```
procedure TSortForm.Heapsort(list : PLongintArray; min, max :
Longint);
var
    i, tmp : Longint;
begin
    // Make a heap (except for the root node).
    for i := (max + min) div 2 downto min + 1 do
        HeapPushDown(list, i, max);

    // Repeatedly:
    //     1. HeapPushDown.
    //     2. Output the root.
    for i := max downto min + 1 do
    begin
        // HeapPushDown.
```

```
        HeapPushDown(list, min, i);

        // Output the root.
        tmp := list^[min];
        list^[min] := list^[i];
        list^[i] := tmp;
    end;
end;
```

The earlier discussion of priority queues showed that initially building the heap takes O(N) steps. After that, it takes O(log(N)) steps to rebuild the heap when an item is swapped into its final position. Heapsort does this N times so it needs a total of O(N) * O(log(N)) = O(N * log(N)) steps to pull the sorted list out of the heap. The total runtime for heapsort is O(N) + O(N * log(N)) = O(N * log(N)).

This is the same as the runtime for mergesort and the average runtime for quicksort. Like mergesort, heapsort does not depend on the values or distribution of the items being sorted. Remember that quicksort has trouble with lists containing many duplicated values; mergesort and heapsort do not.

Even though heapsort is usually a little slower than mergesort, it does not require the temporary scratch space mergesort needs. Heapsort builds the initial heap and moves the items into sorted order within the original list array. For very large lists, mergesort's extra scratch space may force the program to page while it would not using heapsort.

Countingsort

Countingsort is a specialized algorithm that works extremely well if the data items are integers with values that fall within a relatively small range. The algorithm is fast, for example, if all the values lie between 1 and 1000.

As long as the list meets these conditions, countingsort is incredibly fast. In one test on a 133-megahertz Pentium, quicksort sorted 1 million items with values between 1 and 10,000 in 3.93 seconds. To sort the same items, countingsort required only 0.37 seconds—1 / 10th as long.

Countingsort achieves its remarkable speed by not using comparisons to sort the items. Earlier, this chapter mentioned that any sorting algorithm using comparisons must take at least O(N * log(N)) time. By not using comparisons, countingsort is able to sort items in O(N) time.

The complete source code for countingsort is deceptively brief. It is so short that one might think it is simple. Actually, it is short but subtle.

Countingsort starts by creating an array to count the items with each data value. If item values range from 1 to M, the algorithm creates a counts array with lower bound 1 and upper bound M. The algorithm initializes all of the counts entries to zero. If there are M item values, the array holds M entries, so this is an O(M) step.

Next, the algorithm counts the occurrences of each value in the list. It examines each item and increments the value of the corresponding counts entry. When examining item i, the program increments counts^[list^[i]]. The algorithm examines each item once during this process, so this step takes O(N) time.

Finally, the algorithm runs through the counts array placing the appropriate number of items with each value in the sorted array. For each value i between 1 and M, it places counts^[i] items with value i in the array. Because this step places one entry in each position in the array, it takes O(N) steps.

```
type
    TCountArray = array [1..10000000] of Longint;
    PCountArray = ^TCountArray;

procedure Countingsort(list : PLongintArray;
        counts : PCountArray;
        min, max, min_value, max_value : Longint);
var
    i, j, new_index : Longint;
begin
    // Initialize the counts to 0.
    for i := min_value to max_value do counts^[i] := 0;

    // Count the values.
    for i := min to max do
        counts^[list^[i]] := counts^[list^[i]] + 1;

    // Place the values in their correct locations.
    new_index := min;
    for i := min_value to max_value do
        for j := 1 to counts^[i] do
        begin
            list^[new_index] := i;
            new_index := new_index + 1;
        end;
end;
```

The complete algorithm takes O(M) + O(N) + O(N) = O(M + N) steps. If M is small compared to N, this is extremely fast. If M < N, for example, O(M + N) = O(N), which is quite fast. If N = 100,000 and M = 1000, then M + N = 101,000 while N * log(N) = 1.6 million. The steps taken by countingsort are also quite simple compared to those taken by quicksort. These facts combine to make countingsort incredibly quick.

On the other hand, if M is larger than O(N * log(N)), then O(M + N) will be larger than O(N * log(N)). In that case, countingsort may be slower than O(N * log(N)) algorithms like quicksort. In one test, quicksort took 0.016

seconds to sort 10,000 items with values between 1 and 1 million, while countingsort needed 0.16 seconds.

Countingsort relies on the fact that the data values are integers, so the algorithm cannot easily sort noninteger data. In Delphi, you cannot create an array with bounds AAA to ZZZ.

The section *Key Combination and Compression* earlier in this chapter shows how to encode noninteger data using integers. If you can encode your data as integers or long integers, you can still use countingsort.

Bucketsort

Like countingsort, bucketsort does not use comparisons to sort items. It uses the item values to divide the items into buckets. It then sorts the buckets recursively. When the buckets are small enough, the algorithm stops and uses a simpler algorithm like selectionsort to finish sorting.

In a sense, this algorithm is similar to quicksort. Quicksort divides the items into two sublists and recursively sorts the sublists. Bucketsort does the same thing except it divides the list into many buckets instead of just two sublists.

To divide the list into buckets, the algorithm assumes that the data values are evenly distributed, and it divides the items evenly among the buckets. For example, suppose the data items have values ranging from 1 to 100 and the algorithm is using 10 buckets. The algorithm places items with values 1–10 in the first bucket, items with values 11–20 in the second bucket, and so forth. Figure 9.11 shows a list of 10 items with values between 1 and 100 placed in 10 buckets.

If the items are evenly distributed, each bucket receives roughly the same number of items. If there are N items in the list and the algorithm uses N buckets, each bucket receives only one or two items. The program can sort the one or two items in a constant number of steps, so the total runtime for the algorithm is O(N).

In practice, data values are usually not distributed perfectly evenly. Some buckets receive more items and some receive fewer. If the distribution is at all close to uniform, however, each bucket receives only a small number of items.

Even if there is a clump in the data so that one bucket receives many items, the items within the bucket will probably be evenly distributed. When the algorithm

Figure 9.11 Placing items in buckets.

| Unsorted list | 1 | 74 | 38 | 72 | 63 | 100 | 89 | 57 | 7 | 31 |

Bucket number	1	2	3	4	5	6	7	8	9	10
Bucket	1 7		38 31			57	63	74 72	89		100

recursively sorts this large bucket, the items will be divided evenly among the new buckets. The items will be handled easily in the second round of the algorithm.

One case that causes trouble occurs when the list contains few distinct values. If every item has the same value, for example, bucketsort puts them all in the same bucket. If the algorithm does not detect this, it will recursively put them all in the same bucket again and again, causing runaway recursion and using up all of the stack space.

Linked List Bucketsort

You can implement bucketsort in Delphi in several ways. One of the easiest uses linked lists for the buckets. This makes it easy to move items from one bucket to another as the algorithm progresses. The following code shows the linked list bucketsort algorithm.

```
type
    PCell = ^TCell;
    TCell = record
        Value     : Longint; // The data.
        NextCell : PCell;    // The next cell.
    end;
    TCellArray = array [1..1000000] of TCell;
    PCellArray = ^TCellArray;

procedure LLBucketsort(top : PCell);
var
    count, min_value, max_value  : Longint;
    i, value, bucket_num         : Longint;
    cell, nxt                    : PCell;
    bucket                       : PCellArray;
    scale                        : Double;
begin
    cell := top^.NextCell;
    if (cell = nil) then exit;

    // Count the cells and find the min and max values.
    count := 1;
    min_value := cell^.Value;
    max_value := min_value;
    cell := cell^.NextCell;
    while (cell <> nil) do
    begin
        count := count + 1;
        value := cell^.value;
        if (min_value > value) then min_value := value;
```

```
        if (max_value < value) then max_value := value;
        cell := cell^.NextCell;
    end;


    // If min_value = max_value, there is only one value
    // so the list is sorted.
    if (min_value = max_value) then exit;

    // If the list has no more than Cutoff cells, finish
    // with LLInsertionsort.
    if (count <= Cutoff) then
    begin
        LLInsertionsort(top);
        exit;
    end;


    // Allocate the empty buckets.
    GetMem(bucket, count * SizeOf(TCell));
    for i := 1 to count do bucket^[i].NextCell := nil;


    // Move the cells into the buckets.
    scale := (count - 1) / (max_value - min_value);
    cell := top^.NextCell;
    while (cell <> nil) do
    begin
        nxt := cell^.NextCell;
        value := cell^.value;
        if (value = max_value) then
            bucket_num := count
        else
            bucket_num :=
                Trunc((value - min_value) * scale) + 1;
        cell^.NextCell := bucket^[bucket_num].NextCell;
        bucket^[bucket_num].NextCell := cell;
        cell := nxt;
    end;


    // Recursively sort buckets with more than one cell.
    for i := 1 to count do
        if (bucket^[i].NextCell <> nil) then
            LLBucketsort(@bucket^[i]);


    // Merge the sorted lists.
    top^.NextCell := bucket^[count].NextCell;
```

```
for i := count - 1 downto 1 do
begin
    cell := bucket^[i].NextCell;
    if (cell <> nil) then
    begin
        nxt := cell^.NextCell;
        while ((nxt <> nil) and
                (nxt^.value < INFINITY)) do
        begin
            cell := nxt;
            nxt := cell^.NextCell;
        end;
        cell^.NextCell := top^.NextCell;
        top^.NextCell := bucket^[i].NextCell;

        // Free the bottom sentinel if there is one.
        if (nxt <> nil) then Dispose(nxt);
    end;
end;

// Free the memory allocated for the buckets.
    FreeMem(bucket);
end;
```

This method can be cumbersome if the items are originally stored in an array. In that case, you need to move the items from the array into the linked list and back into the array when you are done sorting. It also requires extra memory for the linked list. If the items are originally stored in an array, it is easier and usually faster to use one of the array-based algorithms presented earlier.

However, if the items are already stored in a linked list, bucketsort is quite fast. It is much faster than linked list insertionsort. In a test on a 133-megahertz Pentium, insertionsort took 15.85 seconds to sort 20,000 items; bucketsort took 0.039 seconds. For longer lists, the $O(N^2)$ performance of insertionsort makes the difference even greater.

Summary

Table 9.4 shows the advantages and disadvantages of the sorting algorithms described in this chapter. Taking these into account, here are some rules you can use to help you select a sorting algorithm.

- If you just want to implement some algorithm quickly, use quicksort and switch algorithms later if necessary.

- If your list is more than 99 percent sorted already, use bubblesort.

- If you have a very small list (under 100 items), use selectionsort.

- If your program stores the values in a linked list, use linked list bucket-sort.
- If the items in your list range over a small number of integer values (up to several thousand), use countingsort.

Table 9.4 Advantages and Disadvantages of Sorting Algorithms

Algorithm	Advantages	Disadvantages
Insertionsort	Very simple Fast for small lists	Very slow for large lists
Linked List Insertionsort	Simple Fast for small lists Moves pointers, not data Works with linked lists	Slow for large lists
Selectionsort	Very simple Fast for small lists	Slow for large lists
Bubblesort	Fast for lists that are almost sorted	Very slow for all other lists
Quicksort	Fast for large lists	Trouble if there are lots of duplicate values
Mergesort	Fast for large lists	Requires scratch space Not as fast as quicksort
Heapsort	Fast for large lists No scratch space required	Not as fast as mergesort
Countingsort	Very fast when value range is small	Slower when value range $> \log(N)$ Requires extra memory Only works with integer data
Bucketsort	Very fast with evenly distributed data Handles data spread over wide ranges Works with linked lists	Slower than counting sort

If you understand your data and a variety of different sorting algorithms, you can select the algorithm that best fits your needs. The guidelines in the previous list and the information in Table 9.4 can help you pick the algorithm that will give you the best possible performance.

SEARCHING

10

10

A fter you sort a list of items, you might want to locate a particular item in the list. This chapter describes several algorithms for locating items in sorted lists. The chapter begins by briefly discussing exhaustive searching. Although not as fast as the other algorithms, exhaustive searching is very simple. That makes it easy to program and debug. Its simplicity also makes exhaustive searching faster than other algorithms for very small lists.

Next, the chapter describes binary searching. A binary search repeatedly subdivides the list to locate an item and is much faster than exhaustive search for larger lists. The idea behind binary searching is simple, but the implementation is a little tricky.

The chapter then discusses interpolation searching. Like binary search, interpolation search repeatedly subdivides the list to locate an item. Using interpolation, this algorithm makes a reasonable guess about where the target item should lie, so it is much faster than binary search for evenly distributed lists.

Finally, the chapter discusses hunt and search methods. These techniques sometimes make searching for multiple items faster.

Example Programs

Example program Search demonstrates all the algorithms described in this chapter. Enter the number of items the list should contain. Click the Create List button to make the program create an array-based list where each item is between 0 and 5 greater than the previous item. The program displays the value of the largest item in the list so you know what values you might find.

After you create the list, use the check boxes to select the algorithms you want to use. Enter a target value and click the Search button to make the program locate the value using the algorithms you selected. Because the items are not all consecutive, you may need to search for several different values before you find one that is in the list.

The program also lets you specify the number of times it should repeat each search. Some of the algorithms are very fast, so you may need to use many repetitions if you want to compare their speeds.

Figure 10.1 shows program Search after locating an item with the value 250,000. The item was in position 83,333 in a list of 100,000 items. To find the item, the exhaustive search algorithm examined 83,333 list entries. Binary search examined 15 entries and interpolation search examined just 2.

Exhaustive Search

To perform an *exhaustive* or *linear* search, start at the beginning of the list and examine every item until you find the target item.

```
type
    TLongArray = array [1..10000000] of Longint;
    PLongArray = ^TLongArray;

function LinearSearch(target : Longint; List : PLongArray;
    min, max : Longint) : Longint;
var
    i : Longint;
begin
    for i := min to max do
        if (list^[i] = target) then
        begin
            // We found it.
            Result := i
            exit;
        end;
```

Figure 10.1 Program Search.

```
    // The item is not here.
    Result := 0
end;
```

Because it examines each item in order, this algorithm locates items near the front of the list more quickly than items near the rear. The worst case for this algorithm occurs when the item is near the end of the list or is not present at all. In these cases, the algorithm must search all the items in the list, so it has O(N) worst case behavior.

If the item is in the list, the algorithm must examine N / 2 entries on the average before it finds the target item. This gives the algorithm an average behavior of O(N). Even though this O(N) behavior is not particularly fast, the algorithm is simple enough that it is quite fast in practice. For small lists, the algorithm gives adequate performance.

Searching Sorted Lists

If a list is sorted, you can modify the exhaustive searching algorithm to get slightly better performance. As the algorithm searches the list, if it ever finds an item that has value greater than the target value, the algorithm can stop. Because it has passed the position where the target item would belong if it were in the list, the item must not be present.

For example, suppose you are searching for the value 12 and you come to the value 17. You have passed the position where 12 would be so you know the value 12 is not in the list. The following code shows the improved exhaustive search algorithm.

```
function LinearSearch(target : Longint; List : PLongArray;
    min, max : Longint) : Longint;
var
    i : Longint;
begin
    for i := min to max do
        if (list^[i] >= target) then break;

    if (i > max) then
        Result := 0
    else if (list^[i] = target) then
        Result := i
    else
        Result := 0;
end;
```

This modification makes the algorithm faster when the target item is not in the list. The previous version searches all the way to the end of the list if the target item is not present. The new version stops as soon as it finds an item greater than the target item.

If the target item is randomly positioned between the smallest and largest items in the list, the algorithm will require an average of N / 2 steps to determine that the item is not there. The runtime is still O(N), but the performance in practice is faster. Example program Search uses this version of the algorithm.

Searching Linked Lists

Exhaustive searching is the only way to search a linked list. Because you have access to items only through their NextCell pointers, you must start at the beginning of the list and step through the items one at a time until you find the one you want.

As is the case with exhaustive search in an array, if the list is sorted, you can stop searching when you find an item that has value greater than the target value. Once you have passed the position where the target item would be if it were in the list, you know the item is not there.

```
type
    PCell = ^TCell;
    TCell = record
        Value     : Longint;
        NextCell : PCell;
        PrevCell : PCell;
    end;
```

```
function TSearchForm.LListSearch(target : Longint; top : PCell) :
PCell;
begin
    top := top^.NextCell;
    while (top <> nil) do
    begin
        if (top^.Value >= target) then break;
        top := top^.NextCell;
    end;
    if (top = nil) then
        Result := nil
    else if (top^.Value = target) then
        Result := top
    else
        Result := nil;
end;
```

Example program Search uses this algorithm to locate items within a linked list. The overhead involved in managing object pointers makes this algorithm slightly slower than the array-based exhaustive search.

You can make one more change to the linked list search algorithm to make it a little faster. If you keep a pointer to the bottom of the list, you can add a new cell at the end that contains the target value. This item is called a *sentinel*, and it serves a purpose similar to that of the sentinels used in the lists built in Chapter 2, "Lists." It allows the program to treat a special case as if it were not special.

In this case, adding the sentinel to the end of the list ensures that the algorithm will eventually find the target item. The program cannot run off the end of the list so it need not check the condition top = nil each time the while loop executes.

```
function SentinelSearch(target : Longint; top : PCell) : PCell;
var
    bottom_sentinel : TCell;
begin
    // Add the sentinel.
    BottomCell^.NextCell := @bottom_sentinel;
    bottom_sentinel.Value := target;

    top := top^.NextCell;
    while (top^.Value < target) do
        top := top^.NextCell;
    if ((top^.Value <> target) or
        (top = @bottom_sentinel))
    then
        Result := nil
    else
        Result := top;

    // Remove the sentinel.
    BottomCell^.NextCell := nil;
end;
```

Even though this may seem like a small change, the top = nil test is contained in a frequently executed loop. For large lists, this loop is executed many times and the savings accumulate. In Delphi, this linked list search runs about 10 percent faster than the previous version. Program Search demonstrates both versions of the linked list search algorithms so you can compare the two.

Some algorithms use threads through linked lists to improve searching. For example, pointers within the list cells could organize the cells into a binary tree. Searching for an item using the tree would take $O(\log(N))$ time if the tree is properly balanced. This sort of data structure is not a simple list, so it is not discussed further here. For more information on trees, see Chapter 6, "Trees," and Chapter 7, "Balanced Trees."

Binary Search

As is mentioned in the previous sections, an exhaustive search is very fast for small lists. For larger lists, binary search is much faster. The binary search algorithm examines the item in the middle of the list and compares it to the target item. If the target item is smaller, the algorithm continues searching the first half of the list. If the target item is larger than the middle item, the algorithm searches the second half of the list. Figure 10.2 graphically shows a binary search for the value 44.

Although this algorithm is naturally recursive, it is fairly easy to write without recursion. Because it is easy to understand either way, the algorithm is written nonrecursively here to save the expense of making a lot of function calls.

The general idea behind the algorithm is simple, but the details are a little tricky. The program must keep careful track of the portion of the array that might contain the target item. Otherwise, the algorithm may miss the target.

The algorithm uses two variables, min and max, to keep track of the minimum and maximum indexes of the array entries that could contain the target item. While the algorithm runs, the target will always have an index between min and max. In other words, min <= target index <= max.

During each pass, the algorithm sets middle = (min + max) / 2 and examines the item with index middle. If the middle item has the same value as the target item, the algorithm has found the target and is finished. If the target item is smaller than the middle item, the algorithm sets max to middle – 1 and continues searching. Because the range of indexes that might contain the target item is now min to middle – 1, the program searches the first half of the list.

If the target item is larger than the middle item, the program sets min to middle + 1 and continues searching. The range of indexes that might hold the target item is now middle + 1 to max, so the program searches the second half of the list.

Eventually, the program will either find the item, or it will raise min and lower max until min is greater than max. The program adjusts min and max so the index of the target item is always between them. Because there are no more indexes between min and max at this point, the item must not be in the list.

Figure 10.2 Binary search for the value 44.

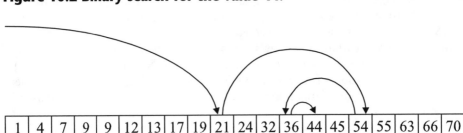

| 1 | 4 | 7 | 9 | 9 | 12 | 13 | 17 | 19 | 21 | 24 | 32 | 36 | 44 | 45 | 54 | 55 | 63 | 66 | 70 |

The following code shows how program Search performs binary search.

```
function BinarySearch(target : Longint; List : PLongArray;
    min, max : Longint) : Longint;
var
    middle : Longint;
begin
    searches := 0;

    // During the search the target's index will be between
    // min and max: min <= target index <= max.
    while (min <= max) do
    begin
        searches := searches + 1;

        middle := Round((max + min) / 2);
        if (target = list^[middle]) then // We found it.
        begin
            Result := middle;
            exit;
        end else if target < List[middle] then
            // Search the left half.
            max := middle - 1
        else
            // Search the right half.
            min := middle + 1;
    end;

    // If we get here the target is not in the list.
    Result := 0;
end;
```

At each step, this algorithm cuts the number of items that still might contain the target item in half. For a list of size N, the algorithm needs at most $O(\log(N))$ steps to locate any given item or to decide that it is not contained in the list. This makes binary search much faster than exhaustive search. To exhaustively search a list of 1 million items would take an average of 500,000 steps. The binary search algorithm would need at most $\log(1,000,000)$, or 20 steps.

Interpolation Search

Binary search is a great improvement over exhaustive search because it eliminates large portions of the list without actually examining all the eliminated values. If you know that the values are fairly evenly distributed, you can use interpolation to eliminate even more values at each step.

Interpolation is the process of using known values to guess where an unknown value lies. In this case, you use the indexes of known values in the list to guess what index the target value should have. For example, suppose you had the same list of values shown in Figure 10.2. This list contains 20 items with values between 1 and 70. Now suppose you wanted to locate the item in this list with value 44. The value 44 is 64 percent of the way between the values 1 and 70. If you assume the values are evenly distributed, you would expect the target item to be about 64 percent of the way through the list at index 13.

If the position chosen by the interpolation is incorrect, the search compares the target value to the value at the chosen position. If the target value is smaller, the search continues to locate the target in the first part of the list. If the target value is larger, the search continues to locate the target in the second part of the list. Figure 10.3 shows an interpolation search graphically.

A binary search subdivides the list by examining the item in the middle of the list. An interpolation search subdivides the list by examining an item that should be close to the target item in the list. The program selects the dividing point by interpolation using the following code.

```
middle := Round(min + ((target - list^[min]) *
    ((max - min) / (list^[max] - list^[min])))));
```

This statement places middle between min and max in a way that reflects where the target value lies between list^[min] and list^[max]. If the target is close to list^[min], the target − list^[min] term is close to 0. Then the complete statement is close to middle = min + 0, so the value of middle is near min. This makes sense. You would expect the item to have an index near min if its value is close to list^[min].

Similarly, if the target is close to list^[max], the target − list^[min] term is about the same as the list^[max] − list^[min] term. These two terms cancel out and the statement is approximately middle = min + (max − min). This simplifies to middle = max and also makes sense. You would expect the item to have an index near max if its value is close to list^[max].

Once the program has computed middle, it compares the item at that position to the target item much as it would during a binary search. If the item matches

Figure 10.3 Interpolation search for the value 44.

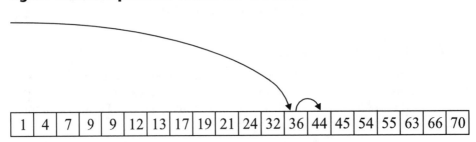

| 1 | 4 | 7 | 9 | 9 | 12 | 13 | 17 | 19 | 21 | 24 | 32 | 36 | 44 | 45 | 54 | 55 | 63 | 66 | 70 |

the target, it has found the target item and is finished. If the target is smaller than this middle item, the program sets max to middle − 1 and continues searching the smaller items in the list. If the target is larger than the middle item, the program sets min to middle + 1 and continues searching the larger items in the list.

Notice that the statement that calculates the new value for middle divides by (list^[max] − list^[min]). If list^[min] and list^[max] have the same value, this statement tries to divide by 0 and the program crashes. This can happen if the list has two identical values in it. Because the algorithm keeps min <= target index <= max, this problem can also occur if min is raised and max is lowered until min = max.

To handle this problem, the program checks whether list^[min] and list^[max] are the same before performing the division. If they are, there is only a single distinct value left to consider. The program simply checks that value to see if it matches the target.

One other detail is that the value calculated for middle is sometimes not between min and max. The simplest case in which this occurs is when the target is outside the range of values in the list. Suppose you are looking for the value 300 in the list 100, 150, 200. The first time the program calculates middle, min = 1 and max = 3. Then middle = 1 + (300 − List(1)) * (3 − 1) / (List(3) − List(1)) = 1 + (300 − 100) * 2 / (200 − 100) = 5. The index 5 is not only outside the range min <= target index <= max, but it is also outside the array bounds. If the program tries to access list^[5], it may crash.

A similar problem can occur if the values between min and max are very unevenly distributed. Suppose you want to locate the value 100 in the list 0, 1, 2, 199, 200. The first time the program calculates middle, it finds middle = 1 + (100 − 0) * (5 − 1) / (200 − 0) = 3. It then compares list^[3] to the target 100. Since List^[3] = 2, which is less than 100, it sets min = middle + 1, so min = 4.

When the program next calculates middle, it finds middle = 4 + (100 − 199) * (5 − 4) / (200 − 199) = −98. The value −98 is outside the range min <= target index <= max and is also far outside the array bounds.

If you look closely at the calculation of middle, you will see that there are two ways in which the new value might be smaller than min or greater than max. First, suppose middle is less than min.

```
min + ((target - list^[min]) *
((max - min) / (list^[max] - list^[min])))
    < min
```

Subtracting min from both sides gives:

```
(target - list^[min]) * ((max - min) / (list^[max] - list^[min]) < 0
```

Because max >= min, the (max − min) term must be greater than 0. Because list^[max] >= list^[min], the (list^[max] − list^[min] term must also be greater than 0. Then the only way the entire value can be less than 0 is if the (target − list^[min]) term is less than 0. That means the target value is less than list^[min].

In that case, the target item cannot be in the list since all of the list entries smaller than list^[min] have already been eliminated.

Now suppose middle is larger than max.

```
min + ((target - list^[min]) *
((max - min) / (list^[max] - list^[min])))
    > max
```

Subtracting min from both sides gives:

```
(target - list^[min]) * (max - min) / (list^[max] - list^[min]) > max
- min
```

Multiplying both sides by (list^[max] – list^[min]) / (max – min) make this become:

```
target - list^[min] > list^[max] - list^[min]
```

Finally, by adding list^[min] to both sides you get:

```
target > list^[max]
```

That means the target value is greater than list^[max]. In that case, the target item cannot be in the list because all the list entries larger than list^[max] have already been eliminated.

Putting these results together, the only way the new value for middle can be outside the range min to max is if the target value is outside the range list^[min] to list^[max]. The algorithm uses this fact whenever it calculates a new value for middle. It first checks to see if the new value is between min and max. If it is not, the target item is not in the list and the algorithm is finished.

The following code shows how program Search performs interpolation search.

```
function InterpolationSearch(target : Longint; List : PLongArray;
    min, max : Longint) : Longint;
var
    middle : Longint;
begin
    while (min <= max) do
    begin
            // Prevent division by zero.
        if (list^[min] = list^[max]) then
        begin
                // This must be the item (if it's in the list).
            if List[min] = target then
                Result := min
            else
                Result := 0;
            exit;
```

```
    end;

        // Compute the dividing point.
    middle := Round(min + ((target - list^[min]) *
            ((max - min) / (list^[max] - list^[min]))));

        // Make sure we stay in bounds.
    if ((middle < min) or (middle > max)) then
    begin
            // It's not in the list.
        Result := 0;
        exit;
    end;

    if target = List[middle] then // We found it.
    begin
        Result := middle;
        exit;
    end else if target < List[middle] then
            // Search the left half.
        max := middle - 1
    else
            // Search the right half.
        min := middle + 1;
    end; // End while (min <= max) do...

        // If we got to this point, the item is not in the list.
    Result := 0;
end;
```

Binary search is very fast, but interpolation search is much faster. In one set of tests, binary search took more than 3 times as long to locate values in a list of 100,000 items. The difference would have been even greater had the data been stored on a hard disk or other relatively slow device. Even though interpolation search spends more time calculating than binary search does, the reduced number of disk accesses saves far more time.

String Data

If the data items in a list are strings, you have a couple of options. The easiest thing to do is use a binary search. Binary search compares items to each other directly, so it can easily handle string data.

Interpolation search, on the other hand, uses the items' numeric data values to compute the index where the target item should be. If the items are strings, the algorithm cannot use the data values directly to compute the target item's location.

If the strings are short enough, you can encode them as integers, long integers, or doubles using the techniques described in the section *Key Combination and Compression* in Chapter 9, "Sorting." Once you have encoded the strings, you can use interpolation search to locate items within the list.

If the strings are too long to encode as doubles, you can still use the string values for interpolation. Begin by finding the first character at which list^[min] and list^[max] differ. Encode the next three characters of each string and the corresponding three characters of the target value using the techniques from Chapter 9, "Sorting." Then use those values for the interpolation.

For example, suppose you are searching for the string TARGET in the list: TABULATE, TANTRUM, TARGET, TATTERED, THEATER. When min = 1 and max = 5, you examine the values TABULATE and THEATER. These values first differ at the second character so you consider the three characters starting with character 2. These are ABU for list^[1], HEA for list^[5], and ARG for the target string.

The encodings of these strings are 804, 5968 and 1222, respectively. Plugging these values into the calculation of middle in the interpolation search algorithm gives:

```
middle = min + (target - List(min)) *
    ((max - min) / (List(max) - List(min)))
       = 1 + (1222 - 804) * ((5 - 1) / (5968 - 804))
       = 1.3
```

This rounds to 1 so the next value for middle is 1. Since list^[1] = TABULATE is less than TARGET, the search continues with min = 2 and max = 5.

Hunting and Searching

If you know your program needs to locate many items within a list and you suspect that each item will be close to the previous one, a hunting technique can make the search faster. Instead of starting the search by considering the entire list, you can use the value from the previous search to begin searching close to the target's correct position.

Binary Hunt and Search

To begin a binary hunt, compare the target value from the previous search to the new target value. If the new target value is smaller, begin hunting to the left. If the new target is larger, begin hunting to the right.

To hunt to the left, set min and max both equal to the index returned by the previous search. Then set min equal to min − 1 and compare the target value to list^[min]. If the target is smaller than list^[min], set max = min and min = min − 2 and try again. If the target is still smaller, set max = min and min = min − 4. If that fails, set max = min and min = min − 8, and so forth. Continue setting max equal to min and subtracting the next power of 2 from min until you find a value for min where list^[min] is less than the target.

Be sure you do not run off the end of the array with min smaller than the lower array bound. If you reach a point where min is smaller, set min equal to the lower array bound. If list^[min] is still larger than the target item, the target is not in the list. Figure 10.4 shows a hunt to the left from the previous target value 44, looking for the new target 17.

A hunt to the right is similar to a hunt to the left. Start by setting min and max both equal to the index returned by the previous search. Then set min = max and max = max + 1, min = max and max = max + 2, min = max and max = max + 4, and so forth until you come to a point where list^[max] is greater than the target. Once again, be sure you do not run past the end of the array.

Once you have finished the hunt phase, you know that the target has index between min and max. You can then use a normal binary search to find the target's exact location. If the new target is close to the old target, a hunt will quickly find the correct values for min and max. If the indexes of the new and old targets are P positions apart, the hunt will take roughly log(P) steps to find the new values for min and max.

Suppose you started a normal binary search for the target without a hunt phase. It would take that search about log(NumItems) – log(P) steps to narrow the search down to the point where min and max were within P positions of each other. That means a hunt and search will be faster than a normal binary search if log(P) < log(NumItems) – log(P). Adding log(P) to both sides of this equation gives 2 * log(P) < log(NumItems). If you exponentiate both sides, you get $2^{2*\log(P)}$ < $2^{\log(NumItems)}$ or $(2^{\log(P)})^2$ < NumItems. This simplifies to P^2 < NumItems.

This shows that a hunt and search will be faster if you are fairly certain that the distance between two consecutive searches will be less than the square root of the number of items in the list. If consecutive searches will be for targets that are farther apart, you will be better off using a normal binary search.

Interpolative Hunt and Search

You can build on the techniques of the previous section to perform a hunt using interpolation. Begin as before by comparing the target value from the previous search to the new target value. If the new target value is smaller, begin a hunt to the left. If the new target is larger, begin a hunt to the right.

Figure 10.4 A binary hunt for the value 17 from the value 44.

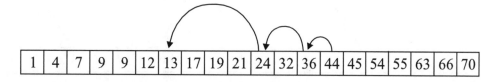

To hunt to the left, you would use interpolation to guess where the value is between the previous target and list^[1]. But this is the same as a normal interpolation search where min = 1 and max is the index returned by the previous search. After a single step, the hunt phase is over, and you can proceed with a normal interpolation search.

A hunt to the right is similar. Simply set max = NumItems and min to the index returned by the previous search. Then continue with a normal interpolation search.

Figure 10.5 shows an interpolation search starting from the previous target value 44, looking for the new target 17.

If the data values are fairly evenly distributed, interpolation search always picks a value near the target in its first step or in any later step. That means starting from a previous value does not improve the algorithm too much. In its first step, without using the result of the previous search, interpolation search will probably pick an index close to the target's true location anyway.

On the other hand, using the previous target value may help protect against unevenness in the data. If you know the new target's value is close to the old target's value, an interpolation starting from the previous search's value will have to give a value near the old target's location. This means using the old target as a starting point may provide some benefit.

The previous search's result also bounds the new target's location a little more tightly than the range 1 to NumItems, so the algorithm might save a step or two. This is especially important if the list is stored on a hard disk or other slow device where every disk access counts. If you can save the results of the previous search in memory, you can at least compare the new target to the previous target without an extra disk access.

Summary

If your items are stored in a linked list, use exhaustive search. If possible, use a bottom sentinel to make the search a little faster.

If you need to occasionally search a list containing a dozen or so items, use an exhaustive search. This will be easier to debug and maintain than a more complicated search technique, and it will provide adequate performance.

Figure 10.5 Interpolation search for the value 17 from the value 44.

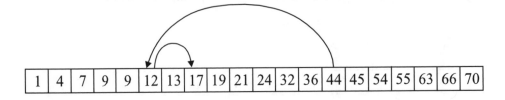

If you need to search a larger list, use an interpolation search. As long as the data values are fairly evenly distributed, interpolation search will give you the best performance. If your list is on a hard disk or other slow storage device, the difference between interpolation search and other search techniques may be quite large.

If the data values are strings, try to encode them as integers, longs, or doubles. Then you can use an interpolation search to locate items. If the data values are too long to fit in doubles, it may be easiest to use a binary search. Table 10.1 summarizes the advantages and disadvantages of each of the different search techniques.

Using binary search or interpolation search, you can locate items within a huge list extremely quickly. If data values are evenly distributed, interpolation search allows you to locate an item in a list containing millions of items in only a few steps.

Such a large list is still difficult to manage if you need to make changes to it. Inserting or removing an item from a sorted list requires O(N) time. If the item is at the beginning of the list, this could be quite time consuming, especially if the list is stored on a slow storage device.

If you need to add and remove items from a large list, you should consider using a different data structure. Chapter 7, "Balanced Trees," discusses data structures that allow you to add and remove items in only O(log(N)) time.

Chapter 11, "Hashing," explains techniques for adding and locating items even more quickly. To achieve this speed, these methods require extra storage space. Hash tables also do not provide information about the ordering of the data. You can add, locate, and remove items from a hash table, but you cannot easily list the items in the table in sorted order.

Table 10.1 Advantages and Disadvantages of Search Techniques

Technique	Advantages	Disadvantages
Exhaustive	Simple	Slow for large lists
	Fast for small lists	
Binary	Fast for large lists	More complicated
	Not dependent on data distribution	
	Easily handles string data	
Interpolation	Very fast for large lists	Very complicated
		Data must be evenly distributed
		Difficult to handle string data

If your list will never change, a sorted list using interpolation search gives excellent performance. If you need to add and remove items from the list, you may want to consider using a hash table. If you also need to list the items in order or move forwards and backwards through the list, balanced trees provide both speed and flexibility. After you decide which operations you must perform, you can pick the algorithm that best suits your needs.

HASHING

Chapter 10, "Searching," describes interpolation search. That algorithm uses interpolation to quickly locate an item within a list. By comparing a target value with values at known locations, the algorithm can guess the position where the target item should be. It essentially creates a function that maps the target value to the index where the item should lie. If the first guess is wrong, the algorithm uses the function again to make a new guess. It continues making guesses until it finds the target item.

Hashing uses a similar concept to map items into a *hash table.* Using the value of a target item, a hashing algorithm uses some sort of function to decide where in the table the item should lie.

For example, suppose you need to store several records that have unique keys with values between 1 and 100. You could create an array of records with 100 entries and initialize the keys of each entry to 0. To add a new record to the array, you simply copy its data into the corresponding position. To add a record with key value 37, you copy the record into the 37th position in the array. To locate a record with a particular key, you examine the corresponding array entry. To remove a record, you simply reset the corresponding array entry's key value to 0. Using this scheme you can add, locate, and remove items from the array in a single step.

Unfortunately, in real applications the key values do not always fit in nice ranges like 1 to 100. Usually, the possible key values span a very wide range. An employee database might use Social Security number as a key. There are 1 billion possible values for nine-digit numbers like Social Security numbers. In theory you could allocate an array with one entry for every possible nine-digit number, but in reality you probably do not have enough memory or disk space. If each employee record required 1 kilobyte of memory, the array would occupy 1 terabyte (1 million megabytes) of memory. Even if you could allocate this much storage, this scheme would be quite wasteful. Unless your company hired more than 10 million employees, the array would always be more than 99 percent empty.

To work around these problems, hashing schemes map a potentially large number of possible keys into a relatively small hash table. If your company employs 700 workers, you might allocate a hash table with 1000 entries. The hashing scheme maps the 700 employee records into the 1000 positions in the table. The hashing function might map records into entries according to the first three digits of the employees' Social Security numbers. An employee with Social Security number 123-45-6789 would map to table position 123.

Of course, if there are more possible key values than there are table entries, some key values must map to the same position in the hash table. For example, the values 123-45-6789 and 123-99-9999 both map to table position 123. If there are 1 billion possible Social Security numbers and if you only have 1000 positions in the table, on the average 1 million records must map to each table position.

To handle this potential problem, a hashing scheme must have a *collision resolution policy* that tells what to do when a key maps to a position that is already occupied by another record. The following sections discuss several different methods for handling collisions.

All the methods discussed follow a similar approach to collision resolution. They first map a record's key to a position in the hash table. If that position is already occupied, they map the key to a new position. If that position is also occupied, they remap the key again until the algorithm finally locates an empty table position. The sequence of positions examined while locating or inserting an item in a hash table is called a *probe sequence*.

To summarize, you need three things to implement hashing:

- A data structure called a hash table to hold the data

- A hashing function to map key values into table entries

- A collision resolution policy that tells what to do when keys map to the same position

The sections that follow describe several different data structures you can use for hashing. Each has a corresponding hashing function and one or more possible collision resolution policies. As is the case with most computer algorithms, each method has its strengths and weaknesses. The final section in the chapter summarizes these so you can pick the best hashing technique for your situation.

Chaining

One method for collision resolution is to store records that map to the same table position in linked lists. To add a new record to the table, you use a hash function to pick the linked list that should hold it. You then add the record to that list.

Figure 11.1 shows an example of chaining in a hash table that contains 10 entries. The hashing function maps a key K into array position K mod 10. Each position in the array contains a pointer to the first item in a linked list. To add an item to the table, you add it to the appropriate list.

To initially create the hash table in Delphi, allocate a zero-based array of cells to act as list sentinels. If the hash table will contain NumChains lists, declare the array with bounds 0 to NumChains – 1. Initialize each of the sentinels' NextCell entries to nil.

Figure 11.1 Chaining.

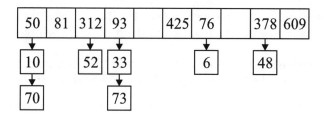

To locate an item with key K in the hash table, compute K mod NumChains. This gives the index of the sentinel of the linked list in which the item may lie. Look through that list until you find the item or you reach the end of the list.

```
var
    cell : PChainCell;
begin
    // See which chain should hold the value.
    cell := ListTops^[value mod NumChains].NextCell;
    while (cell <> nil) do
    begin
        if (cell^.Value = value) then break;
        cell := cell^.NextCell;
    end;

    if (cell <> nil) then
    begin
        // Do something with the cell here.
            :
```

To insert an item with key K into the table, compute K mod NumChains as before to see what list should hold the value. Add the item to the list using the techniques described in Chapter 2, "Lists."

```
procedure InsertItem(value : TTableData);
var
    cell, new_cell : PChainCell;
begin
    // See which chain should hold the value.
    cell := @ListTops^[value mod NumChains];

    // Insert the item at the top of the chain.
    New(new_cell);
    new_cell^.Value := value;
    new_cell^.NextCell := cell^.NextCell;
```

```
    cell^.NextCell := new_cell;
end;
```

Normally, hash tables allow only one entry with a given key. In that case, the InsertItem procedure should check whether the item is already in the table before adding it.

To remove an item from the hash table, compute K mod NumChains to find the item's list. Remove the item from the list using the techniques described in Chapter 2, "Lists."

```
procedure RemoveItem(value : TTableData);
var
    cell, nxt_cell : PChainCell;
begin
    // See which chain should hold the value.
    cell := @ListTops^[value mod NumChains];
    nxt_cell := cell^.NextCell;

    // Find the item.
    while (nxt_cell <> nil) do
    begin
        if (nxt_cell^.Value = value) then break;
        cell := nxt_cell;
        nxt_cell := cell^.NextCell;
    end;

    if (nxt_cell <> nil) then
    begin
        // The cell is here. Remove it.
        cell^.NextCell := nxt_cell^.NextCell;
        Dispose(nxt_cell);
    end;
end;
```

Advantages and Disadvantages of Chaining

One advantage of this method is that chaining hash tables never become full. It is always easy to insert or locate items even if there are many items in the table. In some of the hashing techniques described in later sections, performance drops drastically when the table is almost full.

It is also easy to remove items from a hash table that uses chaining. Simply remove the item's cell from its linked list. In some of the following hashing schemes, removing items is difficult or impossible.

One disadvantage of chaining is that, unless the number of linked lists is relatively large, the chains can grow long. Then to insert or locate an item, you must search down a fairly long chain. If a hash table contains 10 linked lists and you add 10,000 items to the table, the linked lists will have an average length of 1000. Whenever you need to locate an item in the table, you might have to search through 1000 or more cells.

One way you can make the search a little faster is to keep the linked lists in sorted order. Then you can use the techniques presented in Chapter 10, "Searching," to search for items in a sorted linked list. This allows you to stop searching for a target value if you encounter an item with value larger than the target. On the average, you will need to search only half of a linked list before you either find the item or can conclude that it is not present.

```
var
     cell : PChainCell;
begin
     // See which chain should hold the value.
     cell := ListTops^[value mod NumChains].NextCell;
     while (cell <> nil) do
     begin
         if (cell^.Value >= value) then break;
         cell := cell^.NextCell;
     end;

     if (cell <> nil) then
         if (cell.Value = value) then
         begin
                 // Do something with the cell.
                 :
         end;
```

Keeping the lists sorted makes searches a little faster, but it does not address the real problem. The chains are long because the table is too full. A better though more time-consuming solution is to create a larger hash table and rehash the items into the new table so the new linked lists are smaller. This can be a lot of work, particularly if the lists are stored on a hard disk or other slow device rather than in memory.

Example program Chain implements a hash table with chaining. Enter the number of lists you want in the Table Creation area on the form. Check the Sort Lists box if you want the program to use sorted chains. Then click the Create Table button to create the hash table. You can enter new values in this section and click Create Table at any time to create a new hash table.

Because hash tables are often most interesting when they contain lots of items, program Chain allows you to create many random items at the same time. Enter the number of items you want to create and the maximum value those items should have in the Random Items area. Click the Create Items button to make the program add the random items to the hash table.

Finally, enter a value in the Search area. If you click the Add button, the program inserts the item in the hash table if it is not already there. If you click the Find button, the program locates the item in the table. If you click Remove, the program removes the item if present.

After finishing an add, find, or remove operation, the program displays the status of the operation at the bottom of the form. The program tells whether the operation succeeded and shows the number of items examined during the operation.

The status label also tells you the current average length of a successful probe sequence (when the item is in the table) and an unsuccessful probe sequence (when the item is not in the table). The program calculates this average by searching for every number between 1 and the largest number currently in the hash table, then computing the average probe sequence length.

Figure 11.2 shows program Chain after it has successfully located the item 475.

Buckets

Another way to handle collisions is to allocate a number of buckets, each of which can hold several data items. To add an item to the table, you map the item into a bucket and then insert the item in that bucket. If the bucket is full, you use an overflow policy to deal with the new item.

Figure 11.2 Program Chain.

The simplest overflow policy is to place all overflowed items into overflow buckets at the end of the array of normal buckets. When you need more overflow buckets, you must create a new, larger array of buckets and copy the current entries into the new array.

For example, to add a new item K to a hash table containing five buckets, first try to place it in bucket number K mod 5. If that bucket is full, place it in an overflow bucket.

To locate an item K in the table, calculate K mod 5 to see where the item belongs. Then search that bucket. If the item does not appear in the bucket and the bucket is not full, then the item is not present in the hash table. If the item does not appear in the bucket and the bucket is full, search the overflow buckets.

Figure 11.3 shows five buckets numbered 0 through 4 and one overflow bucket. Each bucket can hold five items. In this example, the following items have been added to the hash table in this order: 50, 13, 10, 72, 25, 46, 68, 30, 99, 85, 93, 65, 70. When items 65 and 70 were added, their buckets were already full so they were placed in the first overflow bucket.

To implement a bucket hashing scheme in Delphi, you can use an array of pointers to buckets that are themselves resizable arrays. Then when you need to resize the array, you only need to copy pointers to the old buckets into the new array instead of copying all of the bucket contents.

```
type
    TTableData = Longint;
    TBucket = array [0..1000000] of TTableData;
    PBucket = ^TBucket;
    TBucketArray = array [0..1000000] of PBucket;
    PBucketArray = ^TBucketArray;
```

To locate an item K, calculate the bucket number K mod NumBuckets. Then search that bucket until you find the item, an empty bucket entry, or the end of the

Figure 11.3 Hashing with buckets.

Buckets						Overflow
0	1	2	3	4		
50	46	72	13	99		65
10			68			70
25			93			
30						
85						

bucket. If you find the item, you are finished. If you find an unused entry, you know the item is not in the hash table and you are also finished. If you search the entire bucket and do not find the item or an unused entry, search the overflow buckets.

```
var
    bucket, pos : Integer;
begin
    // See what bucket it belongs in.
    bucket := (value mod NumBuckets);

    // Look for the item or an unused position.
    for pos := 0 to BucketSize - 1 do
    begin
        item_probes := item_probes + 1;
        if (Buckets^[bucket]^[pos] = UNUSED) then
        begin
            // It's not here.
            exit;
        end;
        if (Buckets^[bucket]^[pos] = value) then
        begin
            // We found it. Dome something with it here.
                :
            exit;
        end;
    end;

    // If we haven't found it, check the overflow buckets.
    for bucket := NumBuckets to MaxOverflow do
    begin
        bucket_probes := bucket_probes + 1;
        for pos := 0 to BucketSize - 1 do
        begin
            item_probes := item_probes + 1;
            if (Buckets^[bucket]^[pos] = UNUSED) then
            begin
                // It's not here.
                exit;
            end;
            if (Buckets^[bucket]^[pos] = value) then
            begin
                // We found it. Dome something with it here.
                    :
                exit;
            end;
```

```
        end;
    end;

    // If we still haven't found it, it's not here.
```

Example program Bucket demonstrates this scheme. This program is very similar to program Chain except it uses hashing with buckets instead of chaining. When this program reports probe lengths, it gives the number of buckets it examined followed by the number of items it examined within the buckets. Figure 11.4 shows the program after it successfully located item 793 in the first overflow bucket. In this example, the program examined seven items in two buckets.

Hash Tables on Disk

Most storage devices, like tape drives, floppy drives, and hard disks, can retrieve large chunks of data a block at a time. Usually this block is 512 or 1024 bytes long. It takes the device no more time to read one of these blocks of data than it takes it to read a single byte.

If you have a large hash table stored on a hard disk, you can use this fact to improve performance. Accessing data on a disk takes much longer than accessing it in memory. If you load all of the items in a bucket at once, you may be able to read them all in a single disk access. Once the items are loaded into memory, you can examine them much more quickly than you could if you had to read them one at a time from the disk.

Figure 11.4 Program Bucket.

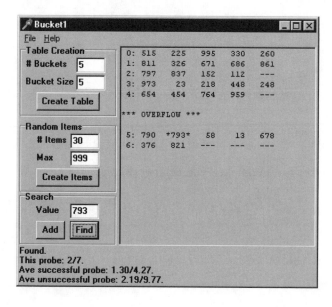

Define a bucket type as an array with a fixed number of elements.

```
const
     BUCKET_SIZE = 5;
type
     TTableData = Longint;
     TBucket = array [0..BUCKET_SIZE - 1] of TTableData;
```

Next, declare the data file to be a file of that type. For the system to know how large the records in the file are, the TBucket type must have a constant size. That is why the size of the buckets is compiled into the program.

```
var
     DataFile : file of TBucket;
```

To create a new data file, the program should use Delphi's AssignFile and Reset procedures. To create a new file, it should use AssignFile and Rewrite.

For convenience, you can write functions to read and write buckets. These functions read and write data from the global variable TheBucket that holds the data for a single bucket. Once you have loaded the data into this variable, you can search the items within the bucket in memory.

```
var
     TheBucket : TBucket;
```

```
// Get a bucket.
procedure GetBucket(num : Longint);
begin
     Seek(DataFile, num);
     Read(DataFile, TheBucket);
end;
```

```
// Save a bucket to file.
procedure PutBucket(num : Longint);
begin
     Seek(DataFile, num);
     Write(DataFile, TheBucket);
end;
```

Using procedures GetBucket and PutBucket, you can rewrite the hash table search procedure to read records from a file.

```
var
     bucket, pos : Integer;
begin
     // Get the bucket it belongs in.
     bucket := (value mod NumBuckets);
```

```
GetBucket(bucket);

// Look for the item or an unused position.
for pos := 0 to BUCKET_SIZE - 1 do
begin
    if (TheBucket[pos] = UNUSED) then
    begin
        // It's not here.
        exit;
    end;
    if (TheBucket[pos] = value) then
    begin
        // We found it. Do something with it here.
            :
        exit;
    end;
end;

// If we haven't found it, check the overflow buckets.
for bucket := NumBuckets to MaxOverflow do
begin
    bucket_probes := bucket_probes + 1;
    GetBucket(bucket);

    for pos := 0 to BUCKET_SIZE - 1 do
    begin
        item_probes := item_probes + 1;
        if (TheBucket[pos] = UNUSED) then
        begin
            // It's not here.
            exit;
        end;
        if (TheBucket[pos] = value) then
        begin
            // We found it. Do something with it here.
                :
            exit;
        end;
    end;
end;

// If we still haven't found it, it's not here.
    :
```

Example program Bucket2 is similar to program Bucket except it stores its buckets on disk. It also does not compute and display average probe sequence lengths because those calculations would require many disk accesses and would slow the program greatly.

Because bucket accesses occur on disk and item accesses occur in memory, the number of buckets accessed is much more important in determining the program's runtime than the total number of items examined.

Each bucket in program Bucket2 can hold up to five items. This makes it easy for you to fill the buckets until they overflow. In a real program, you should try to fit as many items as possible into a bucket while keeping the bucket size a multiple of your disk drive's natural block size. For example, you might decide to read and write data in blocks of 1024 bytes. The following code shows how a program might define buckets using a small employee record.

```
type
    TTableData = record
        LastName   : String[20];
        FirstName  : String[20];
        EmployeeID : Integer;
    end;
const
    ITEM_SIZE = SizeOf(TTableData);
    ITEMS_PER_BUCKET = 1024 div ITEM_SIZE;
type
    TBucket = array [0..ITEMS_PER_BUCKET - 1] of TTableData;
```

Putting more items in each bucket allows you to read more data in a single disk access. It also allows the table to hold more items before you need to use overflow buckets. Accessing overflow buckets requires extra disk accesses, so you should avoid using them whenever possible.

On the other hand, if the buckets are large, they may contain a lot of unused entries. If the data items are not evenly distributed among the buckets, some buckets may overflow and others may be nearly empty. A different arrangement with a larger number of smaller buckets might reduce this problem. Even though some data items will still overflow and some buckets will be nearly empty, the nearly empty buckets will be smaller so they will not contain as many unused entries.

Figure 11.5 shows two bucket arrangements holding the same data. The arrangement on the top uses five buckets containing five items each. It holds all of the data with no overflow buckets and 12 unused item entries. The arrangement on the bottom uses 10 buckets containing two items each. It holds the items with one overflow bucket and contains only nine unused item entries.

This is an example of a space versus time trade-off. In the first arrangement, all the items are located in normal (nonoverflow) buckets so that you can locate

Figure 11.5 Two different bucket arrangements.

Buckets

0	1	2	3	4
50	46	72	18	
10		57	68	
25			93	
35			28	
65			73	

Buckets

0	1	2	3	4	5	6	7	8	9	Overflow
50		72	93		25	46	57	18		28
10			73		35			68		65

them all quickly. The second arrangement saves space but places some of the items in overflow buckets that take longer to access.

Bucket Chaining

A slightly different way to manage full buckets is to chain them to overflow buckets. Each full bucket gets its own set of overflow buckets rather than having all overflow buckets shared. When you search for an item in a full bucket, you do not need to examine any items that have overflowed from other buckets. If there has been a lot of overflow, this can save quite a bit of time.

Figure 11.6 shows the same data in two different hashing schemes. In the top arrangement, items that overflow are added to common overflow buckets. To locate the items 32 or 30, you must access three buckets. First, you examine the bucket in which the item normally belongs. The item is not there so you then examine the first overflow bucket. The item is not there either so you must examine the second overflow bucket. There you finally find the item.

In the bottom arrangement, full buckets are linked to their own overflow buckets. In this arrangement, you can locate every item after accessing, at most, two buckets. As before, you start by examining the bucket where the item normally belongs. If you do not find the item there, you examine that bucket's linked list of overflow buckets. In this example, you need to check only one overflow bucket to find the item.

If the hash table contains many items in its overflow buckets, chaining the overflow buckets may save a lot of time. Suppose you have a moderately large

Figure 11.6 Linked overflow buckets.

hash table containing 1000 buckets holding 10 items each. Suppose also that you have 1000 items in overflow buckets. To hold all of those overflow items, you would need 100 overflow buckets. To locate one of the last items in the overflow buckets, you would have to examine 101 buckets.

Even worse, suppose you wanted to locate an item K that is not in the table but that maps to a full bucket. You would need to search all 100 overflow buckets before you learned that the item was not in the table. If your program often searches for items that are not in the table, it will spend a huge amount of time looking through the overflow buckets.

If you chain overflow buckets, and if the key values are reasonably distributed, you will be able to locate items much more quickly. If the largest number of items that have overflowed out of any single bucket is 10, each bucket will have at most one overflow bucket. In that case, you can locate any item or determine that an item is not in the table by examining, at most, two buckets.

On the other hand, if the hash table is just a little too full, many buckets may have overflow buckets containing only one or two items. To continue this example, suppose 11 items map into each bucket. Because each bucket holds only 10 items, every normal bucket would need an overflow bucket. In this case, you would need 1000 overflow buckets, each containing a single item. Between them all, these overflow buckets would contain 900 unused entries.

This is another example of a space versus time trade-off. Chaining buckets allows you to add and locate items more quickly, but it may also fill the hash table with unused space. Of course, you could probably avoid the problem completely by creating a new, larger hash table and rehashing all the table entries.

Removing Items

Although it is not as easy to remove items from buckets as it is to remove them from chains, it is still possible. First, locate the item you want to remove in the hash table. If its bucket is not full, replace the target item with the last item in the bucket. This will ensure that all of the nonempty bucket entries are stored at the front of the bucket. Later, when you search for an item in the bucket, if you find an unused item, you can conclude that the item is not in the table.

If the bucket containing the target item is full, you must search the overflow buckets to find an item that can replace the target item in this bucket. If none of the items in the overflow buckets belong in this bucket, replace the target item with the last item in the bucket, leaving the bucket's last entry empty.

Otherwise, if there is an item in the overflow buckets that belongs in this bucket, move the chosen overflow item into the target bucket in place of the target item. That will leave a hole in the overflow bucket, but that is easy to fix. Just take the last item from the last overflow bucket and move it to fill in the hole.

Figure 11.7 illustrates the process of removing an item from a full bucket. First, item 24 is removed from bucket 0. Because bucket 0 was full, you must look for an item in the overflow buckets that you can move into bucket 0. In this case, bucket 0 holds all of the even items, so any even item in the overflow buckets will do. The first even item in the overflow buckets is item 14, so you can replace item 24 in bucket 0 with item 14.

That leaves a hole in the third position in the first overflow bucket. Fill in the hole by replacing item 14 with the last item in the last overflow bucket, in this case, item 79. At this point, the hash table is again ready for use.

An alternative method for removing an item is to mark the item as having been removed but to leave it in its bucket. To locate items in that bucket, you should ignore removed items. Later, when you add new items to that bucket, you can reuse the removed item's position.

Figure 11.7 Removing an item from a full bucket.

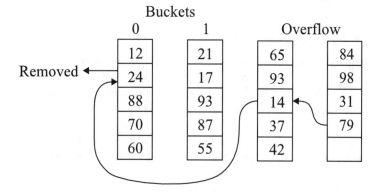

Marking an item as removed is faster and easier than actually removing it from the hash table, but eventually, the table may become full of unused entries. If you add a bunch of items to the hash table and then remove most of them in first-in-first-out order, the buckets will become bottom heavy. Most of the real data will be in the bottom of the buckets and in the overflow buckets. Adding new items to the table will be easy, but you will waste a fair amount of time skipping removed entries when you search for an item.

As a compromise, when you remove an item from a bucket, you can move the last item in the bucket into the emptied position and then mark the last item in the bucket as removed. Then when you search a bucket, you can stop looking through that bucket if you encounter an item that has been marked as removed. You would then search the overflow buckets if there are any.

Advantages and Disadvantages of Buckets

Adding or locating an item in a hash table with buckets is relatively fast, even when the table is completely full. In fact, a hash table using buckets will usually be faster than a hash table using chaining (chaining as described in the previous section, not bucket chaining). If the hash table is stored on a hard disk, a bucket scheme can read an entire bucket of data in one disk access. With chaining, the next item in a chain may not be anywhere near the previous one on the disk. You would need one disk access every time you needed to examine an item.

Removing an item from a table using buckets is harder than removing an item from a table using chaining. To remove an item from a bucket that is full, you may need to examine all the overflow buckets to find a suitable replacement item.

A final advantage to a hash table that uses buckets stored on disk is that it is easy to extend the table when it becomes full. When all the overflow buckets are full, you simply create a new overflow bucket at the end of the file.

If you extend the table in this way too many times, a large fraction of the data will eventually be stored in the overflow buckets. Then to find or insert an item, you must examine many buckets, and performance will suffer. In that case, it may be better to create a new hash table with more initial buckets and rehash the items than to expand the overly full table.

Open Addressing

Sometimes the data items you need to store are too big to fit conveniently in buckets. If you need a list of 1000 items, each occupying 1Mb of disk space, it would be difficult to use buckets that could hold more than one or two items. If the buckets only hold one or two items, you must examine many buckets to add or locate an item.

In open addressing, you use a hashing function to map data items directly into positions in an array. For example, you could use an array with dimensions

0 to 99 for a hash table. Then for a hashing function you could map the key value K to array position K mod 100. You would insert the value 1723 in the table at position 23. Later, if you wanted to locate item 1723, you would look for it at position 23.

Different open addressing schemes use different methods for generating probe sequences. The following sections examine three of the more important methods: *linear probing*, *quadratic probing*, and *pseudo-random probing*.

Linear Probing

When you map a new item into an array position that is already in use, you can simply look through the array from that point until you come to an unoccupied position. This collision resolution policy is called *linear probing* because you search through the table in a linear fashion.

Consider again the example where you have an array dimensioned 0 to 99 and the hashing function maps K to position K mod 100. To insert the item 1723, you first examine array position 23. If that position is full, you try position 24. If it is also in use, you try positions 25, 26, 27, and so on until you find an empty position.

To insert a new item into a hash table, you follow that item's probe sequence until you find an unused entry. To locate an item in the table, you follow the item's probe sequence until you find the item or you find an unused entry. If you find an unused entry first, you know the item is not in the hash table.

You could write a combined hashing and probing function as:

```
Hash(K, P) = (K + P) mod 100        where P = 0, 1, 2, ...
```

Here P is the number of the item in the probe sequence for K. In other words, to hash item K you try Hash(K, 0), Hash(K, 1), Hash(K, 2), and so on until you find an empty position.

You can generalize this idea to build a table of size N using an array dimensioned from 0 to N – 1. The hashing function is:

```
Hash(K, P) = (K + P) mod N          where P = 0, 1, 2, ...
```

The following code shows how you can locate an item using linear probing in Delphi.

```
type
    TLinearReturnValue =
        (linInserted, linFound, linNotFound, linTableFull);

function FindItem(value : TTableData; var probes : Integer)
    : TLinearReturnValue;
var
    new_value : TTableData;
    pos       : Integer;
```

```
begin
    probes := 1;
    pos := (value mod TableSize);
    repeat // Repeat infinitely.
        new_value := HashTable^[pos];

        // If we found the value, we're done.
        if (new_value = value) then
        begin
            Result := linFound;
            exit;
        end;

        // If the entry is unused, the value is not here.
        if (new_value = UNUSED) then
        begin
            Result := linNotFound;
            exit;
        end;

        // Try the next location in the probe sequence.
        pos := (pos + 1) mod TableSize;
        probes := probes + 1;

        // See if we have checked every entry.
        if (probes > TableSize) then
        begin
            Result := linNotFound;
            exit;
        end;
    until (False); // End infinite loop looking for the value.
end;
```

Example program Linear demonstrates open addressing with linear probing. By filling in the Table Size field and clicking the Create Table button, you can create hash tables of different sizes. You can then enter the value of an item and click the Add or Find button to insert or locate the item in the table.

To add several random values to the table all at once, enter the number of items you want to add and the maximum value they should have in the Random Items area. Then click the Create Items button to make the program add the items to the table.

After the program completes each operation, it displays the status of the operation (whether it succeeded or not) and the length of the probe sequence it just followed. It also displays the average lengths of a successful and an unsuccessful probe sequence. The program computes the average probe sequence lengths by searching for every value between 1 and the largest value in the table at that time.

Table 11.1 shows the average lengths of successful and unsuccessful probe sequences produced by program Linear for a table with 100 entries and items in the range 1 to 999. The table shows that the algorithm's performance degrades as the table becomes full. Whether the performance is acceptable to you depends on how you use the table. If a program spends most of its time searching for values that are in the table, performance will be reasonably good even when the table is quite full. If a program often searches for values that are not in the table, performance will be poor if the table is too full.

As a rule, hashing provides reasonable performance without too much wasted space when the table is 50 to 75 percent full. If the table is more than 75 percent full, performance suffers. If the table is less than 50 percent full, it occupies more space than it really needs. This makes open addressing a good example of a space versus time trade-off. By making a hash table larger, you can decrease the time needed to insert and locate items.

Primary Clustering

Linear probing has an unfortunate *primary clustering* property. After you insert many items into the table, the items tend to cluster together to form large groups. When you add more items, the new items tend to collide with the clusters. Then you need to search past the cluster before you find an empty position in the table.

Table 11.1 Lengths of Successful and Unsuccessful Probe Sequences

Entries Used	Successful	Unsuccessful
10	1.10	1.12
20	1.15	1.26
30	1.20	1.50
40	1.35	1.83
50	1.92	2.64
60	2.03	3.35
70	2.61	5.17
80	3.41	8.00
90	3.81	10.74
100	6.51	100.00

To see how clusters form, suppose you begin with an empty hash table that can hold N entries. If you pick a number at random and insert it into the table, there will be a 1 / N chance that the item will end up in any given position P in the table.

When you insert a second randomly chosen item, there is a 1 / N chance that the item maps to the same position P. This collision forces you to put the item in position P + 1. There is also a 1 / N chance that the item maps directly to position P + 1 and a 1 / N chance that it maps to position P – 1. In all three of these cases, the new item ends up next to the previously inserted item. There is a total chance of 3 / N that the new item winds up next to the previous one, starting a small cluster. These odds are slightly greater than the 1 / N odds that the item ends up in any other particular position.

Once a cluster starts to grow, the chance of subsequent items landing on or next to the cluster increases. When a cluster contains two items, there is a 4 / N chance that the next item will add to the cluster. When it contains four items, there is a 6 / N chance that the cluster will grow, and so forth.

Worse still, once a cluster starts to grow, it continues to grow until it bumps into an adjacent cluster. The two clusters join to form an even larger cluster that grows even faster, meets other clusters, and forms still larger clusters.

Ideally, if a hash table is half full, the items in the table will occupy every other array position. Then there is a 50 percent chance that the algorithm immediately finds an empty position for the next item added. There is also a 50 percent chance that it would find an empty position after examining only two table positions. The average probe sequence length is 0.5 * 1 + 0.5 * 2 = 1.5.

In the worst case, all of the items in the table will be grouped together in one giant cluster. There is still a 50 percent chance that the algorithm immediately finds an empty position for the next item added. When it does not find an empty position, however, the algorithm takes much longer to find an open position. If the item lands on the first position in the cluster, the algorithm must search past all the entries in the cluster to find an open position. On average, it takes much longer to insert an item in this arrangement than it does if the items are evenly spaced throughout the hash table.

In practice, the amount of clustering will be somewhere between these extremes. You can use program Linear to see the clustering effect. Run the program and build a hash table with 100 entries. Then randomly add 50 items with values up to 999. You will notice that several clusters have formed. In one test, 38 of the 50 items were part of clusters. If you add another 25 items to the table, most of the items will be part of clusters. In another test, 70 of the 75 items were grouped in clusters.

Ordered Linear Probing

When you perform an exhaustive search of a sorted list, you can stop whenever you find an item with value greater than the value you are seeking. Since you have passed the position where the target item would be if it were in the list, the item must not be present.

You can use a similar idea when searching a hash table. Suppose you can arrange the items in the hash table so the values along every probe sequence are arranged in increasing order. Then as you follow a probe sequence looking for an item, you can stop if you ever find an item greater than the target value. In that case, you have passed the position where the item belongs, so you know it is not in the table.

```
function FindItem(value : TTableData; var probes : Integer)
    : TOrderedReturnValue;
var
    new_value : TTableData;
    pos       : Integer;
begin
    probes := 1;
    pos := (value mod TableSize);
    repeat // Repeat infinitely.
        new_value := HashTable^[pos];

        // If we found the value, we're done.
        if (new_value = value) then
        begin
            Result := ordFound;
            exit;
        end;

        // If the entry is unused, the value is not here.
        if (new_value = UNUSED) then
        begin
            Result := ordNotFound;
            exit;
        end;

        // See if the test entry is larger than the new one.
        if (new_value > value) then
        begin
            Result := ordNotFound;
            exit;
        end;

        // Try the next location in the probe sequence.
        pos := (pos + 1) mod TableSize;
        probes := probes + 1;
```

```
    // See if we have checked every entry.
    if (probes > TableSize) then
    begin
        Result := ordNotFound;
        exit;
    end;
until (False); // End infinite loop looking for the value.
end;
```

For this method to work, you must arrange the items in the hash table so that you encounter them in increasing order whenever you follow a probe sequence. There is a fairly simple method for inserting items that guarantees this arrangement.

When you insert a new item into the table, follow its probe sequence. If you find an empty position, insert the item at that position and you are finished. If you come to an item with value larger than the new item, swap the two items. Then follow the probe sequence for the larger item to find a new location for it in the table. As you search for a new position for the larger item, you may come to another item that is larger still. Swap those items and go on to find a new location for the new, even larger item. Continue this process, possibly swapping several items, until you eventually find an empty position to hold the item you are currently placing.

```
function InsertItem(value : TTableData; var probes : Integer)
    : TOrderedReturnValue;
var
    new_value : TTableData;
    pos       : Integer;
begin
    probes := 1;
    pos := (value mod TableSize);
    repeat // Repeat infinitely.
        new_value := HashTable^[pos];

        // If we found the value, it's already here.
        if (new_value = value) then
        begin
            Result := ordFound;
            exit;
        end;

        // If the entry is unused, the value belongs here.
        if (new_value = UNUSED) then
        begin
```

```
        HashTable^[pos] := value;
        Result := ordInserted;
        NumUnused := NumUnused - 1;
        exit;
    end;


    // See if the test entry is larger than the new one.
    if (new_value > value) then
    begin
            // Swap them and continue.
        HashTable^[pos] := value;
        value := new_value;
    end;


    // Try the next location in the probe sequence.
    pos := (pos + 1) mod TableSize;
    probes := probes + 1;


    // See if we have checked every entry.
    if (probes > TableSize) then
    begin
        Result := ordTableFull
        exit;
    end;
    until (False); // End infinite loop looking for the value.
end;
```

Example program Ordered demonstrates open addressing with ordered linear probing. It is identical to program Linear except it uses an ordered hash table.

Table 11.2 shows average probe sequence lengths of successful and unsuccessful searches using linear and ordered linear probing. The average lengths of successful searches are similar for the two methods. For unsuccessful searches, however, ordered probing is significantly faster. The difference is particularly noticeable when the hash table is more than about 70 percent full.

Both methods require roughly the same number of steps to insert a new item. To add item K to the table, each method starts at position K mod NumEntries and moves through the hash table until it finds an empty position. During ordered hashing, you may need to swap the item you are inserting with others in its probe sequence. If the items are large records, this may be quite time consuming, particularly if the records are stored on a hard disk or other slow storage device.

Ordered linear probing is definitely a better choice if you expect your program to make many unsuccessful searches. If your program will usually search for items that are in the hash table, or if the items in the table are large and difficult to move, you may get better performance using unordered linear probing.

Table 11.2 Lengths of Searches Using Linear and Ordered Linear Probing

Entries Used	Linear Successful	Linear Unsuccessful	Ordered Successful	Ordered Unsuccessful
10	1.10	1.12	1.10	1.04
20	1.15	1.26	1.10	1.09
30	1.20	1.50	1.23	1.13
40	1.35	1.83	1.38	1.23
50	1.92	2.64	1.36	1.35
60	2.03	3.35	1.53	1.56
70	2.61	5.17	1.64	1.76
80	3.41	8.00	2.04	2.18
90	3.81	10.74	3.42	3.88
100	6.51	100.00	6.16	6.20

Quadratic Probing

One way to reduce primary clustering is to use a hashing function like this one:

$Hash(K, P) = (K + P^2) \bmod N$ where $P = 0, 1, 2, \ldots$

Suppose, while inserting an item into a hash table, you map the item into a cluster of other items. If the item maps to a position near the beginning of the cluster, you will have several more collisions before you find an empty position for the item. As the parameter P in the probe function grows, the value of this function changes quickly. That means the final position where you place the item will probably not be adjacent to the cluster.

Figure 11.8 shows a hash table containing a large cluster of items. It also shows the probe sequences that result when you try to insert two different items into positions occupied by the cluster. Both of these probe sequences end in a final position that is not adjacent to the cluster, so the cluster does not grow when you insert these items.

The following code shows how to locate an item using quadratic probing.

```
function FindItem(value : TTableData; var probes : Integer)
     : TQuadraticReturnValue;
var
    new_value : TTableData;
```

Figure 11.8 Quadratic probing.

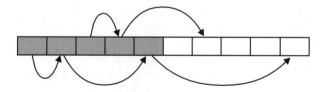

```
    pos         : Integer;
begin
    probes := 1;
    pos := (value mod TableSize);
    repeat // Repeat infinitely.
        new_value := HashTable^[pos];

        // If we found the value, we're done.
        if (new_value = value) then
        begin
            Result := qFound;
            exit;
        end;

        // If the entry is unused, it's not here.
        if (new_value = UNUSED) then
        begin
            Result := qNotFound;
            exit;
        end;

        // Try the next location in the probe sequence.
        pos := (value + probes * probes) mod TableSize;
        probes := probes + 1;

        // See if we have checked every entry.
        if (probes > TableSize) then
        begin
            Result := qNotFound;
            exit;
        end;
    until (False); // End infinite loop looking for the value.
end;
```

Example program Quad demonstrates open addressing with quadratic probing. It is similar to program Linear except it uses quadratic rather than linear probing.

Table 11.3 shows average probe sequence lengths produced by programs Linear and Quad for a hash table with 100 entries and items ranging in value from 1 to 999. Quadratic probing generally gives better results.

Quadratic probing does have some disadvantages. Because of the way the probe sequence is generated, you cannot guarantee that it will visit every item in the table. That means you may sometimes be unable to insert an item even though the table is not completely full. For example, consider a small hash table that holds only six entries. The probe sequence for the number 3 is:

```
3
3 +  1² =    4 = 4 (mod 6)
3 +  2² =    7 = 1 (mod 6)
3 +  3² =   12 = 0 (mod 6)
3 +  4² =   19 = 1 (mod 6)
3 +  5² =   28 = 4 (mod 6)
3 +  6² =   39 = 3 (mod 6)
3 +  7² =   52 = 4 (mod 6)
3 +  8² =   67 = 1 (mod 6)
3 +  9² =   84 = 0 (mod 6)
3 + 10² =  103 = 1 (mod 6)
Etc.
```

Table 11.3 Lengths of Searches Using Linear and Quadratic Probing

Entries Used	Linear Successful	Linear Unsuccessful	Quadratic Successful	Quadratic Unsuccessful
10	1.10	1.12	1.00	1.11
20	1.15	1.26	1.10	1.21
30	1.20	1.50	1.33	1.44
40	1.35	1.83	1.77	1.75
50	1.92	2.64	1.80	2.14
60	2.03	3.35	1.88	2.67
70	2.61	5.17	2.09	3.43
80	3.41	8.00	2.30	5.05
90	3.81	10.74	2.77	15.03
100	6.51	100.00	3.79	101.00

This probe sequence visits the positions 1 and 4 twice each before visiting position 3, and it never visits positions 2 and 5. To see this effect, create a six-entry hash table using program Quad. Then add the items 1, 3, 4, 6, and 9 in that order. The program will tell you that the table is full even though there are two unused entries. The probe sequence for the item 9 does not visit positions 2 and 5, so the program cannot insert the new item in the table.

It can be shown that a quadratic probe sequence will visit at least N / 2 of the table entries if the size of the table N is prime. While this guarantees some level of performance, it may still become a problem when the table is almost full. Because performance drops when the table is almost full anyway, you are probably better off enlarging the hash table rather than worrying about not being able to find the last empty entries.

A more subtle problem with quadratic probing is that, while it eliminates primary clustering, it allows a similar problem called *secondary clustering*. If two items initially hash to the same location, they follow the same probe sequence. If many items initially map to the same table location, they form a secondary cluster that is spread out within the hash table. When a new item with the same initial value appears, it must follow a long probe sequence before it gets past the other items in the secondary cluster.

Figure 11.9 shows a hash table that can hold 10 entries. The table contains the items 2, 12, 22, and 32, all of which map initially to position 2. If you try to add the item 42 to the table, you must follow a long probe sequence that visits each of these other items' positions before finding an empty spot.

Pseudo-Random Probing

Clustering occurs when items that map into a cluster join the cluster. Secondary clustering occurs when items that initially collide at the same location follow the same probe sequence to form a secondary cluster spread through the hash table. You can eliminate both of these effects if you can make different items follow different probe sequences, even if they initially map to the same position.

One way to do this is to use a pseudo-random number generator to provide the probe sequence. To compute the probe sequence of an item, use the item's value to initialize the number generator. Then use the successive numbers produced by the generator to build the probe sequence. This is called *pseudo-random probing*.

Figure 11.9 Secondary clustering.

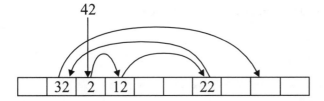

Later, when you want to locate an item in the hash table, reinitialize the random number generator using the item's value. The generator will then produce the same sequence of numbers you used to insert the item into the table. Using these numbers, you can recreate the original probe sequence and find the item.

If your random number generator is good, different item values will produce different random numbers and, therefore, different probe sequences. Even if two item values initially map to the same position, the next positions in their probe sequences will probably be different. In this case, your hash table will not suffer from clustering or secondary clustering.

You can initialize Delphi's random number generator with a seed value using the RandSeed statement. The Random statement generates the same sequence of numbers every time it is initialized with the same seed value.

The following code shows how you can locate an item using pseudo-random probing.

```
function FindOrInsert(value : TTableData; var probes : Integer)
    : TRandomReturnValue;
var
    new_value : TTableData;
    pos       : Integer;
begin
    // Seed the random number generator.
    RandSeed := value;

    probes := 0;
    repeat // Repeat infinitely.
        // Generate the next value in the pseudo-random
        // probe sequence.
        pos := Random(TableSize);
        probes := probes + 1;
        new_value := HashTable^[pos];

        // If we found the value, we're done.
        if (new_value = value) then
        begin
            Result := rndFound;
            exit;
        end;

        // If the entry is unused, it's not here.
        if (new_value = UNUSED) then
        begin
            Result := rndNotFound;
            exit;
```

```
        end;

            // See if we have checked every entry.
        if (probes > TableSize) then
        begin
            Result := rndNotFound;
            exit;
        end;
    until (False); // End infinite loop looking for the value.
end;
```

Example program Rand demonstrates open addressing with pseudo-random probing. It is the same as programs Linear and Quad except it uses pseudo-random rather than linear or quadratic probing.

Table 11.4 shows approximate average probe sequence lengths produced by programs Quad and Rand for a hash table with 100 entries and items ranging from 1 to 999. Pseudo-random probing generally gives the best results, though the difference between quadratic and pseudo-random probing is not as great as the difference between linear and quadratic probing.

Pseudo-random probing also has its drawbacks. Because the probe sequence is chosen pseudo-randomly, you cannot be certain how quickly the algorithm will

Table 11.4 Lengths of Searches Using Quadratic and Pseudo-Random Probing

Entries Used	Quadratic Successful	Quadratic Unsuccessful	Pseudo-Random Successful	Pseudo-Random Unsuccessful
10	1.00	1.11	1.00	1.10
20	1.10	1.21	1.15	1.24
30	1.33	1.44	1.13	1.41
40	1.77	1.75	1.23	1.63
50	1.80	2.14	1.36	1.91
60	1.88	2.67	1.47	2.37
70	2.09	3.43	1.70	3.17
80	2.30	5.05	1.90	4.70
90	2.77	15.03	2.30	9.69
100	3.79	101.00	3.79	101.00

visit every item in the table. If the table is small compared to the number of possible pseudo-random values, there is a chance that the probe sequence will visit the same value repeatedly before it visits other values in the table. It is also possible that a probe sequence will completely miss a table entry, so it will be unable to insert an item even when the table has room.

As is the case with quadratic probing, these effects cause trouble only when the table is mostly full. At that point, enlarging the table provides a much greater performance improvement than worrying about finding the last unused table entries.

Removing Items

Removing items from a hash table that uses open addressing is not as easy as removing items from a table that uses chains or buckets. You cannot simply remove an item from the table because that item may lie in the probe sequence for some other item.

Suppose item A is in the probe sequence for item B. If you remove A from the table, you will no longer be able to find item B. When you search for B, you will find the empty position left by the removal of item A, so you will incorrectly conclude that item B is not in the table.

Instead of removing the item from the hash table, you can mark it as removed. If you later find a position marked as removed while you are adding a new item to the table, you can reuse that position. If you encounter a marked item while you are searching for another item, ignore the removed item and continue following the probe sequence.

After you have marked many items as removed, the hash table may become full of garbage. When you search for items, you will spend a great deal of time skipping over these removed items. Eventually, you may want to rehash the table to reclaim the unused space.

Rehashing

To free removed entries in a hash table, you can rehash the table in place. For this algorithm to work, you must have some way to tell whether an item has already been rehashed. One way to do this is to create an array of Boolean variables that indicate the entries that have not yet been rehashed.

Begin by initializing all these Boolean values to True to indicate that all of the items have yet to be rehashed. Then pass through the table looking for entries that are not marked as removed and that have not yet been rehashed.

When you find such an item, remove it from the table and rehash it. Follow the normal probe sequence for the item. If you come to an entry that is empty or marked as removed, deposit the item there, mark it as rehashed, and continue looking for other items that have not yet been rehashed.

While rehashing an item, if you find an item that is already marked as rehashed, continue following the item's probe sequence.

If you come to an item that has not yet been rehashed, swap the two items, mark the position as rehashed, and start the process over to rehash the new item.

```
type
    TBoolArray = array [0..1000000] of Boolean;
    PBoolArray = ^TBoolArray;

procedure Rehash;
var
    not_rehashed       : PBoolArray;
    i, pos             : Integer;
    value, new_value : TTableData;
begin
    // Allocate space for the rehashed flags.
    GetMem(not_rehashed, TableSize * SizeOf(Boolean));

    // Mark all items as not rehashed.
    for i := 0 to TableSize - 1 do not_rehashed^[i] := True;

    // Look for unrehashed items.
    for i := 0 to TableSize - 1 do
    begin
        if (not_rehashed^[i]) then
        begin
            value := HashTable^[i];
            HashTable^[i] := UNUSED;

            // Don't rehash deleted or unused entries.
            if ((value = DELETED) or (value = UNUSED)) then
                continue;

            // Otherwise follow this value's probe sequence
            // until we find an empty, deleted, or an
            // unrehashed item.
            pos := value mod TableSize;
            repeat // Repeat infinitely.
                new_value := HashTable^[pos];

                // If this spot is empty or deleted, place
                // the item here.
                if ((new_value = UNUSED) or (new_value = DELETED))
then
                begin
                    HashTable^[pos] := value;
                    not_rehashed^[pos] := False;
                    break;
                end;
```

```
        // If this spot holds a non-rehashed item,
        // swap them and continue.
    if (not_rehashed^[pos]) then
    begin
        HashTable^[pos] := value;
        not_rehashed^[pos] := False;
        value := new_value;
        pos := value mod TableSize;
    end else
        pos := (pos + 1) mod TableSize;
    until (False); // End infinite loop.
    end; // End if (not_rehashed^[i]) then ...
    end; // End for i := 0 to TableSize - 1 do ...
end;
```

Resizing Hash Tables

If a hash table becomes too full, performance drops dramatically. In that case, you might want to enlarge the table to improve performance and make room for more entries. Conversely, if a hash table contains very few entries, you might want to make it smaller to free some memory. Using techniques similar to those used to rehash a table in place, you can expand or shrink a hash table.

To resize a hash table, allocate a new hash table array. Then rehash the items, moving them into the new table. Example program Rehash uses open addressing with linear probing. It is similar to program Linear, but it also allows you to mark objects as removed and to rehash the table.

Summary

The different kinds of hash tables described in this chapter each have strengths and weaknesses.

Hash tables that use chaining or buckets are easy to enlarge and allow easy removal of items. Buckets can also take advantage of disk behavior by loading many data items with a single disk access. Both of these methods, however, are slower than open addressing techniques.

Linear probing is simple and allows you to insert and locate items in the hash table fairly quickly. Ordered linear probing allows you to determine that an item is not in the table more quickly than does unordered linear probing. On the other hand, adding items to the table using ordered linear probing is more difficult.

Quadratic probing prevents clustering that affects linear probing, so it gives better performance. Pseudo-random probing avoids clustering and secondary clustering, so it gives better performance still.

Table 11.5 shows a summary of the advantages and disadvantages of the various hashing methods.

Table 11.5 Advantages and Disadvantages of Hashing Methods

Method	Advantages	Disadvantages
Chaining	Easy to enlarge Easy to remove items Contains no unused entries	Slows when lists grow long
Buckets	Easy to enlarge Easy to remove items Works naturally on disks	Slow when there are many overflow buckets Contains unused entries
Bucket chaining	Easy to enlarge Easy to remove items Works naturally on disks	Contains more unused entries
Linear probing	Fast access	Hard to enlarge Hard to remove items Contains unused entries
Ordered linear probing	Fast access Short, unsuccessful probes	Hard to enlarge Hard to remove items Takes longer to insert items Contains unused entries
Quadratic probing	Faster access	Hard to enlarge Hard to remove items Contains unused entries
Pseudo-random probing	Fastest access	Hard to enlarge Hard to remove items Contains unused entries

Which hashing technique is best for a given application depends on the data and the ways in which the data will be used. The different schemes offer different trade-offs in size, speed, and ease of modification. Table 11.5 can help you pick the algorithm that best meets your needs.

NETWORK ALGORITHMS

Chapter 6, "Trees," and Chapter 7, "Balanced Trees," discuss tree algorithms. This chapter covers the more general topic of networks. Networks play important roles in many applications. You can use them to model network-like objects such as streets, telephone facilities, power lines, water pipes, sewers, storm drains, airline connections, and railroad lines. You can also use networks in less obvious ways to solve problems such as districting, critical path scheduling, crew scheduling, and work assignment.

Definitions

Like a tree, a *network* or *graph* is a set of *nodes* connected by a set of *edges* or *links*. Unlike a tree, a network has no concept of ancestors and descendants. Nodes connected to other nodes are neighbors rather than parents or children.

The links in a network may each have an associated direction, in which case the network is called a *directed network*. Each link may also have an associated *cost*. In a street network, for example, the cost might be the time it takes to drive across the section of road represented by the link. In a telephone network, the cost might be the amount of electrical loss across the cable represented by the link. Figure 12.1 shows a small directed network where numbers next to the links show the links' costs.

A *path* between nodes A and B is a series of links that connects the two nodes. If there is at most one link between any two nodes in the network, a path can be described uniquely by listing the nodes along the path. Because that is usually easier to visualize, paths are described in this way if possible. In Figure 12.1, the path containing the nodes B, E, F, G, E, and D is a path connecting nodes B and D.

A *cycle* is a path that connects a node to itself. The path E, F, G, E in Figure 12.1 is a cycle. A path is *simple* if it contains no cycles. The path B, E, F, G, E, D is not simple because it contains the cycle E, F, G, E.

If there is any path between two nodes, then there must be a simple path between the two nodes. You can find this path by removing any cycles from the original path. For example, if you replace the cycle E, F, G, E with the node E in

Figure 12.1 A directed network with link costs.

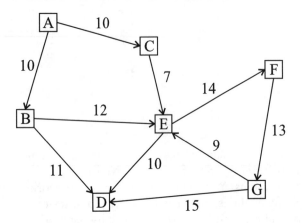

the nonsimple path B, E, F, G, E, D, you get the simple path B, E, D connecting nodes B and D.

A network is *connected* if there is at least one path from every node in the network to every other node. In a directed network, it is not always obvious whether the network is connected. In Figure 12.2, the network on the left is connected. The network on the right is not because there is no path from node E to node C.

Network Representations

Chapter 6, "Trees," described several representations for trees. Most of those representations are useful for manipulating networks as well. For example, the fat node, child list (neighbor list for networks), and forward star representations can all be used to store networks. See Chapter 6 for an explanation of these representations.

Figure 12.2 Connected (left) and disconnected (right) networks.

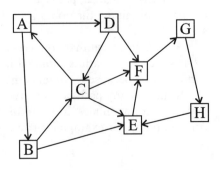

Which network representation is best depends on the application. A fat node representation works well if each node in the network is connected to a limited number of edges. A neighbor list strategy provides more flexibility than a fat node approach. Forward star representations, while harder to modify than the others, may require less storage space.

In addition to these options, several explicit link variations can make certain types of networks easier to manage. These representations use one class or record type to represent nodes and another to represent links. The link class or record makes it easier to work with link properties such as costs.

For example, a directed network with link costs might use the following node and link types. Each link keeps pointers to the nodes where it starts and ends. Each node keeps a linked list of links leaving it. Each node also has a NextNode pointer so the program can keep all of the nodes in the network in a linked list.

```
type
    PLink = ^TLink;
    PNode = ^TNode;
    TLink = record
        ToNode       : PNode;     // The link's end node.
        Cost         : Integer;   // The cost.
        NextLink     : PLink;     // Next link in start node's list
                                  // of links.
    end;
    TNode = record
        Id           : Integer;   // Node ID.
        X            : Integer;   // Position.
        Y            : Integer;
        LinkSentinel : TLink;     // Links out of this node.
        NextNode     : PNode;     // Next node in list of all nodes.
    end;
```

Using these definitions, a program could find the least costly link out of a node using the following code.

```
var
    link, best_link : PLink;
    best_cost       : Integer;
begin
    best_cost := 32767;
    best_link := nil;
    link := node^.LinkSentinel.NextLink;
    while (link <> nil) do
    begin
        if (link^.Cost < best_cost) then
        begin
```

```
            best_link := link;
            best_cost := link^.Cost;
        end;
        link := link^.NextLink;
    end;
```

The node and link classes are often extended for the convenience of particular algorithms. For example, a Marked flag is often added to the node class. When the program visits a node, it sets Marked to True so it will later know that it has already visited the node.

A program managing an undirected network might use a slightly different representation. The node class is the same as before, but the link class includes a pointer to both of the nodes at its end points. The two nodes at each end of the link can both point to the same link structure.

```
type
    TLink = record
        Node1    : PNode;     // One end node.
        Node2    : PNode;     // The other end node.
        Cost     : Integer;   // The cost.
        NextLink : PLink;     // Next link in start node's list
                              // of links.
    end;
```

For an undirected network, the previous representation would need to use two objects to represent each link—one for each of the link's directions. In the new version, each link is represented by a single object.

Figure 12.3 Program NetEdit.

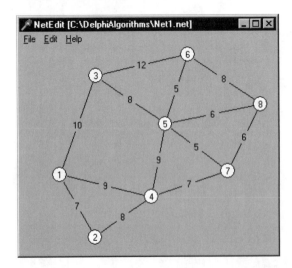

Example program NetEdit uses a similar representation to allow you to manage undirected networks with link costs. The File menu allows you to open and save networks in files. The commands in the Edit menu allow you to add and remove nodes and links. Program NetEdit is shown in Figure 12.3.

Managing Nodes and Links

The root of a tree is unique: It is the only node in a tree that has no parent. From the root node, you can follow child pointers to locate all the other nodes in the tree. This makes the root a convenient handle for the tree. If you store a pointer to the root node in a variable, you can later access all the nodes in the tree.

Networks do not always contain a node in such a unique position. In a disconnected network, there may not be a way to follow links from one node to all of the others. For this reason, network programs often keep a complete list of all the nodes in the network. A program may also keep a list of all the links. These lists make it easy to act on all the links or nodes in the network. For example, if a program keeps linked lists of all of the nodes and links, it can use the following method to draw the network.

```
var
    node : PNode;
    link : PLink;
begin
    // Draw the links first.
    link := top_link;
    while (link <> nil) do
    begin
        // Draw the link.
            :
        link := link^.NextLink;
    end;

    // Draw the nodes.
    node := top_node;
    while (node <> nil) do
    begin
        // Draw the node.
            :
        node := node^.NextNode;
    end;
```

Network Traversals

Traversing a network is similar to traversing a tree. You can traverse a network using either a depth first or breadth first traversal. Depth first traversals are generally similar to preorder traversals in trees, though you could also define postorder and even inorder traversals for a network.

The algorithm for performing a preorder traversal for a binary tree described in Chapter 6, "Trees," is:

1. Visit the node.

2. Recursively traverse the left subtree in preorder.

3. Recursively traverse the right subtree in preorder.

In a tree, there is a parent-child relationship between nodes that are connected. Because the algorithm starts at the root and always works downward through the child nodes, it will never visit a node twice.

On the other hand, in a network, nodes are not necessarily linked in a top-down manner. If you try to implement this preorder traversal algorithm in a network, you may stumble into a cycle and enter an infinite loop.

To prevent this, when the algorithm reaches a node, it should mark the node as visited. When the algorithm searches neighboring nodes, it visits only the nodes that are not yet marked. When the algorithm finishes, all the nodes in the network will be marked as visited (if the network is connected). The preorder network traversal algorithm is:

1. Mark the node.

2. Visit the node.

3. Recursively traverse the node's neighbors that are not yet marked.

In Delphi, you can add a Visited flag to the TNode type.

```
type
    TNode = record
        Id            : Integer;   // Node ID.
        X             : Integer;   // Position.
        Y             : Integer;
        LinkSentinel  : TLink;     // Links out of this node.
        NextNode      : PNode;     // Next node in list of all nodes.
        Visited       : Boolean;   // Has the node been visited?
    end;
```

The following code shows how a procedure can visit all of the nodes reachable from a given node that have not yet been visited. If the network is connected, the resulting traversal will visit every node in the network.

```
procedure Traverse(node : PNode);
var
    link     : PLink;
    neighbor : PNode;
begin
    // Mark this node as visited.
```

```
node^.Visited := True;

// Visit unmarked neighbors.
link := node^.LinkSentinel.NextLink;
while (link <> nil) do
begin
    // See which node is the neighbor.
    if (link^.Node1 = node) then
        neighbor := link^.Node2
    else
        neighbor := link^.Node1;

    // Visit the neighbor if it's not yet marked.
    If (not neighbor^.Visited) then Traverse(neighbor);

    // Examine the next link.
    link := link^.NextLink;
    end;
end;
```

Because this procedure does not visit any node twice, the collection of links traversed does not contain any cycles. That makes this collection a tree.

If the network is connected, the tree will reach every node in the network. Because the tree spans every node in the network, it is called a *spanning tree*. Figure 12.4 shows a small network with a spanning tree rooted at node A drawn in bold lines.

You can use a similar node marking technique to convert the breadth first tree traversal algorithm into a network algorithm. The tree traversal algorithm begins by placing the tree's root node in a queue. It then removes the first node from the queue, visits it, and places its children at the end of the queue. It repeats this process until the queue is empty.

Figure 12.4 A spanning tree.

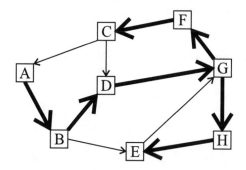

In the network traversal algorithm, you must make certain that a node is not placed in the queue if it has been visited before or if it is currently in the queue. To do this, mark each node as you place it in the queue. The network version of the algorithm is:

1. Mark the first node (this will be the root of the spanning tree) and add it to the end of the queue.

2. Repeat until the queue is empty:
   a. Remove the first node from the queue and visit it.
   b. For each of the node's neighbors that are not yet marked, mark the neighbor and add it to the end of the queue.

The following procedure prints a list of network nodes in breadth first order.

```
procedure BreadthFirstPrint(root : PNode);
var
    queue          : TNodeQueue;
    node, neighbor : PNode;
    link           : PLink;
begin
    // Put the root in the queue.
    root^.Marked := True;
    queue.EnterQueue(root);

    // Repeatedly process the top item in the
    // queue until the queue is empty.
    while (queue.NumItems > 0) do
    begin
        // Get the next node from the queue.
        node := queue.LeaveQueue;

        // Print the node's ID here.
            :

        // Add the node's unmarked neighbors to the queue.
        link := node^.LinkSentinel.NextLink;
        while (link <> nil) do
        begin
            // See which node is the neighbor.
            if (link^.Node1 = node) then
                neighbor := link^.Node2
            else
                neighbor := link^.Node1;
```

```
          // If the neighbor has not yet been
          // visited, add it to the queue.
          if (not neighbor.Visited) then queue.EnterQueue(neighbor);

          // Go to the next link.
          link := link^.NextLink;
      end; // End checking links from this node.
    end; // End checking nodes in the queue.
  end;
```

Minimal Spanning Trees

Given a network with link costs, a *minimal spanning tree* is a spanning tree where the total cost of all the links in the tree is as small as possible. You can use a minimal spanning tree to pick the least costly way to connect all the nodes in a network.

For example, suppose you need to design a telephone network connecting six cities. You could build a trunk between every pair of the cities, but that would be needlessly expensive. A less costly solution would be to connect the cities along the links contained in a minimal spanning tree. Figure 12.5 shows six cities with a possible trunk drawn between each pair of cities. A minimal spanning tree is drawn in bold.

Notice that a network may contain more than one minimal spanning tree. Figure 12.6 shows two pictures of one network with two different minimal spanning trees drawn in bold. The total cost of both of these trees is 32.

There is a simple algorithm for finding a minimal spanning tree for a network. Start by placing any node in the spanning tree. Then find the least costly link that connects a node in the tree to a node that is not yet in the tree. Add that

Figure 12.5 Telephone trunks connecting six cities.

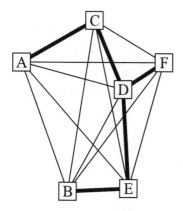

Figure 12.6 Two different minimal spanning trees for the same network.

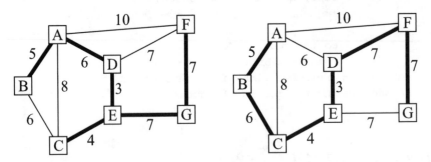

link and the corresponding node to the tree. Repeat this procedure until you have added all the nodes to the tree.

In a way, this algorithm is similar to the hill climbing heuristic described in Chapter 8, "Decision Trees." At each step, both algorithms modify the solution to improve it as much as possible. At each step, the spanning tree algorithm selects the smallest link that adds a new node to the tree. Unlike the hill climbing heuristic, which does not always find an optimal solution, this algorithm is guaranteed to find a minimal spanning tree.

Algorithms like this, which reach globally optimal solutions by making locally optimal decisions, are called *greedy algorithms*. You can think of greedy algorithms as hill climbing algorithms that are not heuristics—they are guaranteed to find the best solution possible.

The minimal spanning tree algorithm uses a linked list to store the candidate links that might be added to the spanning tree. Initially, the algorithm places the links out of the root node in the candidate list. It then searches the list for the link with the smallest cost. If the node at the other end of that link is not already in the spanning tree, the program adds both it and the link. It then adds the links leaving the new node to the candidate list so they will be considered in the future.

The algorithm uses the variable BeenInList in the link record to indicate whether a link has been in the candidate list before. Once a link has been on the list, it will not be added to the list again.

It is possible that the candidate list will empty completely before all the nodes have been added to the spanning tree. In that case, the network is not connected. There is no path from the root node to all the other nodes in the network.

```
type
    PLink = ^TLink;
    PNode = ^TNode;
    TLink = record
        Node1       : PNode;
        Node2       : PNode;
```

```
            Cost            : Integer;
            NextLink        : PLink;    // Next link in the node's list
                                        // of links.
            BeenInList      : Boolean;  // Has it been in the candidate
                                        // list?
            InTree          : Boolean;  // Is it in the spanning tree?
        end;
    TNode = record
        Id              : Integer;
        X               : Integer;
        Y               : Integer;
        LinkSentinel    : TLink;    // Links out of this node.
        NextNode        : PNode;    // Next node in list of all nodes.
        InTree          : Boolean;  // Is it in the spanning tree?
    end;

        // Cell for candidate linked list.
        PCandidate = ^TCandidate;
        TCandidate = record
            Link            : PLink;
            NextCandidate   : PCandidate;
        end;

procedure FindSpanningTree(root : PNode);
const
    INFINITY = 32767;
var
    candidate_sentinel          : TCandidate;
    new_candidate, before       : PCandidate;
    best_before                 : PCandidate;
    best_node, from_node        : PNode;
    link                        : PLink;
    best_cost                   : Integer;
begin
    if (root = nil) then exit;

    // Reset all nodes' InTree flags and all links'
    // BeenInList and InTree flags.
    ResetSpanningTree;

    // Start with the root in the spanning tree.
    RootNode := root;
    candidate_sentinel.NextCandidate := nil;
    root.InTree := True;
    best_node := root;
```

```
    // Loop infinitely examining the candidate list.
repeat
        // Add best_node's links to the candidate list.
    link := best_node^.LinkSentinel.NextLink;
    while (link <> nil) do
    begin
        if (not link^.BeenInList) then
        begin
                // Add the link to the candidate list.
            GetMem(new_candidate, SizeOf(TCandidate));
            new_candidate^.NextCandidate :=
                candidate_sentinel.NextCandidate;
            candidate_sentinel.NextCandidate :=
                new_candidate;
            new_candidate^.Link := link;
            link^.BeenInList := True;
        end;
        link := link^.NextLink;
    end;


        // Find the shortest link in the candidate list
        // that leads to a node not yet in the tree.
    before := @candidate_sentinel;
    best_before := before;
    new_candidate := before^.NextCandidate;
    best_cost := INFINITY;
    while (new_candidate <> nil) do
    begin
        link := new_candidate^.Link;
        if (link^.Node2^.InTree) then
        begin
                // This node is already in the tree.
                // Remove the link from the list.
            before^.NextCandidate :=
                new_candidate^.NextCandidate;
            FreeMem(new_candidate);
            new_candidate := before^.NextCandidate;
        end else begin
                // See if the link has the lowest cost.
            if (link^.Cost < best_cost) then
            begin
                best_before := before;
                best_cost := link^.Cost;
            end;
```

```
            before := new_candidate;
            new_candidate := new_candidate^.NextCandidate;
        end;
    end; // End examining the candidates.

    // If there are no usable links, we are done.
    // At this point the candidate list is empty.
    if (best_cost = INFINITY) then break;

    // Add the link and its node to the spanning tree.
    new_candidate := best_before^.NextCandidate;
    link := new_candidate^.Link;
    link^.InTree := True;
    best_node := link^.Node2;
    best_node^.InTree := True;

    // Remove the entry from the candidate list.
    best_before^.NextCandidate :=
        new_candidate^.NextCandidate;
    FreeMem(new_candidate);

    // Add the reverse link to the spanning tree.
    from_node := link^.Node1;
    link := best_node^.LinkSentinel.NextLink;
    while (link <> nil) do
    begin
        if (link^.Node2 = from_node) then break;
        link := link^.NextLink;
    end;
    if (link <> nil) then
    begin
        link^.InTree := True;
        link^.BeenInList := True;
    end;
    until (False); // End infinite loop examining the candidate
                   // list.

// Redraw the network.
GotTree := True;
DrawNetwork;
end;
```

This algorithm examines each link at most once. As each link is examined, it is added and then later removed from the candidate list. If the candidate list is stored in a linked list as in the previous code, it takes O(N) time to locate the least costly link in the list. That makes the total runtime for the algorithm O(N²). If N is relatively small, this performance is reasonable.

If the candidate list were stored as a heap-based priority queue, it would take O(log(N)) time to add or remove an item from the queue where N is the number of links in the network. In that case, the total runtime for the algorithm would be O(N * log(N)). If the number of links in the network is large, this could be a substantial savings.

Example program Span uses this algorithm to find minimal spanning trees. The program is similar to program NetEdit. It lets you load, edit, and save network files. When you are not adding or removing a node or link, you can click on a node to make the program find and display a minimal spanning tree rooted at that node. Figure 12.7 shows program Span displaying a minimal spanning tree rooted at node 9.

Shortest Paths

The types of shortest path algorithms discussed in the following sections find all the shortest paths from a single point to every other point in the network, assuming the network is connected. The collection of links used by all of the shortest paths forms a *shortest path tree*.

Figure 12.8 shows a network where the shortest path tree rooted at node A is drawn in bold. This tree shows the shortest path from node A to every other node

Figure 12.7 Program Span.

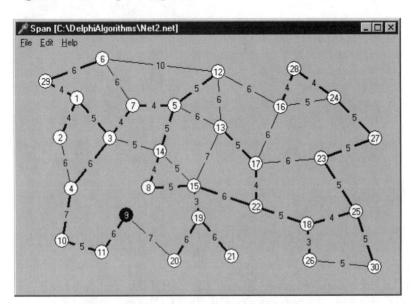

in the network. The shortest path from node A to node F, for example, follows
the path A, C, E, F.

Most shortest path algorithms start with an empty shortest path tree and then
add links one at a time to the tree until the tree is complete. These algorithms can
be divided into two categories according to how they select the next link to add
to the growing shortest path tree.

Label setting algorithms always select a link that is guaranteed to be part of the
final shortest path tree. This is similar to the way the minimal spanning tree algorithm works. Once a link has been added to the tree, it will not be removed later.

Label correcting algorithms add links that may or may not be part of the
final shortest path tree. As the algorithm progresses, it may discover that a different link should have been added instead of one that is already in the tree. In that
case, the algorithm replaces the old link with the new one and continues.
Replacing a link in the tree may make new paths possible that were not possible
before. To check for these paths, the algorithm must reexamine any paths it previously added to the tree using the link that was removed.

The label setting and the label correcting algorithms described in the following sections use similar record types to represent nodes and links. The TNode
type includes a Dist field that indicates the distance from the root to the node in
the growing shortest path tree. In a label setting algorithm, Dist is correct once a
node has been added to the tree and it will not be changed later. In a label correcting algorithm, Dist may be revised later when the algorithm replaces a link
with a different one.

Figure 12.8 A shortest path tree.

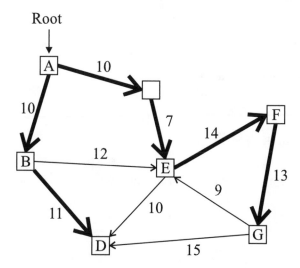

The TNode class also includes a Status field that indicates whether the node is currently in the shortest path tree, in a candidate list, or in neither. The InLink field indicates the link that leads to the node in the growing shortest path tree.

```
var
      TStatus = (nsNotInList, nsWasInList, nsNowInList);

      TNode = record
            Id            : Integer;
            X             : Integer;
            Y             : Integer;
            LinkSentinel  : TLink;     // Links out of this node.
            NextNode      : PNode;     // Next node in list of all nodes.
            Status        : TStatus;   // Has it been in the tree?
            Dist          : Integer;   // Distance from root.
            InLink        : PLink;     // The link into this node.
      end;
```

Using the InLink fields, a program can list the nodes in the path from the root to a node in reverse order using the following code.

```
procedure ListPath(node : PNode);
var
      prev_node : PNode;
begin
      while (True) do // Repeat infinitely.
      begin
            // List the node here.
              :

            if (node = RootNode) then break;

            // Go to the next node up the tree.
            if (node^.InLink^.Node1 = node) then
                node := node^.InLink^.Node2
            else
                node := node^.InLink^.Node1;
      end;
```

The TLink record type includes an InTree field that indicates whether the link is part of the shortest path tree.

```
type
      TLink = record
            Node1     : PNode;
```

```
    Node2     : PNode;
    Cost      : Integer;
    NextLink  : PLink;    // Next link in the node's list of
                          // links.
    InTree    : Boolean;  // Is it in the shortest path tree?
  end;
```

Both label setting and label correcting algorithms use a candidate list to keep track of nodes that might be added to the shortest path tree. The algorithms differ in the ways they manage the candidate list. Label setting algorithms add candidates to the tree using links that are guaranteed to be part of the shortest path tree. The label correcting algorithm described here selects whatever node is at the top of the candidate list.

Label Setting

This algorithm begins by initializing all nodes' Status fields to nsNotInList and their Dist fields to INFINITY. Then it sets the root node's Dist value to 0 and places the root node in the candidate list. It sets the root's Status value to nsNowInList to indicate that it is currently in the candidate list.

The algorithm then searches the list for the node with the smallest Dist value. Initially, that will be the root node because it is the only node in the list.

The algorithm removes the selected node from the candidate list. It sets the node's Status entry to the value nsWasInList to indicate that the node is now a permanent part of the shortest path tree. Its Dist and InLink fields have their correct final values. For the root node, InLink is nil and Dist is zero.

Next, the algorithm examines each of the links leaving the selected node. If the neighbor node at the other end of a link has never been on the candidate list before, the algorithm adds the neighbor to the list. It sets the neighbor's Status value to nsNowInList. It sets the neighbor's Dist value to the distance from the root node to the selected node plus the cost of the link. Finally, it sets the neighbor's InLink value to indicate the link connecting it to the selected node.

As the algorithm examines the links leaving the selected node, if a neighbor node has Status value nsNowInList, it is already in the candidate list. The algorithm compares the neighbor's current Dist value to see if the new path via the selected node would be shorter. If so, it updates the neighbor's InLink and Dist entries and leaves it in the candidate list.

The algorithm repeats this process, removing nodes from the candidate list, examining their neighbors, and adding neighbors to the candidate list, until the list is empty.

Figure 12.9 shows a partial shortest path tree. At this point, the algorithm has considered nodes A and B, has removed them from the candidate list, and has examined their links. It has added nodes A and B to the shortest path tree, and the candidate list now contains nodes C, D, and E. The bold arrows in Figure

Figure 12.9 A partial shortest path tree.

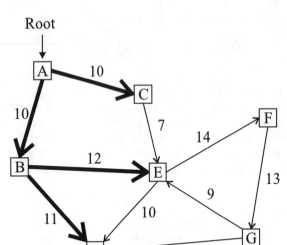

12.9 indicate the InLink values at this point. For example, the InLink value for node E currently connects nodes E and B.

Next, the algorithm searches the candidate list for the node with the smallest Dist value. At this point, the Dist values of C, D, and E are currently 10, 21, and 22, respectively, so the algorithm selects node C. It removes node C from the candidate list and sets the node's Status value to nsWasInList. Now node C is part of the shortest path tree, and its Dist and InLink entries have their correct final values.

The algorithm then examines the links leaving node C. The only link leaving node C goes to node E. Node E is currently in the candidate list, so the algorithm does not add it to the list again.

The current shortest path from the root to node E is the path A, B, E, with a total cost of 22. But the path A, C, E has a cost of only 17. This is lower than the current cost of 22, so the algorithm updates the InLink value for node E and sets node E's Dist entry to 17.

```
procedure FindPathTree(root : PNode);
var
    candidate_sentinel   : TCandidate;
    new_candidate        : PCandidate;
    before, best_before  : PCandidate;
    best_dist, new_dist  : Integer;
    node, to_node        : PNode;
    link                 : PLink;
begin
    if (root = nil) then exit;
```

```
RootNode := root;

// Reset the tree.
ResetPathTree;

// Start with the root in the shortest path tree.
root^.Dist := 0;
root^.InLink := nil;
root^.Status := nsNowInList;
GetMem(new_candidate, SizeOf(TCandidate));
candidate_sentinel.NextCandidate := new_candidate;
new_candidate^.NextCandidate := nil;
new_candidate^.Node := root;

// Repeat until the candidate list is empty.
while (candidate_sentinel.NextCandidate <> nil) do
begin
    // Find the candidate closest to the root.
    best_dist := INFINITY;
    best_before := nil;
    before := @candidate_sentinel;
    new_candidate := before^.NextCandidate;
    while (new_candidate <> nil) do
    begin
        new_dist := new_candidate^.Node^.Dist;
        if (new_dist < best_dist) then
        begin
            best_before := before;
            best_dist := new_dist;
        end;
        before := new_candidate;
        new_candidate := before^.NextCandidate;
    end;

    // Add this node to the shortest path tree.
    new_candidate := best_before^.NextCandidate;
    node := new_candidate^.Node;
    node^.Status := nsWasInList;

    // Remove the node from the candidate list.
    best_before^.NextCandidate :=
        new_candidate^.NextCandidate;
    FreeMem(new_candidate);
```

```
// Examine the node's neighbors.
link := node^.LinkSentinel.NextLink;
while (link <> nil) do
begin
        to_node := link^.Node2;
        // If the node hasn't been in
        // the candidate list, add it.
        if (to_node^.Status = nsNotInList) then
        begin
                // Update the node's status and distance.
                to_node^.Status := nsNowInList;
                to_node^.Dist := best_dist + link^.Cost;
                to_node^.InLink := link;

                // Add it to the list.
                GetMem(new_candidate, SizeOf(TCandidate));
                new_candidate^.Node := to_node;
                new_candidate^.NextCandidate :=
                    candidate_sentinel.NextCandidate;
                candidate_sentinel.NextCandidate :=
                    new_candidate;
        end else if (to_node^.Status = nsNowInList) then
        begin
                // If the node is now in the candidate list,
                // update its Dist and InLink values.
                new_dist := best_dist + link.Cost;
                if (new_dist < to_node.Dist) then
                begin
                        to_node.Dist := new_dist;
                        to_node.InLink := link;
                end;
        end;

        link := link^.NextLink;
    end; // End examining the node's neighbors.
  end; // End while (candidate list is not empty) ...
end;
```

It is important that the algorithm update the InLink and Dist entries only for nodes with Status nsNowInList. For many networks, there will be no improvement possible for a node unless it is in the candidate list. If the network contains a cycle of negative total length, however, the algorithm will find that it can improve the distances to some nodes that are already in the shortest path tree. This connects two branches of the shortest path tree so that it is no longer a tree.

Figure 12.10 Incorrect shortest path tree for a network with a negative cost cycle.

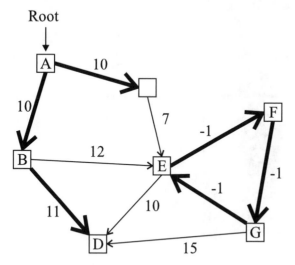

Figure 12.10 shows a network with a negative cost cycle and the shortest path tree that would result if the algorithm updated the costs of nodes already in the tree.

Example program PathS uses this label setting algorithm to compute shortest paths. It is similar to programs NetEdit and Span. If you are not adding or removing a node or link, you can click on a node to make the program find and display a shortest path tree rooted at that node. Figure 12.11 shows program PathS displaying a shortest path tree rooted at node 3.

Label Setting Variations

The main bottleneck in this algorithm is in locating the node in the candidate list that has the smallest Dist value. Several variations of this algorithm use different data structures for storing the candidate list. For example, you could store the candidate list as a sorted linked list. Using this method, it would take only a single step to find the next node to add to the shortest path tree. The list would always be sorted, so the node at the top would always be the one to add.

This would make finding the correct node in the list easier, but it would also make adding a node to the list harder. Instead of placing the node at the beginning of the list, you would need to add it at its proper position.

You would also sometimes need to move nodes around in the list. If, by adding a node to the shortest path tree, you reduce the best distance to another node that is already in the list, you need to move that node closer to the top of the list.

The previous algorithm and this new variation represent two extremes for managing the candidate list. The first stores the list in a totally unordered way

Figure 12.11 A shortest path tree rooted at node 3.

and spends a lot of time looking for nodes in the list. The second spends a lot of effort maintaining a sorted linked list, but can select nodes very quickly. Other variations use intermediate strategies.

For example, you could store the candidate list in a heap-based priority queue. Then you could easily select the next node from the top of the heap. Adding a new node to the heap and rearranging the heap would be faster than performing the same operations on a sorted linked list. Other strategies use clever arrangements of buckets to keep the best candidates easy to find.

Some of these variations are quite complicated. The extra complication often makes these algorithms slower than simpler algorithms for small networks. For very large networks or networks in which each node has a very large number of links, these algorithms may be worth the extra complication.

Label Correcting

Like the label setting algorithm, this algorithm begins by setting the root node's Dist value to 0 and placing the root node in the candidate list. It initializes the Dist values of the other nodes to infinity. It then selects the first node in the candidate list to add to the shortest path tree.

Next, the algorithm examines each of the neighbors of the selected node. It checks whether the distance from the root to the selected node plus the cost of the link is less than the neighbor's current Dist value. If it is, the algorithm updates the neighbor's Dist and InLink entries so the best path to the neighbor goes through the selected node. If the neighbor is not currently in the candidate list, the algorithm also adds it. Notice that this algorithm does not check whether the item has been on the list before. If there is improvement in the path from the root to the neighbor, the algorithm always adds the node to the candidate list.

The algorithm continues removing nodes from the candidate list, examining their neighbors, and adding neighbors to the candidate list until the list is empty.

If you compare the label setting and label correcting algorithms carefully, you will find that they are very similar. The only difference is in how each selects a node from the candidate list to add to the shortest path tree.

The label setting algorithm always picks a link that is guaranteed to belong in the shortest path tree. Once it removes a node from the candidate list, that node has been permanently added to the tree and will not be placed in the candidate list again.

The label correcting algorithm always selects the first node from the candidate list. That node may not always be the best choice. The node's Dist and InLink entries may not hold the best possible values. In that case, the algorithm will eventually examine a node in the candidate list that gives a better path to the node than the one originally chosen. The algorithm then updates the incorrect node's Dist and InLink entries, and it places the updated node back in the candidate list.

The algorithm may be able to use the new path to form other paths that it might have missed earlier. By placing the updated node back in the candidate list, the algorithm ensures it will consider the node again and find any such paths.

```
procedure FindPathTree(root : PNode);
var
     top_candidate        : PCandidate;
     new_candidate        : PCandidate;
     node_dist, new_dist  : Integer;
     node, to_node        : PNode;
     link                 : PLink;
begin
     if (root = nil) then exit;

     // Reset the tree.
     ResetPathTree;

     // Start with the root in the shortest path tree.
     root^.Dist := 0;
     root^.InLink := nil;
     root^.Status := nsNowInList;
     GetMem(new_candidate, SizeOf(TCandidate));
     top_candidate := new_candidate;
     new_candidate^.NextCandidate := nil;
     new_candidate^.Node := root;
```

```
    // Repeat until the candidate list is empty.
while (top_candidate <> nil) do
begin
      // Add the first candidate to the tree.
      // Remove the entry from the candidate list.
    node := top_candidate^.Node;
    new_candidate := top_candidate;
    top_candidate := top_candidate^.NextCandidate;
    FreeMem(new_candidate);

    node_dist := node^.Dist;
    node^.Status := nsNotInList;

      // Examine the node's neighbors.
    link := node^.LinkSentinel.NextLink;
    while (link <> nil) do
    begin
          // See if there's an improved path using this node.
        to_node := link^.Node2;
        new_dist := node_dist + link.Cost;
        if (new_dist < to_node.Dist) then
        begin
              // It's better. Update Dist and InLink.
            to_node^.InLink := link;
            to_node^.Dist := new_dist;

              // Add to_node to the candidate list if
              // it's not already there.
            if (to_node.Status = nsNotInList) then
            begin
                GetMem(new_candidate, SizeOf(TCandidate));
                new_candidate^.NextCandidate := top_candidate;
                top_candidate := new_candidate;
                new_candidate^.Node := to_node;
                to_node.Status := nsNowInList;
            end;
        end; // End if (new_dist < to_node.Dist) then.

          // Examine the node's next link.
        link := link^.NextLink;
    end; // End examining the node's links.
  end; // End while (candidate list is not empty) ...
end;
```

Unlike the label setting algorithm, this algorithm cannot handle networks that contain negative cost cycles. If it finds such a cycle, the algorithm enters an infinite loop following the links in the cycle. Each time it passes through the cycle, it reduces the distances to the nodes it is examining. As it reduces their distances, it places the nodes back in the candidate list so it can update other paths. When it examines the nodes again, it reduces their distances further. This process continues until the distances to these nodes underflow with values less than –32,768 if the program uses integers for its calculations. If you know that your network contains negative cycles, the easiest thing to do is to use label setting instead of label correcting.

Example program PathC uses this label correcting algorithm to compute shortest paths. It is similar to program PathS except it uses label correcting instead of label setting.

Label Correcting Variations

This label correcting algorithm can select a node from the candidate list very quickly. It can also add a node to the list in only one or two steps. The trouble with this algorithm is that, when it selects a node from the candidate list, it may not make a very good choice. If the algorithm selects a node before that node's Dist and InLink fields reach their final values, it must correct the fields later and place the node back in the candidate list. The more often the algorithm places nodes back in the candidate list, the longer it takes.

Variations on this algorithm try to improve the quality of the node selections without creating a lot of additional work. One technique that works well in practice is to add nodes to both the front and back of the candidate list. If a node has never been on the candidate list before, the algorithm adds it at the back of the list as usual. If the node has previously been on the candidate list but is not now, the algorithm adds it at the front of the list. This makes the algorithm revisit that node quite soon, probably the next time it selects a node.

The idea behind this approach is that, if the algorithm has made a mistake, it should fix the mistake as soon as possible. If the mistake is left uncorrected, the algorithm may use the incorrect information to build long false paths that must be corrected later. By reexamining the node quickly, the algorithm may be able to reduce the number of incorrect paths it needs to rebuild. In the best case, if the node's neighbors are still in the candidate list, reexamining this node before examining its neighbors prevents any incorrect paths from starting.

Other Shortest Path Problems

The previous shortest path algorithms compute all of the shortest paths from a single root node to all of the other nodes in the network. There are many other types of shortest path problems. This section examines three: *point-to-point shortest paths*, *all pairs shortest paths*, and *shortest paths with turn penalties*.

Point-to-Point Shortest Path

In some applications, you may want to find the shortest path between two points, but you may not care about all of the other shortest paths stored in a complete shortest path tree. One easy way you can find a point-to-point shortest path is to compute the complete shortest path tree using either a label setting or label correcting algorithm. Then use the shortest path tree to find the shortest path between the two points.

Another method is to use a label setting algorithm that stops when it finds a path to the destination node. A label setting algorithm never adds links to the shortest path tree that do not belong there. When it adds the destination node to the shortest path tree, the algorithm has found a correct shortest path. In the algorithm described earlier, this occurs when the algorithm removes the destination node from the candidate list.

The only change you need to make in the label setting algorithm comes right after the algorithm has found the node in the candidate list with the smallest Dist value. Before removing the node from the candidate list, the algorithm should check whether the node is the destination node. If so, the shortest path tree already holds a correct path from the start node to the destination node, so the algorithm can stop early.

```
// Find the candidate closest to the root.
    :

// See if this is the destination node.
if (node = destination) then break;

// Add this node to the shortest path tree.
    :
```

In practice, if the two points are far apart in the network, this algorithm will usually take longer than computing the entire shortest path tree. Checking for the destination node each time the loop executes makes the algorithm slower. On the other hand, if the nodes are close together in the network, this algorithm may be much faster than building a complete shortest path tree.

For some networks, like street networks, you may be able to guess how far apart the two points are and then decide which version of the algorithm to use for those points. If your network contains all the streets in southern California and the two points are 10 miles apart, you should use the version that stops when it removes the destination from the candidate list. If the points are 100 miles apart, it will probably be faster to compute the entire shortest path tree.

All Pairs Shortest Paths

Some applications may require you to quickly find the shortest path between any pair of nodes in the network. If the application requires you to compute a large fraction of the possible N^2 paths, it may be faster to precompute all of the possible shortest paths rather than finding each as you need it.

You can store the shortest paths using two two-dimensional arrays, Dists and InLinks. Dists[i, j] holds the shortest distance from node i to node j. InLinks[i, j] holds the link that leads to node j in the shortest path from node i to node j. These values are similar to the Dist and InLink values stored in the node class in the previous algorithms.

One way to find the shortest path information is to build the shortest path tree rooted at each node in the network using one of the previous algorithms. Then save the results in the Dists and InLinks arrays.

Another method for computing all of the shortest paths successively constructs paths through the network using more and more nodes. First, the algorithm finds all the shortest paths that use only the first node plus the end nodes in the path. In other words, for nodes j and k, the algorithm finds the shortest path between nodes j and k that uses only node number 1 plus nodes j and k, if any such paths exist.

Next, the algorithm finds all the shortest paths that use only the first two nodes. It then builds paths using the first three nodes, the first four nodes, and so forth until it has built all the shortest paths using all the nodes. At this point, because the shortest paths can use any node, the algorithm has found all the shortest paths in the network.

Notice that the shortest path from node j to node k, using only the first i nodes, includes the node i only if Dist[j, k] > Dist[j, i] + Dist[i, k]. Otherwise, the shortest path will be whatever path was shortest using only the first i − 1 nodes. That means when the algorithm adds the node i into consideration, it needs to check only whether Dist[j, k] > Dist[j, i] + Dist[i, k]. If so, the algorithm updates the shortest path from node j to node k. Otherwise, the old shortest path between these two nodes is still the shortest.

Turn Penalties

Some networks, particularly street networks, are more useful if you add turn penalties and turn prohibitions. In a street network, a car must slow down before it turns. It may also take longer to turn left than to turn right or to go straight. At some intersections, certain turns may be illegal or impossible due to a center median. You can handle these details by adding turn penalties to the network.

Few Turn Penalties

Often only a few key turn penalties are important. You might like to prevent illegal or impossible turns and place turn penalties on a few key intersections, without placing turn penalties on every intersection in the network. In that case, you can break each node that should have turn penalties into subnodes that implicitly take the penalties into account.

Suppose you want to add a turn penalty for entering an intersection and turning left, and a different penalty for entering the intersection and turning right. Figure 12.12 shows an intersection where you might like to place these penalties. The numbers next to each link are the link's cost. You want to place penalties for entering node A along link L_1 and then leaving along the links L_2 or L_3.

To add turn penalties to node A, break the node into one subnode for each of the links leaving it. In this example, there are two links leaving node A, so you should break node A into two subnodes, A_1 and A_2. Replace the links leaving node A with corresponding links leaving these subnodes. You can think of the subnodes as representing the action of entering node A and turning onto the corresponding link.

Next, replace the link L_1 entering node A with links entering each of the subnodes. These links should have costs equal to the original cost of link L_1, plus any turn penalty you want to assign to the corresponding turn. Figure 12.13 shows the intersection with turn penalties added. This figure shows a turn penalty of 5 for the left turn out of node A and a turn penalty of 2 for a right turn.

By placing turn penalty information directly in the network, you avoid the need to modify your shortest path algorithms. Those algorithms will correctly find shortest paths taking the turn penalties into account.

You still need to modify your programs slightly to deal with the fact that some nodes have been split into subnodes. Suppose you want to find the shortest path between nodes i and j, but node i has been split into subnodes. Assuming you are allowed to leave node i along any link, you can create a dummy node to use as the root node in the shortest path tree. Connect that node to each of the subnodes of node i using zero cost links. Then when you build the shortest path tree rooted at the dummy node, you will have found all the shortest paths that use any of the subnodes. Figure 12.14 shows the intersection from Figure 12.13 connected to a dummy root node.

Figure 12.12 An intersection.

Figure 12.13 An intersection with turn penalties.

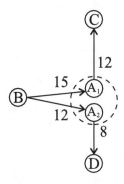

It is easier to deal with the case of finding a path to a node that has been split into subnodes. If you want to find the shortest path between nodes i and j, and node j has been split into subnodes, first find the shortest path tree rooted at node i as usual. Then check each of the subnodes of node j to see which is closest to the tree's root. The path to that subnode is the shortest path to the original node j.

Many Turn Penalties

If you want to add turn penalties to most of the nodes in your network, the previous method is not very efficient. A better method is to create a completely new network to include the turn penalty information.

- For each link in the original network connecting nodes A and B, create a node AB in the new network.

- Create a link between two nodes if the corresponding links were connected in the original network. For example, suppose in the original network one link connects nodes A and B and another link connects nodes B and C. Then you should make a link in the new network connecting the node AB to the node BC.

- Set the cost of the new link to be the cost of the second link in the original network plus the turn penalty. In this example, the cost of the link from node AB to node BC should be the cost of the link connecting nodes B and C in the original network plus the turn penalty for moving from node A to B to C.

Figure 12.15 shows a small network and the corresponding new network representing the turn penalties. Left turns carry a penalty of 3, right turns carry a penalty of 2, and going straight carries no penalty. For example, because the turn from node B to E to F in the original network is a left turn, the link between nodes BE and EF in the new network carries a turn penalty of 3. The cost of the

Figure 12.14 An intersection connected to a dummy root.

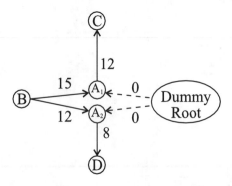

link connecting nodes E and F in the original network is 3, so the total cost of the new link is 3 + 3 = 6.

Now suppose you want to find the shortest path tree rooted at node D in the original network. To do this in the new network, create a dummy root node. Build links connecting that node to all the links that leave node D in the original network. Give these links the same costs as the corresponding links in the original network. Figure 12.16 shows the new network from Figure 12.15 with a dummy root node corresponding to node D. The shortest path tree through this network is drawn in bold lines.

Figure 12.15 A network and corresponding turn penalty network.

Figure 12.16 Shortest path tree in a turn penalty network.

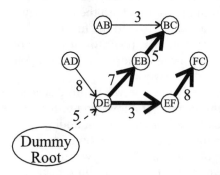

To find the shortest path from node D to node C, examine all the nodes in the new network that correspond to links ending at node C. In this example, those are the nodes BC and FC. The node that is closest to the dummy root gives the shortest path to node C in the original network. The nodes in the shortest path in the new network correspond to the links in the shortest path in the original network.

In Figure 12.16, the best path goes from the dummy root node, to node DE, to node EF, to node FC, and has a total cost of 16. This path corresponds to the path D, E, F, C in the original network. Adding one left turn penalty for the E, F, C turn, this path also has a cost of 16 in the original network.

Notice that you would not have found this path if you had built a shortest path tree in the original network. Without turn penalties, the shortest path from node D to node C would be D, E, B, C with a total cost of 12. With turn penalties, that path has a cost of 17.

Shortest Path Applications

Shortest path calculations are used in many applications. Finding the shortest route between two points in a street network is an obvious example. Many other applications use shortest paths through networks in less obvious ways. The following sections describe a few of these applications.

Districting

Suppose you have the map of a city that shows the locations of all fire stations. You might want to determine, for every point in the city, which is the closest fire station. At first glance, this might seem like a difficult problem. You might try computing the shortest path tree rooted at every node in the network to see which fire station was closest to each node. You might compute the shortest path tree rooted at each fire station and record how close each node is to each fire station. There is a much faster method.

Create a dummy root node and connect it with zero cost links to each of the fire stations. Then find the shortest path tree rooted at this dummy node. For each point in the network, the shortest path from the root node to the point will pass through the fire station that is closest to that point. To find the fire station closest to a point, simply follow the shortest path from that point toward the root until it reaches one of the fire stations. By building a single shortest path tree, you can find the closest fire station to every point in the network.

Example program Distr uses this algorithm to divide a network into districts. Like PathC and other programs described in this chapter, it allows you to load, edit, and save undirected networks with link costs. When you are not adding or deleting nodes or links, you can select stations for districting. Click on nodes with the left mouse button to add a node to the list of stations. Click anywhere on the form with the right button to make the program divide the network into districts.

Figure 12.17 shows the program districting a network with three stations at nodes 3, 18, and 20. The districting shortest path trees are drawn with bold lines.

Critical Path Scheduling

In many projects, including large programming projects, certain tasks must be completed before certain others can begin. When building a house, for example, the land must be graded before the foundation is poured, the foundation must be dry before the framing can begin, the framing must be finished before the electrical, plumbing, and roofing work can start, and so forth.

Figure 12.17 Program District.

Some of these tasks can be performed at the same time while others must happen one after another. The electrical and plumbing work, for example, can be done at the same time.

A *critical path* is one of the longest sequences of tasks that must occur to finish the project. Items that lie along a critical path are important because a slip in any of their schedules will change the completion time of the entire project. If the foundation is poured a week late, the house will be finished a week late. You can use a shortest path algorithm, modified to find longest paths, to identify the critical path tasks.

First, create a network that represents the scheduling relationships among the project tasks. Create a node for each task. Create a link between task i and task j if task i must be completed before task j can begin. Set the cost of the link between task i and task j equal to the length of time it will take to complete task i.

Next, create two dummy nodes, one to represent the start of the project and one to represent the completion. Create zero cost links connecting the start node to every node in the project that has no links leading into it. These nodes correspond to tasks that can begin immediately without waiting for the completion of any other tasks.

Then create zero cost dummy links connecting every node that has no links leaving it to the finish node. These nodes represent tasks for which no other task must wait. Once all of these tasks have been finished, the entire project is completed.

By finding the longest path between the start and finish nodes in this network, you can find a critical path for the project. The tasks along this path are the critical tasks. For example, consider a simplified sprinkler installation project with five tasks. The tasks and their precedence relationships are shown in Table 12.1. The network for this installation project is shown in Figure 12.18.

In this simple example, it is easy to see that the longest path through the network follows the sequence of tasks: dig trenches, install pipe, bury pipe. Those are the critical tasks, and if any of them is delayed, the project completion will be delayed.

Table 12.1 Sprinkler Installation Tasks

Task	Time	Must Start After
A. Buy pipe	1 day	(nothing)
B. Dig trenches	2 days	(nothing)
C. Cut pipe	1 day	A
D. Install pipe	2 days	B, C
E. Bury pipe	1 day	D

Figure 12.18 A sprinkler installation task network.

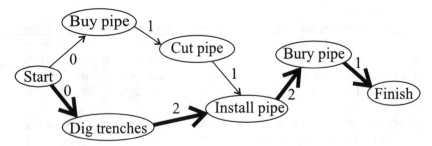

The length of this critical path gives the expected completion time of the project. In this case, if all the tasks are completed on schedule, the project will take five days. This also assumes that tasks are performed at the same time whenever possible. For example, one person should dig trenches while another buys pipe.

In a larger project, like building a skyscraper or producing a movie, there may be thousands of tasks, and the critical paths may be much less obvious.

Crew Scheduling

Suppose you can hire any of several part-time contractors to answer your phone. Each has a certain number of available hours, and each costs a different amount per hour. You want to hire the least expensive combination of contractors who can answer your phone between 9:00 A.M. and 5:00 P.M. Table 12.2 lists the contractors' prices and hours of availability.

To build a corresponding network, create a node to represent each hour of the day. For each contractor, build links representing the hours that contractor is available. If a contractor is available between 9:00 and 11:00, make a link between the 9:00 node and the 11:00 node. Set the link's cost to the total cost for that contractor working during that period. If the contractor charges $6.50 per hour and the period is two hours long, the cost of the link is $13.00. Figure 12.19 shows the network corresponding to the data in Table 12.2.

The shortest path from the first node to the last node gives the least expensive combination of contractors. Each link in the path corresponds to a contractor working a particular time period. In this case, the shortest path from the 9:00 node to the 5:00 node passes through the 11:00, 12:00, and 3:00 nodes. The corresponding employment schedule is this: A works 9:00–11:00, D works 11:00–12:00, A works 12:00–3:00, and E works 3:00 to 5:00. The total cost of this work schedule is $52.15.

Maximum Flow

In many networks, links have *capacities* in addition to costs. Each link can carry a *flow* that is no greater than its capacity. For instance, the streets in a street network

Figure 12.19 A crew scheduling network.

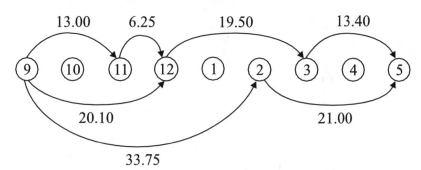

can carry only a certain number of cars per hour. If the number of cars on a link exceeds the link's capacity, the result is a traffic jam. A network with capacities on its links is called a *capacitated network*. Given a capacitated network, the maximum flow problem is to determine the largest flow possible through the network from a specific *source* node to a specific *sink* node.

Figure 12.20 shows a small capacitated network. The numbers next to the links in this network are the link capacities rather than the link costs. In this example, the maximum flow is 4 and can be produced by flowing two units along the path A, B, E, F, and two units along the path A, C, D, F.

The algorithm described here starts with no flows on the links and then incrementally modifies the flows to improve the solution it has found so far. When it can make no more improvements, the algorithm is finished.

To find ways to increase the total flow, the algorithm examines the *residual capacities* of the links. The residual capacity of the link between nodes i and j is the maximum additional net flow that you could send from node i to node j using

Table 12.2 Employee Availability and Costs

Contractor	Hours Available	Cost per Hour
A	9–11	$6.50
	12–3	
B	9–2	$6.75
C	2–5	$7.00
D	11–12	$6.25
E	9–12	$6.70
	3–5	

Figure 12.20 A capacitated network.

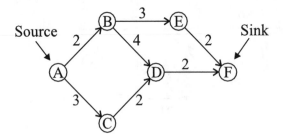

the link between i and j and the link between j and i. This net flow can include additional flow across the i-j link if that link has unused capacity. It can also include removing flow from the j-i link if that link is carrying flow.

For example, suppose there is a flow of 2 on the link connecting nodes A and C in Figure 12.20. Because that link has a capacity of 3, you could add an additional flow of 1 to that link so its residual capacity is 1. Even though the network shown in Figure 12.20 does not have a C–A link, there is a residual capacity for that link. In this example, because there is a flow of 2 units across the A–C link, you could remove up to 2 units of that flow. This would increase the net flow from node C to node A by 2, so the residual capacity of the C–A link is 2.

The network consisting of all the links with positive residual capacities is called the *residual network*. Figure 12.21 shows the network in Figure 12.20 with flows assigned to each link. For each link, the first number is the flow across the link, and the second is the link's capacity. The label "1 / 2," for example, means the link holds a flow of 1 and has capacity 2. The links carrying flows greater than 0 are shown in bold.

Figure 12.22 shows the residual network corresponding to the flows shown in Figure 12.21. Only the links that might actually have residual capacity have been drawn. For example, no links between nodes A and D have been drawn. The original network does not contain an A–D link or a D–A link, so those links will always have zero residual capacity.

Figure 12.21 Network flows.

Figure 12.22 Residual network.

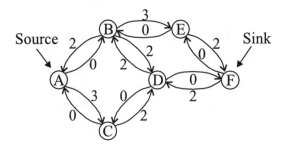

A key fact about residual networks is that any path using links with residual capacities greater than 0, that connects the source to the sink, shows a way to increase the flow in the network. Because this path shows how to increase or augment the flow, this type of path is called an *augmenting path*. Figure 12.23 shows the residual network in Figure 12.22 with an augmenting path drawn in bold.

To update the solution using an augmenting path, find the smallest residual capacity along the path. Then adjust the flows along the path by this amount. In Figure 12.23, for example, the smallest residual capacity of any link along the augmenting path is 2. To update the flows in the network, you add a flow of 2 to any link i–j along the path. You also subtract a flow of 2 from any link j–i where the reversed i–j link is in the path.

Rather than actually adjusting the flows and then rebuilding the residual network, it is easier to simply adjust the residual network. Then, when the algorithm is finished, you can use the result to compute the final flows for the links in the original network.

To adjust the residual network in this example, follow the augmenting path. Subtract 2 from the residual capacity of any link i–j along the path and add 2 to the residual capacity of the corresponding link j–i. Figure 12.24 shows the updated residual network for this example.

Figure 12.23 An augmenting path through a residual network.

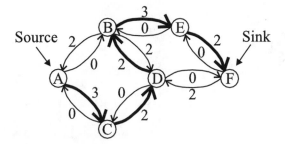

Figure 12.24 Updated residual network.

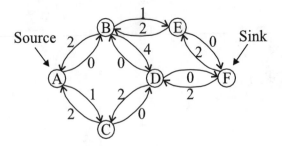

When you can find no more augmenting paths, you can use the residual net-work to compute the flows for the original network. For each link between nodes i and j, if the residual flow between nodes i and j is less than the capacity of the link, then the flow should equal the capacity minus the residual flow. Otherwise, the flow should be 0.

For instance, in Figure 12.24, the residual flow from node A to node C is 1 and the capacity of the A–C link is 3. Because 1 is less than 3, the flow across this link should be 3 – 1 = 2. Figure 12.25 shows the network flows corresponding to residual network in Figure 12.24.

So far the algorithm does not have a method for finding augmenting paths in the residual network. One method is similar to a label correcting shortest path algorithm. Start by placing the source node in a candidate list. Then, while the candidate list is not empty, remove an item from the list. Examine any neighbor-ing nodes connected to the selected node by a link that has a remaining residual capacity greater than 0. If the neighbor has not yet been placed in the candidate list, add it to the list. Continue this process until the candidate list is empty.

There are two ways in which this method differs from a label correcting shortest path algorithm. First, this method does not follow links with residual

Figure 12.25 Maximum flows.

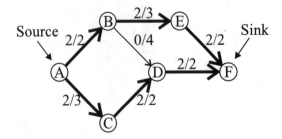

capacity 0. The shortest path algorithm will examine any link, no matter what its cost.

Second, this algorithm examines each node, at most, once. The label correcting shortest path method will update a node and place it back in the candidate list if it later finds an improved path from the root to that node. In this algorithm, you do not care how short the augmenting path is, so you do not need to update paths and place nodes back in the candidate list.

The following code shows how a program can compute maximum flows. This code is designed to work with undirected networks similar to the ones used by the example programs described in this chapter. When the algorithm is finished, it sets the cost of a link to the negative of the flow across the link if the link is used backwards. In other words, if the network contains an i–j link, and the algorithm determines that flow should occur across the j–i link, it sets the flow across the i–j link to be the negative of the flow that should occur across the j–i link. This allows the program to determine the direction of flow using the existing node record types.

```
procedure FindMaxFlows;
var
     top_candidate, candidate  : PCandidate;
     node, to_node             : PNode;
     link, rev_link            : PLink;
     min_residual              : Integer;
begin
     if ((SourceNode = nil) or (SinkNode = nil)) then exit;

     // Initially residual value equals capacity.
     node := NodeSentinel.NextNode;
     while (node <> nil) do
     begin
         link := node^.LinkSentinel.NextLink;
         while (link <> nil) do
         begin
             link^.Residual := link^.Capacity;
             link := link^.NextLink;
         end;
         node := node^.NextNode;
     end;

     // Repeat until we can find no more augmenting paths.
     repeat
         // Find an augmenting path in the residual network.
         // Reset the nodes' NodeStatus and InLink values.
```

```
node := NodeSentinel.NextNode;
while (node <> nil) do
begin
    node^.Status := nsNotInList;
    node^.InLink := nil;
    node := node^.NextNode;
end;

// Put the source on the candidate list.
SourceNode^.Status := nsNowInList;
GetMem(top_candidate, SizeOf(TCandidate));
top_candidate^.Node := SourceNode;
top_candidate^.NextCandidate := nil;

// Repeat until the candidate list is empty.
while (top_candidate <> nil) do
begin
    // Remove the top candidate from the list.
    node := top_candidate^.Node;
    node^.Status := nsWasInList;
    candidate := top_candidate^.NextCandidate;
    FreeMem(top_candidate);
    top_candidate := candidate;

    // Examine the links out of this node.
    link := node^.LinkSentinel.NextLink;
    while (link <> nil) do
    begin
        // See if the residual > 0 and this node
        // has never been on the list.
        to_node := link^.Node2;
        if ((link^.Residual > 0) and
            (to_node^.Status = nsNotInList)) then
        begin
            // Add it to the list.
            to_node^.Status := nsNowInList;
            to_node^.InLink := link;
            GetMem(candidate, SizeOf(TCandidate));
            candidate^.Node := to_node;
            candidate^.NextCandidate := top_candidate;
            top_candidate := candidate;
        end;
        link := link^.NextLink;
    end; // End examining links out of the node.
```

```
        // Stop if the sink has been labeled.
        if (SinkNode.InLink <> nil) then break;
end; // End while (top_candidate <> nil) do ...

    // Stop if we found no augmenting path.
    if (SinkNode.InLink = nil) then break;

    // Trace the augmenting path from SinkNode back to
    // SourceNode to find the smallest residual.
    min_residual := INFINITY;
    to_node := SinkNode;
    while (to_node <> SourceNode) do
    begin
        link := to_node^.InLink;
        if (link^.Residual < min_residual) then
            min_residual := link^.Residual;
        to_node := link^.Node1;
    end;

    // Update the residuals using the augmenting path.
    to_node := SinkNode;
    while (to_node <> SourceNode) do
    begin
        link := to_node^.InLink;
        link^.Residual := link^.Residual - min_residual;

        // Find and update the reverse link.
        node := link^.Node1;
        rev_link := to_node^.LinkSentinel.NextLink;
        while (rev_link <> nil) do
        begin
            if (rev_link^.Node2 = node) then break;
            rev_link := rev_link^.NextLink;
        end;
        if (rev_link <> nil) then
            rev_link^.Residual :=
                rev_link^.Residual + min_residual;

        // Update the next link in the augmenting path.
        to_node := link^.Node1;
    end;

    // Free any items remaining in the candidate list.
    while (top_candidate <> nil) do
```

```
        begin
            candidate := top_candidate^.NextCandidate;
            FreeMem(top_candidate);
            top_candidate := candidate;
        end;
    until (False); // End infinite loop looking for augmenting
paths.
    // The loop ends when there are no more augmenting paths.

    // Calculate the flows from the residuals.
    node := NodeSentinel.NextNode;
    while (node <> nil) do
    begin
        link := node^.LinkSentinel.NextLink;
        while (link <> nil) do
        begin
            if (link^.Capacity > link^.Residual) then
                link^.Flow := link^.Capacity - link^.Residual
            else
                    // Negative to indicate backwards flow.
                link^.Flow := link^.Residual - link^.Capacity;
            link := link^.NextLink;
        end;
        node := node^.NextNode;
    end;

    // Calculate the total flow.
    TotalFlow := 0;
    link := SourceNode^.LinkSentinel.NextLink;
    while (link <> nil) do
    begin
        TotalFlow := TotalFlow + link^.Flow;
        link := link^.NextLink;
    end;
end;
```

Example program Flow uses the augmenting path technique to compute maximal flows through a network. It is similar to the other programs described in this chapter. When you are not adding or removing a node or link, use the left mouse button to select the source node. Use the right mouse button to select the sink node. When you have selected a source and a sink, the program calculates and displays the maximum flows. Figure 12.26 shows the program displaying the flows for a small network.

Figure 12.26 Program Flow.

Maximum Flow Applications

Maximum flow calculations are used in many applications. Although maximal flows may be directly useful for some networks, they are most often used indirectly to calculate results that may seem at first to have little relation to network capacity.

Disjoint Paths

Redundancy is important in large communications networks. Given a network like the one shown in Figure 12.27, you might like to know how many disjoint paths there are between the source node and the sink node. If there are many paths between the two nodes that do not share a common link, there will still be a path between the nodes even if several links in the network fail.

Figure 12.27 A communications network.

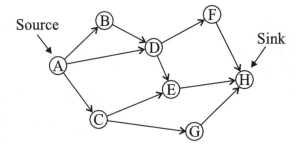

You can determine how many different paths there are using a maximum flow calculation. Create a network with nodes and links corresponding to those in the communications network. Set the capacity of each link to 1.

Next, perform a maximum flow calculation on the network. The maximum flow will be the same as the number of different paths from the source to the sink. Because each link can hold a flow of only 1, none of the paths used by the maximum flow calculation can share a common link.

A stricter definition of redundancy might require that the different paths share no links and no nodes. By modifying the previous network slightly, you can still use a maximum flow calculation to solve this problem. Divide each node, except the source and sink nodes, into two subnodes connected by a single link with capacity 1. Connect the first subnode to all the links entering the original node. Connect all the links leaving the original node to the second subnode. Figure 12.28 shows the network in Figure 12.27 with the nodes divided in this way. Now find the maximal flow for this new network.

If a path used by the maximal flow calculation passes through a node, it must use the link that connects the two corresponding subnodes. Because that link has a capacity of 1, no two paths used by the maximum flow calculation can cross this connecting link, so no two paths can use the same node in the original network.

Work Assignment

Suppose you have a group of employees with certain skills. Suppose you also have a collection of jobs that require the attention of an employee who has a particular set of skills. The assignment problem is to match the employees to the jobs, so each job is assigned to an employee who has the skills to work that job.

To convert this problem into a maximum flow calculation, create a network with two columns of nodes. In the left column, place one node to represent each employee. In the right column, place one node to represent each job.

Figure 12.28 Transformed communications network.

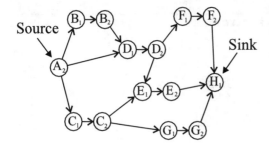

Next, compare the skills of each employee with the skills needed to perform each job. Create links between each employee and every job the employee can work. Set the capacities of all these links to 1.

Create a source node and connect it to every employee with a link of capacity 1. Then create a sink node and connect every job to it, again using links of capacity 1. Figure 12.29 shows the assignment network for a four-person, four-job assignment problem.

Now find the maximum flow from the source node to the sink node. Each resulting unit of flow must pass through one employee node and one job node. That flow represents the assignment of that employee to that job.

If the employees have the proper skills to work all the jobs, the maximum flow calculation will find a way to assign all of the jobs. If it is not possible to work all the jobs, the maximum flow calculation will assign employees to jobs so that as many jobs as possible are worked.

Example program Work uses this algorithm to assign work to employees. Enter employee names followed by their skills in the left text box. Enter jobs followed by required skills in the middle text box. When you click the Assign button, the program uses a maximum flow network to assign work to the employees. Figure 12.30 shows the program displaying a work assignment. In this example, the employees did not have the right combination of skills to work all of the jobs so one is unassigned.

Summary

You can apply some network algorithms directly to network-like objects. For example, you can use shortest path algorithms to find the best route through a street network. You can use a minimal spanning tree to determine the least expensive way to build a communications network or to connect cities with railroad track.

Figure 12.29 A work assignment network.

Figure 12.30 Program Work.

Many other network algorithms are used in less obvious ways. For example, you can use shortest path algorithms for districting, critical path scheduling, or crew scheduling. You can use maximum flow algorithms to perform work assignment. These less obvious uses for network algorithms usually prove more challenging and more interesting.

OBJECT-ORIENTED TECHNIQUES

13

Functions and procedures allow a programmer to break the logic of a large program into manageable pieces. Arrays and user-defined data structures allow a programmer to group data items in ways that make data management easier.

Classes allow a programmer to group logic and data in a different way. A class lets you combine data and logic in a single object. This additional method for managing program complexity allows you to view algorithms from a different perspective.

This chapter explains some of the more important issues raised by Delphi classes. It describes the advantages of object-oriented programming (OOP) and tells how you can maximize the benefits of OOP in Delphi. It then explains an assortment of useful object-oriented paradigms you can use to help manage complexity in your applications.

Benefits of OOP

The traditional benefits of object-oriented programming are *encapsulation*, *polymorphism*, and *reuse*. The following sections explain these benefits and outline how you can best take advantage of them in Delphi.

Encapsulation

An object defined by a class encapsulates the data it contains. Other parts of a program can use the object to manipulate the data without understanding exactly how the data values are stored or modified. The object provides public procedures and functions that allow the program to view and manipulate the data indirectly. Because this keeps the data abstract from the program's point of view, this is also called *data abstraction*.

Encapsulation allows your program to treat objects as black boxes. The program can use the objects' public methods to examine and modify values without needing to understand what happens inside the box.

Because the internal workings of the objects are hidden from the main program, the object's implementation can change without forcing changes to the main program. Changes to the object's internals occur only in the class module.

For example, suppose you have a FileDownload class that retrieves files from the Internet. The program passes a FileDownload object the location of the file and the object returns a string containing the file's contents. In this case, the program does not need to know how the object retrieves the file. It might fetch the file using a direct Internet connection or a dial-up connection. It might even load some of the files from a local disk cache. The program knows only that the object returns a string when it is passed a file location.

Maintaining Encapsulation

To maximize encapsulation, a class should not allow direct access to its data. If a variable is declared public within the class, other parts of the program can directly view and modify the data. Later, if the data representation changes, any parts of the program that interact directly with the data must also be changed. This removes one of the main benefits of encapsulation.

To maintain the separation between the program and the data, the class can declare its data variables private or protected. It can then allow the main program to access the values indirectly through public procedures. I use the term *property procedures* for these routines because, in a sense, they allow the main program to modify the properties of the class. This is also the term used for a similar concept in the Visual Basic programming language.

The following code shows how a TTemperature class might allow other parts of a program to view and modify a DegreesFahrenheit value.

```
interface

type
    TTemperature = class(TObject)
        private
            // The private data variable.
            p_DegreesFahrenheit : Single;

        public
            function DegreesFahrenheit : Single;
            procedure SetDegreesFahrenheit(new_value : Single);
    end;

implementation

// Return the temperature in degrees Fahrenheit.
function TTemperature.DegreesFahrenheit : Single;
begin
```

```
      Result := p_DegreesFahrenheit;
end;
```

// Set the temperature in degrees Fahrenheit.
```
procedure TTemperature.SetDegreesFahrenheit(new_value : Single);
begin
    p_DegreesFahrenheit := new_value;
end;
```

At this point, there is little practical difference between using property procedures and declaring p_DegreesFahrenheit to be a public variable. The procedures allow the class to be easily modified later, however.

For example, suppose you decided to store temperature in degrees Kelvin instead of in degrees Fahrenheit. You could modify the class to use the new storage method without changing parts of the program that use the DegreesFahrenheit property procedures. You could also add error-checking code to ensure that the program does not give the object invalid values.

```
interface

uses SysUtils;

type
    TTemperature = class(TObject)
        private
```
            // The private data variable.
```
            p_DegreesKelvin : Single;

        public
            function DegreesFahrenheit : Single;
            procedure SetDegreesFahrenheit(new_value : Single);
    end;

implementation
```

// Return the temperature in degrees Fahrenheit.
```
function TTemperature.DegreesFahrenheit : Single;
begin
    Result := (p_DegreesKelvin - 273.15) * 1.8;
end;
```

// Set the temperature in degrees Fahrenheit.
```
procedure TTemperature.SetDegreesFahrenheit(new_value : Single);
var
    new_kelvin : Single;
```

```
begin
    new_kelvin := (new_value / 1.8) + 273.15;
    if (new_kelvin < 0) then
        // Raise an error.
        raise ERangeError.CreateFmt(
            'Temperature %f must be above absolute zero',
            [new_value]);

    p_DegreesKelvin := new_kelvin;
end;
```

The programs described throughout this book flagrantly violate the principle of encapsulation by using public class variables. This is not particularly good programming style, but it keeps the algorithms a little simpler. It allows you to concentrate on the algorithms without a bunch of property procedures getting in the way.

Polymorphism

The second major benefit of object-oriented programming is *polymorphism,* which means "having many forms." In Delphi, it means a procedure can sometimes manipulate an object without really knowing what it is. For example, suppose you create a TReport class. From that you derive TBudgetReport and TExpenditureReport classes. The two derived classes inherit some of the capabilities defined by the TReport class.

Now if you write a procedure that takes as a parameter a TReport object, you can pass it a TReport object, a TBudgetReport object, or a TExpenditureReport object. As long as the procedure invokes only methods of the TReport class, it does not need to know which kind of object it is manipulating.

In some cases, a base class may define a method but not implement it. The implementation is left completely up to the derived classes. The reason the method is in the base class at all is to define the form of the method that will be implemented by the derived classes. Defining the method in the base class allows the program to treat objects of the derived classes polymorphically.

The base class can create an empty implementation of the deferred method. Alternatively it can declare the method with the abstract keyword. This tells Delphi that the base class will not provide an implementation of the method.

```
type
    TReport = class(TObject)
        public
            procedure PrintReport; virtual; abstract;
    end;
```

An abstract virtual method not only allows a class to declare the method without defining it, it also controls the program's ability to use the base class. If the program creates an instance of the base class, the compiler generates a warning indicating that the program is creating an object with an abstract method. The program can still create the object and use its non-abstract methods. If it tries to use the abstract method, however, the program generates an exception. The Singleton paradigm described later uses this exception to control access to an object that should be unique.

Reuse and Inheritance

Functions and procedures support *reuse*. Instead of writing a bunch of code whenever you need to use it, you can place the code in a procedure. Rather than rewriting the code, you simply invoke the procedure.

Similarly, you can create a class that makes a procedure available throughout the program. Using an object that is an instance of the class, the program can use the procedure.

Inheritance is the object-oriented version of code reuse. Classes that inherit functionality from their parent classes do not need to reimplement that functionality.

The virtual keyword provides a particularly effective means of reuse through inheritance. The parent class declares some of its methods as virtual. Derived classes can then use the override keyword to replace those methods in the derived class. The new method can use the inherited keyword to call the parent's version of the method.

For example, suppose the TReport class has a PrintReport method that sends various headers to the printer. The TBudgetReport overrides the PrintReport method to print budget information. It uses the inherited keyword to make the parent class provide the same headers for the budget report.

```
interface

type
    TReport = class(TObject)
        protected
            procedure PrintReport; virtual;
    end;

    TBudgetReport = class(TReport)
        protected
            procedure PrintReport; override;
    end;

implementation

// Print a header.
procedure TReport.PrintReport;
begin
```

```
    // Print the header here.
        :
end;


// Print a budget report.
procedure TBudgetReport.PrintReport;
begin
    // Use the parent's PrintReport method
    // to print the header.
    inherited PrintReport;

    // Print the rest of the report here.
        :
end;
```

This technique is quite powerful when combined with polymorphism. Since the PrintReport method is declared virtual, a procedure can invoke the object's most developed form of the PrintReport routine without knowing what kind of object it is.

For example, suppose a procedure takes a TReport object as a parameter. If it is passed a TBudgetReport object and it invokes the PrintReport method, it is the TBudgetReport version of the method that executes. Without knowing exactly what kind of object it is manipulating, the procedure gets the benefit of the object's version of the method.

OOP Paradigms

Chapter 1, "Fundamental Concepts," defined an algorithm as "a set of directions for performing a particular task." A class can certainly use this sort of algorithm in its procedures and functions. For instance, you can use a class to provide a wrapper encapsulating the behavior of an algorithm. Several of the programs described in earlier chapters use classes to encapsulate complicated algorithms.

Classes also allow a new style of programming where several objects work together to perform a task. In that case, providing a set of directions for performing the task may not make sense. It is more appropriate to provide a model of the objects' behaviors than to reduce the task to a list of steps. To differentiate these collections of behavior from more traditional algorithms, I call them *paradigms*.

The following sections describe some useful object-oriented paradigms. Many of these have been drawn from other object-oriented languages such as C++ and Smalltalk, but they can also be used in Delphi.

Command

Command objects are also known as action objects, function objects, and functors. A command object represents an action. A program can use the object's

Execute method to make the object perform its action. The program does not need to know anything about the action; it just knows the object has an Execute method.

Commands can be used in many interesting ways. A program can use commands to implement the following:

- Generic interfaces

- Macros

- Journaling and recovery

- Undo and redo features

To build a generic interface, a form might build an array of buttons. At runtime, the form can load the captions displayed by the buttons and create a corresponding array of command objects. When the user clicks on a button, the button's event handler code only needs to invoke the corresponding command object's Execute method. The details of what happens are inside the command object classes, not in the event handler.

Example program Cmd1 uses command objects to provide a generic interface for several unrelated functions. When you click on a button, the program invokes the corresponding command object's Execute procedure.

A program can use command objects to create user-defined macros. The user specifies a series of actions that the program saves as Command objects stored in an array or other data structure. Later, when the user invokes the macro, the program calls the Execute method of the corresponding command object in the array.

Command objects can provide journaling and recovery. Every time a command object executes, it can store information about itself in a log file. If the program crashes, it can later use the log information to recreate the command objects and execute them to repeat the commands it executed before the crash.

Finally, a program can use a series of command objects to provide undo and redo features. Example program Cmd2 allows you to draw rectangles, ellipses, and lines on a drawing area. Each time you draw a shape, the program stores a drawing Command object in a linked list. To draw the picture, the program replays the commands in an array.

This program's TDrawingCommand class defines variables used by each of the drawing command types. The TRectangleCmd, TEllipseCmd, and TLineCmd classes inherit from the TDrawingCommand class and implement their own drawing methods. The main program's Commands array stores up to 1000 TDrawingCommand objects. They are represented polymorphically as TDrawingCommand objects, but each is actually an instance of one of the specific shape-drawing classes. This program uses a simple array with 1000 entries to hold the drawing commands. A more robust program would use a linked list or resizable array to hold any number of commands.

Program Cmd2 uses the variable LastCommand to keep track of the last valid command object in the array. When the user selects the Draw menu's Undo command, the program decreases LastCommand by 1. When the program next draws the picture, it invokes only the objects up to object number LastCommand.

When the user selects the Draw menu's Redo command, the program increases LastCommand by 1 if any commands have recently been undone. When the program draws the picture, it applies one more command object than it did before so the restored shape is displayed.

When the user adds a new shape, the program removes any commands from the array that lie after position LastCommand. It then adds the new drawing command at the end and disables the Redo command since there are no commands available to redo. Figure 13.1 shows the Cmd2 program after a new shape has been added.

Visitor

A *visitor* object visits the items in an *aggregate* object. A procedure implemented by the aggregate class takes as a parameter a visitor object. It traverses the aggregate's objects passing each as a parameter to the visitor.

For example, suppose an aggregate object stores items in a linked list. The following code shows how its Visit method traverses the list passing each item as a parameter to a TVisitor object's Visit method.

```
procedure TAggregate.Visit(visitor : TVisitor);
var
    cell : TCell;
begin
```

Figure 13.1 Program Cmd2.

```
    cell := TopCell;
    while (cell <> nil) do
    begin
        visitor.Visit(cell.Value);
        cell := cell.NextCell;
    end;
end;
```

The following code shows how the Visit method in the TVisitor class might display the values of the list items in a series of dialog boxes.

```
procedure TVisitor.Visit(value : String);
    ShowMessage(value);
end;
```

When using the visitor paradigm, the aggregate class determines the order in which the items are visited. The visitor has no control over the order.

An aggregate can define more than one method for visiting the items it contains. For example, a tree class might provide VisitPreorder, VisitPostorder, VisitInorder, and VisitBreadthFirst methods to allow visitors to traverse the items in different orders.

Iterator

An *iterator* provides an alternative method for visiting the items in an aggregate object. An iterator object reaches into an aggregate to traverse the items it contains. Here the iterator defines the order in which the items are visited. Multiple iterator classes can be associated with an aggregate class to provide different traversals of the items.

To traverse the items, the iterator must understand the way in which the items are stored so it can define its own traversal. If the aggregate is a linked list, the iterator object must know that items are stored in a linked list, and it must know how to maneuver through the list. Because the iterator knows details of the list's internals, it breaks the aggregate's encapsulation.

Rather than make every class that needs to examine the aggregate's items implement its own traversal, you can associate an iterator class with the aggregate class. The iterator should provide simple MoveFirst, MoveNext, EndOfList, and CurrentItem procedures to allow indirect navigation through the list. New classes can include an instance of the iterator class and use the iterator's methods to traverse the aggregate. Figure 13.2 shows conceptually how the new object uses the iterator object to communicate with the list.

The Iter program, described later in the section *Factory*, uses iterators to traverse a complete binary tree. The Traverse procedure takes a parameter that indicates the kind of traversal to perform. It uses the tree object's CreateIterator factory method (described later) to create an iterator object. The iterator is an object from one of several classes derived from the TIterator class. Procedure

Figure 13.2 Using an iterator to communicate indirectly with a list.

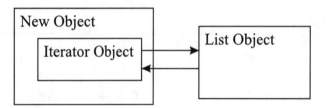

Traverse uses polymorphism to treat the object as if it were of type TIterator. It uses the EndOfTree, CurrentNode, and MoveNext methods provided by the iterator to list the nodes in the tree.

```
// Display a traversal.
procedure TIterForm.Traverse(it_type : TIteratorType);
var
    trav : TIterator;
    txt  : String;
begin
    // Create the iterator using a factory method.
    trav := TheTree.CreateIterator(it_type);

    // Use the iterator to traverse the tree.
    txt := '';
    while (not trav.EndOfTree) do
    begin
        txt := txt + IntToStr(trav.CurrentNode) + ' ';
        trav.MoveNext;
    end;
    ResultLabel.Caption := txt;

    // Destroy the iterator.
    trav.Free;
end;
```

Iterators break the encapsulation of their aggregates, but new classes that contain the iterators do not. Considering the iterator to be an extended part of the aggregate can help limit potential confusion. In program Iter, the main form routines do not understand how the tree is stored. Only the iterators need to know the internal structure of the tree. The iterators are defined inside the same code module as the tree class to make their relationship clear.

In this example, it is also necessary that the iterators be defined in the same code module as the tree class. The tree class defines the CreateIterator factory method that returns an iterator object. All the iterator classes use references to the tree class. In Delphi, classes that contain circular references to each other like this must be defined in the same type statement.

Visitors and iterators provide similar functions using different approaches. Because the visitor paradigm keeps the aggregate's details within the aggregate, it provides better encapsulation. Iterators can be useful if the order of traversal must change frequently or if it must be determined at runtime. For example, the aggregate can use a factory method (described later) to create an iterator object at runtime. The class containing the iterator does not need to know how the iterator is created—it just uses the iterator's methods to access the aggregate's items.

Friend

Many classes work closely with other classes. For example, an iterator class works closely with an aggregate class. To perform its job, the iterator must break the encapsulation of the aggregate. Although these related classes must sometimes break each other's encapsulation, other classes should not.

A *friend* class is a class that has special permission to break another's encapsulation. For example, an iterator class is a friend of the aggregate it traverses. It is allowed to look inside the aggregate even though other classes are not.

The simplest way to implement friends in Delphi is to make an agreement that only friend classes will break each other's encapsulation. If all developers stick to the agreement, the project will be manageable. The temptation to reach directly inside an aggregate class may be strong, however, and there will always be a possibility that someone will become lazy or careless and break the encapsulation.

An alternative strategy is to make the friend object pass itself as a parameter to the other class. By passing itself as a parameter, the friend proves it is of the correct class. Delphi will verify that the parameter is an object of the correct type.

It is still possible to corrupt this method and break the object's encapsulation. A program can create an object of the friend class and use it as a parameter to trick the other object's procedures. This is a rather awkward process, however, so it is unlikely that a developer would do this accidentally.

Interface

In this paradigm, one object acts as an interface between two others. One object can use the properties and methods of the first object to interact with a second. An interface is sometimes called an *adapter*, *wrapper*, or *bridge*. Figure 13.3 shows how an interface works conceptually.

An interface allows the two objects on either side of it to evolve independently. For example, if the methods of the object on the left in Figure 13.3 change, the interface must be modified but the object on the right need not be.

Often in this paradigm, the procedures used by the two objects are maintained by the developers who maintain those objects. Whoever manages the object on the left also manages the interface procedures that interact with the object on the left.

Figure 13.3 An interface.

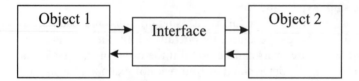

Do not confuse the interface paradigm with the notion of a class with abstract methods. As is described in the section *Polymorphism* earlier, you can use a base class with abstract methods to define the functionality of derived classes. Often the base class is said to define the interface for its derived classes. The interface paradigm defines the way two classes work together. A class with an abstract method defines the interface between that method and the rest of the program.

Facade

A *facade* is similar to an interface except it provides a simple interface to a complicated object or group of objects. A facade is also sometimes called a *wrapper*. Figure 13.4 shows graphically how a facade works.

The difference between a facade and an interface is mainly conceptual. The focus of an interface is on allowing objects to interact indirectly so they can evolve independently. A facade's main purpose is to make using something complicated easier by hiding details.

Factory

A *factory* is an object that creates other objects. A factory method is a procedure or function that creates an object.

Figure 13.4 A facade.

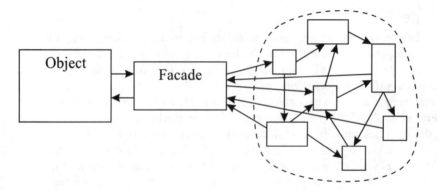

Factories are most useful when two classes must work closely together. For example, an aggregate class can provide a factory method that creates iterators for itself. The factory method can initialize the iterator so that it is ready to work with the specific instance of the aggregate that created it.

Example program Iter creates complete binary trees stored in an array. When you click one of the traversal buttons, the program uses the CreateIterator factory method of the TCompleteTree class to create an appropriate kind of iterator depending on the button you clicked.

The CreatIterator factory method is quite simple. It creates an appropriate iterator object passing itself to the object's constructor. The iterator's constructor saves the tree object for later reference and initializes its position in the tree. The following code shows the CreateIterator factory method and the constructor for the TIterator base class. The individual iterator subclasses TPreorderIterator, TInorderIterator, TPostorderIterator, and TBreadthFirstIterator inherit this constructor without making any changes.

```
// This factory method creates and returns an
// appropriate iterator.
function TCompleteTree.CreateIterator(it_type : TIteratorType) :
TIterator;
begin
    case (it_type) of
        itPreorder:
            Result := TPreorderIterator.Create(Self);
        itInorder:
            Result := TInorderIterator.Create(Self);
        itPostorder:
            Result := TPostorderIterator.Create(Self);
        itBreadthFirst:
            Result := TBreadthFirstIterator.Create(Self);
    else
            Result := nil;
    end;
end;


// Save the tree and order its nodes for the traversal.
constructor TIterator.Create(tree : TCompleteTree);
begin
    inherited Create;
    TheTree := tree;
    OrderNodes;
    CurrentIndex := 0;
end;
```

After it has created the appropriate iterator object, program Iter uses the iterator to traverse the tree and list the nodes in the proper order. Figure 13.5 shows program IterTree displaying a tree's postorder traversal.

Singleton

A *singleton* is an object that is unique in an application. For example, Delphi defines a Printer object that represents the currently selected system printer. Because there is only one selected printer at a time, Printer is a singleton object.

One way to create a singleton is to define a function that returns a specific object defined in a program module. To prevent the main program from instantiating more instances of the singleton class, it should declare a virtual abstract constructor. If the program tries to instantiate an object of this class directly, the undefined constructor will be invoked and the program will generate an exception.

To allow the singleton to be created, the module should create a derived class that is defined in its implementation section. That makes the derived object visible to routines within the module but hidden from the outside. The derived class should provide a non-abstract constructor so the routine in the module can instantiate the singleton.

Example program Single implements a singleton class that returns a list of all of the top-level windows running in Windows. Since the computer has only one monitor, this object can be a singleton. The following code shows how the program provides a singleton TWindowLister object. Figure 13.6 shows program Single displaying a list of windows.

Figure 13.5 Program IterTree displaying a postorder traversal.

Figure 13.6 Program Single.

```
type
    // Because it has a virtual abstract constructor,
    // the program cannot instantiate this class directly.
    TWindowLister = class(TObject)
        public
            constructor Create; virtual; abstract;
            function WindowList : String;
    end;

// Public function that returns the singleton.
function WindowLister : TWindowLister;

implementation

type
    // This subclass can be instantiated
    // but it is visible only in this module.
    TAWindowLister = class(TWindowLister)
        public
            constructor Create; override;
    end;
```

```pascal
// The single instance of TAWindowLister.
var
    TheWindowLister : TAWindowLister;


// ---------------------------------------------------------
// A public function that instantiates and returns the
// singleton.
// ---------------------------------------------------------
function WindowLister : TWindowLister;
begin
    if (TheWindowLister = nil) then
        TheWindowLister := TAWindowLister.Create;

    Result := TheWindowLister;
end;


// ---------------------------------------------------------
// TWindowLister
// ---------------------------------------------------------
// Return the window list.
function TWindowLister.WindowList : String;
const
    CR = #13#10;
    MAX_CHAR = 256;
var
    desktop_hWnd, next_hWnd, buflen : Longint;
    buf : array [0..MAX_CHAR] of Char;
begin
    Result := 'hWnd        Title' + CR + '---------- -----';

    // Get the desktop window handle.
    desktop_hWnd := GetDesktopWindow;

    // Get the first of the desktop's child windows.
    next_hWnd := GetWindow(desktop_hWnd, GW_CHILD);
    while (next_hWnd <> 0) do
    begin
        buflen := GetWindowText(next_hWnd, @buf, MAX_CHAR);
        if (buflen > 0) then
        begin
            Result := Result + CR +
                Format('%10d %s', [next_hWnd, String(buf)]);
        end;
        // Get the next child window.
```

```
            next_hWnd := GetWindow(next_hWnd, GW_HWNDNEXT);
        end;
    end;


    // --------------------------------------------------------
    // TAWindowLister
    // --------------------------------------------------------
    // A do nothing constructor.
    constructor TAWindowLister.Create;
    begin

    end;
```

The WindowLister singleton object is available throughout the project. The following code shows how the main program uses this object's WindowList property to display a list of the windows currently running.

```
ListMemo.Text := WindowLister.WindowList;
```

Serialization

Many applications store objects and later rebuild them. For example, an application may save a representation of its objects in a text file. The next time the program runs, it reads the file and reloads the objects.

An object could provide procedures that read and write it into a file. A more general strategy is to provide procedures that save and restore the object's data using a string. Because storing an object's data in a string converts the object into a series of characters, this process is sometimes called *serialization*.

Serializing an object into a string allows the main program greater flexibility. It can save and restore the object using a text file, a database, or a memory location. It can send the serialization across a network or make it available on a Web page. A program or ActiveX control at the other end can use the serialization to recreate the object. The program can also add extra processing to the string. For example, it can encrypt the string after serialization and decrypt it before deserialization.

One approach to serializing an object is to let it write all its data into a string in a predetermined format. For example, suppose a TBox class has the properties x1, y1, x2, and y2. The following code shows how the class might define its Serialization property procedures.

```
function TBox.Serialization : String;
begin
    Result :=
        Format('%d;%d;%d;%d;', [x1, y1, x2, y2]);
end;
```

```
procedure TBox.SetSerialization(txt : String);
var
    pos1 : Integer;
begin
    pos1 := Pos(';', txt);
    x1 := StrToInt(Copy(txt, 1, pos1 - 1));
    txt := Copy(txt, pos1 + 1, Length(txt - pos1));

    pos1 := Pos(';', txt);
    y1 := StrToInt(Copy(txt, 1, pos1 - 1));
    txt := Copy(txt, pos1 + 1, Length(txt - pos1));

    pos1 := Pos(';', txt);
    x2 := StrToInt(Copy(txt, 1, pos1 - 1));
    txt := Copy(txt, pos1 + 1, Length(txt - pos1));

    pos1 := Pos(';', txt);
    y2 := StrToInt(Copy(txt, 1, pos1 - 1));
    txt := Copy(txt, pos1 + 1, Length(txt - pos1));
end;
```

This method is relatively simple, but it is not very flexible. As the program evolves, changes to the object's structure will force you to translate any previously stored serializations. If you have objects stored in files or databases, you will need to write conversion programs to load the old data and store it in the new format.

A more flexible method is to store the names of the object's data items together with their values. When the object reads serialized data, it uses the item names to determine what values to set. If you later add or remove items from the object's definition, you do not need to translate old serialized data. When a new object loads old data, it simply ignores any values that it no longer supports.

By defining default item values, you can sometimes make object serializations shorter. The Serialization property procedure saves only the items with values that differ from their defaults. Before SetSerialization begins processing a serialization, it initializes all the object's items to default values. Those with nondefault values are updated as the procedure processes the serialized data.

Example program Serial uses this method to save and restore pictures containing ellipses, lines, and rectangles. The following code shows the TDrawingCommand object's serialization property procedures. The GetToken procedure is a helper routine that removes the first token from a string and returns the token's name and value. Each token is stored in the string as a name followed by a value in parentheses as in token_name(token_value). The SetSerialization procedure ignores blank space and carriage returns so function Serialization uses them to make the results more readable.

```
const
    // Constants for serializing and deserializing.
    DEF_x1 = 0;
    DEF_y1 = 0;
    DEF_x2 = 100;
    DEF_y2 = 100;
    DEF_color = clBlack;
    DEF_style = bsSolid;

// Return the basic serialization that stores the
// position color, and style information.
function TDrawingCommand.Serialization : String;
const
    CR = #13#10;
begin
    Result := '';
    if (x1 <> DEF_x1) then
        Result := Result + Format('  x1(%d)', [x1]) + CR;
    if (y1 <> DEF_y1) then
        Result := Result + Format('  y1(%d)', [y1]) + CR;
    if (x2 <> DEF_x2) then
        Result := Result + Format('  x2(%d)', [x2]) + CR;
    if (y2 <> DEF_y2) then
        Result := Result + Format('  y2(%d)', [y2]) + CR;
    if (color <> DEF_color) then
        Result := Result + Format('  color(%d)', [Integer(color)]) +
CR;
    if (style <> DEF_style) then
        Result := Result + Format('  style(%d)', [Integer(style)]) +
CR;
end;

// Load position color, and style information from a
// basic serialization.
procedure TDrawingCommand.Deserialize(txt : String);
var
    token_name, token_value : String;
begin
    // Set default values.
    x1 := DEF_x1;
    y1 := DEF_y1;
    x2 := DEF_x2;
    y2 := DEF_y2;
```

```
    color := DEF_color;
    style := DEF_style;

    while (txt <> '') do
    begin
        // Read a token from the serialization.
        GetToken(txt, token_name, token_value);

        // See which token it is.
        if (token_name = 'x1') then
            x1 := StrToInt(token_value)
        else if (token_name = 'y1') then
            y1 := StrToInt(token_value)
        else if (token_name = 'x2') then
            x2 := StrToInt(token_value)
        else if (token_name = 'y2') then
            y2 := StrToInt(token_value)
        else if (token_name = 'color') then
            color := TColor(StrToInt(token_value))
        else if (token_name = 'style') then
            style := TBrushStyle(StrToInt(token_value));
    end;
end;
```

MVC

The Model/View/Controller (MVC) paradigm allows a program to orchestrate complex relationships between objects that store, objects that display, and objects that manipulate data. For example, a finance application might display expense data in a table, pie chart, or bar graph. If the user changes the value in a table, the application should automatically update all displays. It might also write the modified data to a hard disk.

For complicated systems, managing the interactions between objects that store, display, and manipulate data can be quite confusing. The MVC paradigm decouples the interactions so that they are easy to handle individually. MVC manages data using three kinds of objects: *models*, *views*, and *controllers*.

Models

A *model* represents the data. It provides methods other objects use to examine and modify the data. In a finance application, the model stores the expense data. It provides procedures for viewing and changing expense values and creating new values. It might also provide functions that compute aggregate values such as total expenses, total expenses by department, average expenses per month, and so forth.

The model should also provide AddView and RemoveView procedures that add and remove view objects from a list. The views can be stored in a linked list or some other dynamic data structure. Whenever the data is modified, the model notifies the views in its list. The views then update their displays appropriately.

Views

A *view* displays the data represented by a model. Because views usually display the data to the user, views are often closely associated with forms.

When the program creates a new view, it should add it to the model's view collection. One way to do that is to make the view's constructor take a model as a parameter. The constructor can then call the model's AddView procedure to register itself with the model.

The view should call the model's RemoveView procedure in its destructor. That allows the model to remove the view from its list of views. Unless the view is removed, the model will later try to notify the destroyed view when the data changes.

Controllers

A *controller* modifies the data in a model. A controller must always access a model's data through its public methods. Those methods can then notify the views that a change has occurred. If a controller modifies the data directly, the model cannot notify its views.

View/Controllers

Many objects both display and modify data. For example, a text box allows the user to view and modify data. A form containing a text box can be used as both a view and a controller. Option buttons, check boxes, scroll bars, and many other user interface elements also allow the user to view and manipulate data.

View/controllers are easiest to manage if you separate the view and controller functions as much as possible. When the object changes the data, it should not update its own display. Later, when the model notifies it as a view that the change has occurred, it can update itself.

For example, imagine a draggable bar chart. It displays data visually, and the user can click and drag the bars to modify the data values. When the user clicks and drags, the chart object uses the model's public data access routines to modify the data. The model then notifies the views, including the bar chart. At that point, the bar chart updates its display to show the new value the user has selected.

This technique is awkward for standard user interface objects such as text boxes. When the user types in a text box, the text box is immediately updated and its OnChange event handler executes. The event handler can notify the model of the change. The model then notifies the view/controller (acting as a view) that the change has occurred. If the object updates the text box, it will generate a new OnChange event. It will then notify the model that a change has occurred, and the program will enter an infinite loop.

To prevent this problem, the model's data modification methods should take an optional parameter indicating the controller object that caused the change. When it notifies its views of the change, the model skips that controller. If a view/controller like the bar chart must be notified of a change it causes, it should pass the value nil to the update procedure. A view/controller using a text box can pass itself as a parameter to avoid notification of the change it is causing.

Example program Mvc, shown in Figure 13.7, uses the Model/View/Controller paradigm to display some randomly generated expense data. In Figure 13.7, the program shows three different kinds of views. The TMvcPieView class implements a pie chart view. It is a reasonably straightforward view that simply displays the model's data.

The TMvcTableView class is a table view/controller. It displays expense category names and values in text boxes, and it modifies the model's data when the text boxes are changed. Because the text boxes both display and modify data values, objects of this class pass themselves as parameters to the model when they update the data. The model then skips notifying the object that caused the change.

The TMvcGraphView class is a bar chart view/controller. It displays the data graphically in a bar chart. The user can modify the model's data by clicking and dragging on a bar. This class does not immediately update its display when it changes the data acting as a controller. Instead, it passes the value nil to the

---

Figure 13.7 Program ExpMvc.

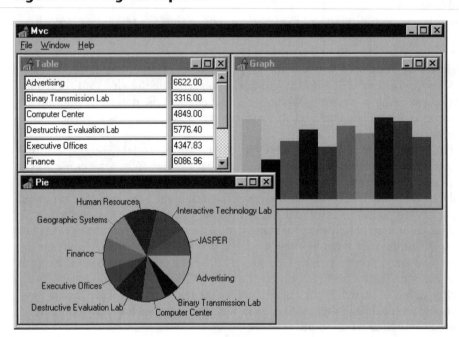

model's data modification routines. That makes the model notify the bar chart that the value has changed, and the chart updates its display at that time acting as a view.

You can create any number of table, pie chart, and bar chart windows in the program. If you change the data using any of the table or bar charts, all of the windows update automatically.

Summary

Classes allow Delphi programmers to think about old problems in new ways. Instead of thinking about long lists of tasks performed in sequential order to accomplish a task, you can think of a group of objects that work in concert to perform the task. If the task is partitioned properly, each of the classes separately may be quite simple, though together they perform a complex function. Using the paradigms described in this chapter, you can decouple the classes so they are individually as simple as possible.

Using the CD-ROM

A

T his appendix outlines the contents of the accompanying CD-ROM and explains how you can use the programs. Appendix B lists and briefly describes the programs.

What's on the CD-ROM

The CD-ROM contains the Delphi 3 source code for the algorithms and example programs described in this book.

The example programs described in each chapter are contained in separate subdirectories. For example, programs demonstrating algorithms described in Chapter 3, "Stacks and Queues," are stored in the Ch3 subdirectory. Appendix B, "List of Example Programs," details the programs described in this book.

Hardware Requirements

To run and modify the example applications, you need a computer that is reasonably able to run Delphi 3. You also need a compact disk drive to load the programs from the CD-ROM.

Algorithms run at different speeds on different computers with different configurations. A 200-megahertz Pentium Pro with 64Mb of memory will be faster than a 386-based computer with 4Mb of memory. You will quickly learn the limits of your hardware.

Installing Source Code

You can load the example programs into the Delphi development environment using the Open command in the File menu. You can select the files directly from the CD-ROM, or you can copy them onto your hard disk first.

Files on a CD-ROM are always marked read only because you cannot normally write files to a compact disk. If you copy files from the CD-ROM onto your hard disk, the copies are also marked as read only. If you want to modify the files, you must give yourself write permission first.

You can do this with the Windows Explorer. First, copy the files you want onto your hard disk. Then select the files and invoke the Properties command in Windows Explorer's File menu. Uncheck the Read Only check box, and click the Ok button. At this point, you can make changes to the copied files and save the changes to your hard disk. Do not worry about making mistakes and accidentally ruining the copied source code. You can always copy the files again from the CD-ROM.

Running the Example Programs

One of the most useful ways to run the example programs is using Delphi's debugging capabilities. Load the source code into Delphi. Using breakpoints, watches, and other debugging features, you can study the internals of the algorithms in action. This can be particularly helpful for understanding more complicated algorithms, such as those presented in Chapter 7, "Balanced Trees," and Chapter 12, "Network Algorithms."

Some of the example programs create data or temporary scratch files. These programs place the files in an appropriate directory. For example, some of the sorting programs presented in Chapter 9, "Sorting," create data files in the Ch9 directory. All of these files have a .dat extension so you can find and remove them if you like.

The example programs are for demonstration purposes only. They are intended to help you understand particular algorithmic concepts, and they do not spend a great deal of time validating data and trapping errors. If you enter invalid data, the programs may crash. If you have trouble figuring out what data to enter, use the program's Help menu to get instructions.

User Assistance and Information

The software accompanying this book is being provided as is without warranty or support of any kind. Should you require basic installation assistance, or if your media is defective, please call the Wiley product support number at (212) 850-6194 weekdays between 9 A.M. and 4 P.M. Eastern Standard Time. You can also contact product support via email at: wprtusw@wiley.com.

To place additional orders or to request information about other Wiley products, please call (800) 879-4539.

You can send comments or questions to the author at RodStephens@delphi-helper.com. Visit www.delphi-helper.com or the Wiley Web page www.wiley.com/compbooks/stephens to learn more about books written by Rod Stephens. These pages include updates and patches to the material presented in the books, as well as descriptions of things readers have done with the material in them.

If you use the material in this book in an interesting way, send email to RodStephens@delphi-helper.com. Your achievements may be added to the sites so others can see what you have accomplished.

List of Example Programs

The CD-ROM accompanying this book contains 72 Delphi 3.0 example programs. This appendix lists the programs and briefly describes the concepts each demonstrates.

Chapter 1—Fundamental Concepts
Pager   Paging and thrashing

Chapter 2—Lists
SizeArr   Resizing arrays
SimList   Simple resizable array-based list
Garbage   Resizable array-based list with garbage collection
LList1   Linked list encapsulated in a class
LList2   Linked list with MoveFirst and MoveNext routines
DblList   Doubly linked list
Threads   Threaded linked list

Chapter 3—Stacks and Queues
AStack   Array-based stack
LStack   Linked list stack
ArrayQ   Array-based queue
CircleQ   Circular queue
LinkedQ   Linked list queue
PriorQ   Linked list priority queue
HeadedQ   Multi-headed queue simulation

Chapter 4—Arrays
Triang   Triangular array class
Poly   Linked lists of polygons that contain linked lists of points
Sparse   Sparse arrays
VSparse   Very sparse arrays

Chapter 5—Recursion

Facto1   Recursive factorials
Gcd1   Recursive GCD
Fibo1   Recursive Fibonacci numbers
Hilb1   Recursive Hilbert curves
Sierp1   Recursive Sierpinski curves
BigAdd1   Recursive addition
Facto2   Nonrecursive factorials using tail recursion removal
Gcd2   Nonrecursive GCD using tail recursion removal
BigAdd2   Nonrecursive addition using tail recursion removal
Fibo2   Nonrecursive Fibonacci numbers using a lookup table
Fibo3   Nonrecursive Fibonacci numbers using a prefilled lookup table
Fibo4   Nonrecursive Fibonacci numbers using bottom-up calculation
Hilb2   Nonrecursive Hilbert curve
Sierp2   Nonrecursive Sierpinski curves

Chapter 6—Trees

Binary   Binary tree
NAry   N-ary tree using resizable child arrays
FStar   N-ary tree using forward star
Trav1   Tree traversals for a complete binary tree
Trav2   Tree traversals for an N-ary tree
TrSort   Sorted binary tree
Qtree   Quadtree

Chapter 7—Balanced Trees

AVL   AVL trees
Btree   B-tree
Bplus   B+tree

Chapter 8—Searching Decision Trees

TicTac   Game tree searching with precomputed initial moves
              and responses
BandB   Exhaustive and branch and bound searching
Heur   Heuristics

Chapter 9—Sorting

Encode   String encoding
Sort   Sorting
Unsort   Randomizing arrays
HeapQ   Heap-based priority queue

Chapter 10—Searching
Search   List searching

Chapter 11—Hashing
Chain   Hash table with chaining
Bucket   Hash table with buckets
Bucket2   Hash table with buckets on disk
Linear   Open addressing with linear probing
Ordered   Open addressing with ordered linear probing
Quad   Open addressing with quadratic probing
Rand   Open addressing with pseudo-random probing
Rehash   Open addressing with linear probing, deletion, and rehashing

Chapter 12—Network Algorithms
NetEdit   Network editor
Span   Minimal spanning tree
PathS   Label setting shortest paths
PathC   Label correcting shortest paths
Distr   Districting using shortest path trees
Flow   Maximum network flow
Work   Work assignment using maximum network flow

Chapter 13—Object-Oriented Techniques
Cmd1   User interface using command objects
Cmd2   Undo/redo using command objects
Iter   Iterators and factory methods for a complete binary tree
Single   Using a singleton to list windows
Serial   Shape drawing using serializable command objects
Mvc   Model/view/controller paradigm

INDEX

CUSTOMER NOTE: IF THIS BOOK IS ACCOMPANIED BY SOFTWARE, PLEASE READ THE FOLLOWING BEFORE OPENING THE PACKAGE.

To use this CD-ROM, your system must meet the following requirements:

Platform/Processor/Operating System. Personal computer with a 486 or higher processor running Microsoft Windows 95 or Windows NT version 4.0 or later operating system; Delphi 3.0 or later.

RAM. 8 MB of memory (12 MB recommended) if running Windows 95; 16 MB (20 MB recommended) if running Windows NT.

Hard Drive Space. You can install none, some, or all of the programs on the CD-ROM. Total tools and information on the CD-ROM: 20 MB.

Peripherals. CD-ROM drive; VGA or higher resolution monitor (SVGA recommended); Microsoft Mouse or compatible pointing device.